Pauline Sangster.

STUDYING
CHILDREN
IN CONTEXT

STUDYING CHILDREN IN CONTEXT

Theories, Methods, and Ethics

M. Elizabeth Graue
Daniel J. Walsh

With
Deborah Ceglowski
Anne Haas Dyson
David E. Fernie
Rebecca Kantor
Robin Lynn Leavitt
Peggy J. Miller
Hsueh-Yin Ting

SAGE Publications
International Educational and Professional Publisher
Thousand Oaks   London   New Delhi

For information:

SAGE Publications, Inc.
2455 Teller Road
Thousand Oaks, California 91320
E-mail: order@sagepub.com

SAGE Publications Ltd.
6 Bonhill Street
London EC2A 4PU
United Kingdom

SAGE Publications India Pvt. Ltd.
M-32 Market
Greater Kailash I
New Delhi 110 048 India

Printed in the United States of America

Library of Congress Cataloging-in-Publication Data

Graue, M. Elizabeth, 1956–
    Studying children in context: Theories, methods, and ethics/
by M. Elizabeth Graue and Daniel J. Walsh with Deborah Ceglowski et al.
    pp.   cm.
    Includes bibliographical references and index.
    ISBN 0-8039-7256-3 (cloth: acid-free paper).—ISBN 0-8039-7257-1
(pbk.: acid-free paper)
    1. Children—Research—Methodology. 2. Children—Research—
United States. 3. Context effects (Psychology) in children—Research—
United States. I. Walsh, Daniel J. II. Title.
HQ767.85.G73   1997
305.23'072—dc21   97-338

98 99 00 01 02 03 04 10 9 8 7 6 5 4 3 2 1

Acquiring Editor:	Peter Labella
Editorial Assistant:	Corrine Pierce
Production Editor:	Diana E. Axelsen
Production Assistant:	Denise Santoyo
Typesetter:	Marion Warren
Indexer:	Mary Mortensen
Print Buyer:	Anna Chin

CONTENTS

PREFACE

Writing this book challenged us in many ways—technically as we dealt with the physical distance between Urbana, Illinois, and Madison, Wisconsin; theoretically as we negotiated differing perspectives on research; and stylistically as we struggled with authorial voice. We met the first challenge with e-mail, phone calls, and 4-hour drives. The other two were more difficult.

We met and talked a number of times while we planned and wrote the book, but we never actually sat down at a keyboard together. When we wrote, we wrote individually. The first draft of each page was written by one of us and then passed on to the other.

Each "we," then, in this volume began as one of us speaking for both of us and waiting to see if the other agreed. Take this brief preface. We met and talked about how we would present ourselves as authors and came to something of an agreement, but one of us (Daniel) initially translated that agreement into text—the first draft of what you are now reading.

We are very different people, with dissimilar styles of writing, distinct ways of presenting ourselves, and, often, conflicting ideas about what research is and how it should proceed. These differences were an important factor in our decision to write this book together. We saw our different viewpoints, experiences, and writing styles as a strength. We wanted not to present ourselves as a homogeneous magisterial "we." We wanted to keep the tension of our discussions in the writing. We attempted to maintain the tension by forging a style that lay between choral writing and cacophony. Tobin and Davidson (1990) used the term *polyvocality*. Our goal was a functional bivocality, complex but not so muddled as to hinder communication. The proof of our efforts will be in the reading.

We indicate at the beginning of each chapter who took primary responsibility for writing the chapter. We do so to identify for the reader the underlying "I" in each chapter. A few chapters were passed back and forth so often that they became very much dual efforts, and those also have been noted. At times, we speak in an identified first person singular, for example, "I (Daniel)." At other times, when agreement is strong, as now, we shift to the first person plural. No chapter that either of us wrote escaped the careful attention of the other.

We extended our voices by bringing in valued colleagues to describe their field experiences. These short narratives illuminate key issues in many chapters. Our ambition has been to produce a text that is accessibly and usefully complex. Many thanks to Deb Ceglowski, Anne Haas Dyson, David Fernie, Rebecca Kantor, Robin Lynn Leavitt, Peggy J. Miller, and Hsueh-Yin Ting for adding an important layer of polyvocality.

We are both indebted to many people who helped and guided us in our development as researchers. Without their tutelage, we would not have written this book. We owe its strengths to them. They should not be faulted for its weaknesses nor identified with its idiosyncrasies.

I (Daniel) owe much to George and Louise Spindler, who first introduced me to ethnography, and to many valued colleagues, particularly Buddy Peshkin, Liora Bresler, Peggy Miller, John D'Amato, Norm Denzin, Joe Tobin, and Gary King. I have learned much from afar from the inimitable Ray McDermott and the peerless Fred Erickson. I have also had the opportunity to associate with many gifted graduate students in recent years. Working with them on research and on their dissertations has taught me a great deal. An incomplete list includes Natalie Baturka, Robin Leavitt, Hui-Fen Lin, Hsueh-Yin Ting, J. C. Chen, Deb Ceglowski, Teresa Vasconcelos, Jean Wolf, Yonghee Hong, Patricia Clark Brown, Min-Ling Tsai, Shunah Chung, Anya Enos, Mugyeong Ryu, Kyunghwa Lee, Carol Owles, Judy Davidson, and Jaesook Lee. Thanks also to Randy Bost for help on the references. Finally, I thank the students who have taken my Child Study and Methods of Educational Inquiry courses, in which many of the ideas in this book were first tried out. My work on this book was facilitated by support from the Bureau of Educational Research at the University of Illinois at Urbana-Champaign.

I (Beth) will always be indebted to Bob Stake, who lured me into the land of qualitative research, and to Margaret Eisenhart and Lorrie Shepard, who through their very different approaches taught me that there were many ways to interpret the world. Thanks also to Mary Lee Smith. Colleagues at Wisconsin have supported and challenged my learning. Special thanks to Mary Louise Gomez, Michael Apple, and Tom Popkewitz. Many grad students have taught me in various courses on interpretive research and have come back for more—thanks to Patti O'-Toole, Matthew Weinstein, Deb Ceglowski, Monica Miller Marsh, Ellen Ansell, and Tamara Lindsey. This work was made possible in part by the support of the Wisconsin Alumni Research Foundation's Graduate School Research Grant Program.

*   *   *

We dedicate this book to our colleague and dear friend Mary Catherine Ellwein, who died in June of 1994 at the age of 36, taken much too young and much too alive by cancer. She was a wonderful woman, strong and smart. She was a extraordinary researcher. And she was good to be with.

Beth and Mary Catherine were graduate students together at the University of Colorado. Daniel and Mary Catherine were colleagues at the University of Virginia. We met each other through Mary Catherine. Were she still alive and working with us, this would be a much better book. Much of what we know about research we learned from her, in particular, the need to be respectful of the multiple layers of intention and commitment required to work with children. We had much left to learn from her when she died.

We both miss her very much.

Beth Graue
Daniel J. Walsh

INTRODUCTION

Don't make up what you could find out.
—*Howard Becker (1996, p. 59)*

Some years ago, I heard Lee Shulman assert that the purpose of research is to get smarter about the world in order to make it a better place. It is, as the Irish say, a "grand" statement. I used it to introduce my research methods courses. I used it to justify my own work, perhaps even to feel grand about it—I was getting smarter about the world, and I was making it a better place.

Maybe I have become smarter about the world, at least about some very small corner of it, but it is presumptuous to think that I have made it a better place. James Garbarino's (1995) argument that contemporary America is raising its children in a "socially toxic environment" is compelling, and it is disturbing to parents of young children, as we both are (two each). When I read, for example, this morning in *Time* that Libya's ruling thug, M. Khadafy, is building an impregnable factory that will produce huge amounts of nerve gas, I thought first of my children and feared for them and the world into which they have been brought.

AUTHORS' NOTE: This introduction was written by Daniel.

Even in the liberal democracy in which we live, agreement would be hard to reach about what would make the world a better place for children. My own research on schools (Walsh, 1991, 1992, 1993) has convinced me that well-intentioned people have very different views about what would make the world better for children—views that are based on deeply embedded beliefs about how the world works and how children should fit into that world.

Believing that we are making the world a better place can make us smug, even arrogant—WE researchers (and not you ordinary folks) are going to improve the world. We can hope, but I think that researchers face a more pressing and mundane challenge, that is, to find it out. The reason we should be finding it out is because the alternative to finding it out is *not* not finding it out, but instead making it up, or, as is more often the case, having it made up for you. Right now, when it comes to children and what we know as a culture about children, those who make it up dominate.

This book is about the process of finding it out. Finding it out is labor-intensive and expensive. One must go out and look and listen and soak and poke and then do it all again and again. Long hours are required to construct a data record from the raw data generated in the field. Finding it out challenges the researcher in her analysis to explore critically not only that part of the world being studied but the very research process itself. Ultimately, all that labor produces knowledge that is uncertain and that will change, but it produces knowledge. The "it" found out will never have the certainty or the universality of the "it" made up. That is how it should be. The construction of knowledge is a human endeavor. It will never be certain.

Finding it out about children is exceptionally difficult—intellectually, physically, and emotionally. Physical, social, cognitive, and political distances between the adult and the child make their relationship very different from the relationships among adults. In doing research with children, one never becomes a child. One remains a very definite and readily identifiable "other."

In marked contrast to finding it out, making it up presents fewer challenges, takes much less time, and, as a short visit to Barnes and Noble will confirm, is more lucrative. Why spend prolonged time with children in classrooms or homes or playgrounds when one can simply pull an anecdote from here, a little theory from there, and a little "common sense" from one's experience as a parent or a teacher? Explaining what children are like by appealing to some authority is much easier than actually going out and finding out. If an anecdote is required, a visit to the local university lab school or an elite preschool allows one to avoid the less pristine conditions in which the vast majority of contemporary children spend their daily lives.

Those who make it up take many forms. Self-styled "experts" may well make the requisite bows to research (as in "the research says") but essentially proclaim how children are and how they should be. Less obvious are people who know something about children but who then move into areas in which they have no particular expertise. Consider, for example, how much of what we as a culture know about children, particularly young children, comes from pediatricians and clinical psychologists who write not about children's mental or physical health but about children in general.

Also contributing to made-up knowledge are researchers who fail to recognize that there is more to the world than the part that they are examining. For example, under the hegemony of a rather narrow measurement orientation, much research done in the context of schooling has ignored aspects of children and childhood that cannot be quantified. Another example: Piaget studied children with extreme care, but most often within the context of contrived and meaningless tasks. From this research, he drew conclusions about children in general, conclusions that have not stood up when researchers examined children doing meaningful tasks in familiar situations (e.g., Donaldson, 1978; Gelman, 1979; Hatano & Inagaki, 1986).

Entire categories of children have been made up. Finlan (1994) argued that there is no empirical evidence for learning disabilities as traditionally defined. LD children nevertheless exist as a cultural construct and in the laws of the land. One can go into any school and find them identified and labeled. Vellutino (1987) concluded that no evidence exists that children, or anyone, see letters or words or, for that matter, anything backwards, but the dyslexic child who sees print backwards stands out in our cultural collection of images of children. Walk up to any reasonably educated person on the street and ask him or her about dyslexia and you will hear about children who see letters backwards.

Ironically, the American cultural obsession with being practical works against finding it out. We tend to dismiss that which cannot be immediately applied—"Just find out what works." We see ourselves as "doers." Within such a context, those who make it up thrive. If one is going to make it up anyway, why not make up what people want to know? One cannot guarantee that what is found out is what people want or expect, or that it will lead immediately to practice. In fact, finding it out tends to challenge what a culture knows as well as what it wants to know.

Truly finding it out requires researchers to look in avoided places and in unfamiliar ways. Research has most often been distanced, focused on what Denzin (1989) calls issues, which "have to do with public matters, and institutional structures," as opposed to troubles, which are "personal matters" (p. 18). Researchers do studies, for example, of day care but ignore the lived realities of the many children who, from a very early age, spend most of their waking hours in institutional care. The result is, as Wolf (1995) points out, findings about academic outcomes for children who have been in day care, the academic backgrounds of day care teachers, how everything about day care that can be measured correlates with everything else that can be measured (whether it makes sense or not)—everything about day care except what it is like for children, and adults, to be there day after day, week after week. Questions such as what it means for children to be in institutional care for most of their early life, and what the implications are for society, are ignored.

Why study children? Our answer: To find it out. And to keep finding it out, because if we do not find it out, someone will make it up. In fact, someone probably has already made it up, and what they make up affects children's lives; it affects how children are viewed and what decisions are made about them. Finding it out challenges dominant images. Making it up maintains them.

Themes

Six themes run through this book. The first is the importance of finding it out in context. The "it" we seek to find out is situated, historically, socially, and culturally. Meaning making is situated.

A second, related, theme is the situated nature of the research process—subjects, researchers, the whole endeavor (Wertsch, 1989, p. 15). The researcher—in fact, the research community—is situated historically, socially, and culturally. Many chapters present short reflections by researchers, each exploring a different aspect of the process in terms of her or his own work.

The third theme is the centrality of social interaction. We are interested in what goes on between children, how children function in groups, and how they transact and interact. The research literature on children teems with within-child explanations. Our focus is on "between," not "within."

A fourth theme is the social nature of research. We refer not only to the interactional nature of fieldwork, but, also as important, to the interactions away from the field and one's desk—with colleagues, family, and friends. One does not do research to inform only oneself. One does it to inform others. Informing others should begin early in the process of finding it out and should never stop.

The fifth theme is the centrality of kids, which may seem obvious given the nature of this book. We emphasize that research should keep coming back to the kids. The meanings sought are kids' meanings, not adults'. One difficulty that people who work with children have when they begin to study children is that they focus on the adults' actions toward children; what was intended to be a study of children becomes an evaluation of adults' interactions with children. Adults are unquestionably part of the children's context, but the research is about the kids.

The final theme is the situatedness of methods. We explore methodology extensively in this book, but methods become actualized only in practice. For this reason, we present many detailed examples as well as working researchers' reflections on their work. One can discuss interviewing children, but it is only when one sits down and actually interviews specific children that interviewing becomes a way of generating data. A method is a tool. One can learn much about tools in general, but how and when to use what kind of tool cannot be determined in the absence of a specific context.

An ongoing challenge in writing this book was deciding to what extent it should deal with general issues of doing research and to what extent it should focus only on research with children. In some ways, all research—whether with children, adults, peonies, or quarks—is similar. In other ways, each research study is its own peculiar genre. If stepping in the same river twice is not possible, neither is doing the same research twice. As Comic Brother Dave Mason commented, "You can't do something again. You can do something similar. But you can't do it again."[1]

Our strategy is to direct the reader to treatments of topics on which we cannot improve. We apologize in advance for unwittingly going over what others have done better. We assume that the reader has some background in doing research and in interpretive research in particular. To the extent that we can, we will deal with generic research issues succinctly, pointing out where work with children presents its own challenges. We will discuss in detail perspectives we present that differ in some ways from, or challenge, commonly held ones.

Occasionally, we present lessons of experience from our own fieldwork as short pieces of advice—set off by bullets and in bold print. The short sections contributed by colleagues illustrate key issues in fieldwork with children. Throughout the text are boxes containing lists of references on various topics as well as other useful lists.

The book has three sections. In the first section, we look across the research process, conceptualizing it as a holistic activity. Chapter 1 critiques the dominant research paradigm on children. Chapter 2 presents a view of research as an interpretive science. Chapter 3 explores theory, Chapter 4 examines ethics, and Chapter 5 discusses the role of the researcher. The second section focuses on fieldwork. Chapter 6 examines strategies for generating data, and Chapter 7 addresses the construction of a data record. The final section interrogates the interpretive process and writing—Chapters 8 and 9 respectively. In the conclusion, we struggle to tie everything together.

No one will learn how to do research on children by reading this book. To learn how, one must do it. Someone with a basic grasp of the research endeavor, however, will come away with a stronger sense of the issues involved in trying to understand children's worlds.

This book was written for people who want to find out what the world is like for today's children and how they construct meaning in it. Our focus is on the society in which we live—late 20th century America. Finding it out is not something that one can do about children in general, but rather about specific groups of children in particular contexts.

We fear that the world is becoming a tougher place for children and that this society neither knows enough about children nor appears to want to know enough to help children negotiate that world. A society that avoids knowing about its children has already made an ominous decision about its priorities.

Note

1. I have tried without success to locate the album to reference it. I first heard the line in 1966 from Jim Mudd. As far as I could tell, he knew the album by heart.

1

THE CHILD AS OBJECT

The literature related to young children is filled with reports of studies in which children have been the objects of inquiry. Given the amount of work focused on children, it is surprising how little we know about their lives. Little if any attention is paid to the contexts in which children live. Where are those young ones whose actions change so much from home to school to playground? Where is the understanding of, or even interest in, children's lived experiences?

It would be easy to blame this distanced view on the dominance of quantitative research. Although the prevailing quantitative approaches certainly have contributed to the problem, one must not forget that much of what we think we know about children stems from Piaget's markedly nonquantitative inquiry.

Instead, the distance stems from the dominance of a particular psychological perspective in which researchers see children as either windows onto universal psychological laws or as indicators of treatment effects. In both cases, the children themselves are simply instruments. The quest has not been to understand children but to pursue the lofty academic goals of the absolute universal law and the ultimate treatment.

As windows to universal laws, children, most often examined in laboratories, become raw materials for the construction of theories of development and learning. Although we have come a long way from the bizarre recapitulationism of G. Stanley Hall, who believed that by listening carefully to children one could hear the distant calls of our ancestors (Kliebard, 1986), the quest for universal laws remains alive and well, as is evidenced by the remarkable tenacity of Piagetian theory.

As indicators of treatment effects, children, most often in institutional settings, provide pre- and post-test results. These results are then used to justify or reject some new form of pedagogy or discipline, some new program for teaching math or social skills, or even some new parenting strategy. In this work, children are simply vehicles for measuring outcomes.

In neither case are children, in their here and now, of interest. Children may be used as exhibits to demonstrate the laws or the treatment effects; for example, countless children have been required to pour water from short, fat beakers to long, tall beakers (or is it the other way around?). Who the specific children are, beyond coded demographic characteristics such as age, gender, and race, is immaterial. Their experiences in a particular program or classroom are certainly never sought or considered.

For the purposes of our critique, we have subdivided this dominant psychological perspective into two categories—Piagetian and quantitative. The categories are arbitrary, constructed to facilitate our discussion. They are not intended to be definitive or mutually exclusive.

The Persistence of Piaget

Piagetian theory has had near hegemonic influence on perspectives on young children, particularly in the field of early childhood education, for the past three decades. It continues to exhibit remarkable persistence in the face of a growing body of disconfirming evidence. We will not present this evidence here. Effective critiques have been made elsewhere (e.g., Bruner, 1986, 1990; Bruner & Haste, 1987; Donaldson, 1978; Gelman, 1979; Gelman & Baillargeon, 1983; Hatano & Inagaki, 1986; Inagaki, 1992; Walsh, 1991). We note only that although the work of Piaget and colleagues often has been richly descriptive, it has been singularly inattentive to context or children's experience.

For the most part, Piagetian descriptions have been of children in laboratory settings doing "novel, nonsignificant problems . . . [requiring] coherent justification according to formal logic" (Hatano & Inagaki,

1986, p. 265). The Genevan school has ignored the influence of culture, as it has ignored the influence of what Donaldson (1978) called the child's "human sense," that meaningful understanding of the world the child has constructed through her culturally mediated experience with it. For the Genevans, the child has been a window onto universal laws, laws that operate independently of culture and context. For a perspective that has the reputation for taking an interactivist view of children, its conceptualization of the child is vacuum-like, disconnecting individuals from their heritages.

The Narrowness of Numbers

The bulk of published research on young children has been quantitative (thumb through, for example, the recent *Handbook of Research on the Education of Young Children*, Spodek, 1993). In this country, even Piagetians have tended to be quantitative.

Focused as it is on instrumental measures of difference and outcome, quantitative research relies on entities that are amenable to measurement. As a result, researchers often reduce the complex realities of children's lives to scores on instruments and questionnaires, to counts of individual behaviors, or to behaviors in contrived settings. Readiness for school, for example, has been measured by the number of teeth lost and the ability to identify shapes and colors.

The methodological focus in these studies, then, is on the technical issues of measurement—how well the instruments capture the proxy for the characteristic of interest rather than on how well the proxy captures that characteristic. The theoretical link between the topic of interest and its measured representation often seem to fade into the background in the rush for technical elegance. This ignores the distinction between *precision*—how well the operationalization is being described, in this case by measurement, and *accuracy*—how well the actual phenomenon of interest is being described (King, Keohane, & Verba, 1994). Instead, precision is presented as accuracy, when, more often than not, more precise measures are likely to be less accurate. For example, counting how many times children poke each other is relatively easy, but it will not give an accurate description of aggression in children. A colleague described being flabbergasted when told by a child that a friend was somebody who steps on your shoes in line and pokes you. In adult eyes, poking is aggression; in some children's eyes, it is often a sign of friendship. Human life, in its complexity, simply cannot be pinned down so easily.

Consider the following operationalizations from one issue of *Early Childhood Research Quarterly*: A discussion of friendship defines peer contact as being "within 3 feet of a peer and at least engaged in parallel activity with mutual awareness" (Howes, 1988, p. 24); social problem-solving skills are assessed by showing children a series of pictures and inquiring about hypothetical situations (Holloway & Reichhart-Erickson, 1988); and children's curiosity is analyzed in "four six-minute episodes in a semistructured setting," which were scored in 10-second intervals (Bradbard, Halperin, & Endsley, 1988, p. 95).

We can learn something from such efforts, but what we learn is severely limited by the distance between the operationalization of the construct, which must be narrow to be technically defensible, and the construct as lived by children, which is inherently complex in children's lives. The examples above provide fine measures of something, but those somethings are at best tangential to children's friendships, their ability to interact socially, or their curiosity. Precision-oriented researchers rarely mention the limitations of their efforts, and they talk as though they have actually studied, for example, children's friendship.

Observing children and coming away with nothing but numbers (or worse, standardized numbers) has told us little about the day-to-day interactions of children. It has led us to believe that such interactions indeed can be reduced to computations. Those aspects of children's lives that cannot be readily measured, but that instead must be described in text and *interpreted*, have been ignored or operationalized in very suspect fashion.

Summary

Both approaches described create the illusion that we know more about young children than we actually do. We have systematically, but narrowly, studied children in this country for more than 100 years, dating back to Hall's 1883 publication, "The Content of Children's Minds." Hall himself concluded from his research that "[t]he guardians of the young should strive first of all to keep out of nature's way" (1901, p. 474). It's not clear that we have moved much beyond that prescription. Until we take seriously the charge to study children in context, our knowledge of children will continue to be severely limited. For the rest of this chapter, we struggle with the issue of context.

Context

How does one study children in context? Beginning with a grounding in interpretive research methodology is a first step. We have approached the process of constructing this book with the assumption that the reader will be at least slightly familiar with the general theory and methods of interpretive research. We focus our discussion in a way that is quite simple and commonsensical, yet as complex as everyday life.

To study children in context, we pay close and systematic attention to children in their local contexts—the playground, school, backyard, or after-school program. We attend to the "concrete particulars" (Erickson, 1986) of their lives in these contexts, and we record those particulars in painstaking detail.

In traditional research on children, the context in which the child acts is irrelevant beyond its specification as a variable in a research design. Indeed, the goal is to standardize the context as much as possible, thus the popularity of laboratory or laboratory-like rooms—the contextless context. There, children are supposedly buffered from history and culture. Other, less bufferable factors such as gender, social class, and intelligence are either ignored, as by Piaget, or are dealt with methodologically, for example, by partitioning variance.

The concern for standardization and objectivity has required the researcher to maintain distance between herself and children through strategies such as one-way mirrors and hidden checklists of behavior. Researchers even lie to children about what they are doing so that the data will remain pristine. It is assumed that child activity is exactly as it appears on the adult-perceived surface. No attention is paid to the meaning or underlying motive—the goal is to capture the behavior.

We propose that researchers think of children as living in *specific* settings, with *specific* experiences and life situations. We suggest that researchers spend less time attempting to develop grand theories and more time learning to portray the richness of children's lives across the many contexts in which children find themselves. In this "post-everything" world (Erickson, 1992), grand theories do not carry the weight they once did, or at the very least, there are fewer people willing to carry around that weight.

A growing body of interpretive research focuses on children in context (for a review of studies related to young children, see Walsh, Tobin, & Graue, 1993; see Box 1.1 for a partial list of our favorite individual studies). This trend mirrors the larger research community's effort to broaden its approaches to inquiry. The interpretive record of children's contextualized lives nevertheless remains underdeveloped. There is not enough of it. It is too school focused, and it is very often undercontextualized. We address the second of these concerns briefly before turning to the third, the topic of this chapter.

The majority of the interpretive studies on children have focused on school-related issues or have taken place in school environments. As a result, we have a very incomplete record of vast portions of children's day-to-day experiences. Sociologists and anthropologists have studied children in Little Leagues and on playgrounds (see Fine & Sandstrom, 1988, for examples), but we know much more about children in schools or school-like settings than elsewhere.

Consider, for example, how many children in this society spend large portions of their lives in some form of child care. We suspect that many readers of this book have had their lives driven at some point by the search for and the maintenance of child care. Many children spend 80% or more of their waking weekday lives in child care—in many places, for much of the year, from before the sun comes until well after it sets. For all its pervasive presence in children's lives, try to find thick descriptive accounts of children's experiences when they leave home and enter the child care situation. They are amazingly few, and, at times, discomfiting to read (e.g., Leavitt, 1994; Wolf, 1994). We suspect that the present discourse on child care would be dramatically changed if a body of interpretive studies of child care existed.

The emerging body of interpretive research represents a significant improvement over much of the earlier research on children. We believe, however, that we still have much to learn about studying children in context.

What Is a Context?

Children's contexts have changed dramatically in recent years as social, cultural, and economic factors have modified the resources and

Box 1.1
Interpretive Studies of Children—A Resource

Bennett deMarrais, K. P., Nelson, P., & Baker, J. (1992). Meaning in mud: Yup'ik Eskimo girls at play. *Anthropology and Education Quarterly, 23,* 120-144.

Bissex, G. (1980). *Gnys at wrk: A child learns to write and read.* Cambridge, MA: Harvard University Press.

Boggs, S. T. (1985). *Speaking, relating, and learning: A study of Hawaiian children at home and at school.* Norwood, NJ: Ablex.

Clark, C. D. (1995). *Flights of fancy, leaps of faith: Children's myths in contemporary America.* Chicago: University of Chicago Press.

Corsaro, W. A., & Miller, P. J. (Eds.). (1992). *Interpretive approaches to children's socialization.* San Francisco: Jossey-Bass.

Cox, S. T. (1990). Who the boss? Dynamic tensions in oral storybook reading. *International Journal of Qualitative Studies in Education, 3*(3), 231-252.

D'Amato, J. (1988). "Acting": Hawaiian children's resistance to teachers. *The Elementary School Journal, 88,* 529-544.

Davies, B. (1989). *Frogs and snails and feminist tales.* St Leonards, Australia: Allen & Unwin.

Davies, B. (1993). *Shards of glass: Children reading and writing beyond gendered identities.* Cresskill, NJ: Hampton.

Dyson, A. H. (1993). *Social worlds of children learning to write in an urban primary school.* New York: Teachers College Press.

Fine, M. (1991). *Framing dropouts: Notes on the politics of an urban school.* Albany: State University of New York Press.

Hatch, J. A. (Ed.). (1995). *Qualitative research in early childhood settings.* Westport, CT: Praeger.

Kantor, R., Elgas, P., & Fernie, D. (1989). First the look and then the sound: Creating conversations at group time. *Early Childhood Research Quarterly, 4,* 433-440.

Kelly-Byrne, D. (1989). *A child's play life: An ethnographic study.* New York: Teachers College Press.

Leavitt, R. L. (1994). *Power and emotional in infant-toddler day care.* Albany: State University of New York Press.

Lubeck, S. (1985). *Sandbox society.* Philadelphia: Falmer.

Mayall, B. (Ed.). (1994). *Children's childhoods observed and experienced.* London: Falmer.

Miller, P. (1982). *Amy, Wendy, and Beth: Learning language in South Baltimore.* Austin: University of Texas Press.

Box 1.1
Continued

Polakow, V. (1993). *Lives on the edge: Single mothers and their children in the other America.* Chicago: University of Chicago Press.
Taylor, D. (1991). *Learning denied.* Portsmouth, NH: Heinemann.
Thorne, B. (1993). *Gender play: Girls and boys in school.* New Brunswick, NJ: Rutgers University Press.
Tobin, J. J., Wu, D. Y. H., & Davidson, D. H. (1989). *Preschool in three cultures: Japan, China, and the United States.* New Haven, CT: Yale University Press.
Wolf, S. A., & Heath, S. B. (1992). *The braid of literature: Children's worlds of reading.* Cambridge, MA: Harvard University Press.

---

tools in their lives. Different relationships are available to children now as compared to previous generations—as varied as play-group peers to Barney the Dinosaur—and different knowledge is available to them—from computer savvy to thinking about AIDS.

Children cannot possibly remain untouched by their contexts. Just as their contexts are shaped by their presence, children and their contexts mutually constitute each other. To try to think about children without considering their life situations is to strip children and their actions of meaning. Michael Cole (1996) suggests thinking of contexts in terms of a weaving metaphor:

> An "act in its context" understood in terms of the weaving metaphor requires a *relational* interpretation of mind; objects and contexts arise together as part of a single bio-social-cultural process of development. (p. 136)

This image of the interweaving of object and context provides a situated and complex portrayal of inquiry. Why have we not attended closely to these experiences in very local contexts, in a specific culture, at one point in historical time?

To answer—no, to even consider—this question, we must think of children differently from how we have in the previously dominant research paradigm. Rather than sampling subjects to represent a population, we must be fiercely interested in individuals, particular individuals. The focus of inquiry must become intensely local. If, as Tip O'Neill noted, all politics is local, then certainly daily life is as well. The lens of research must zoom in to a shot of the situated child. Her context is more than an interchangeable backdrop—it is part of the picture, lending life to the image portrayed by the researcher. An example is provided by Cole (1996):

> A large, orange, striped, furry leg with a cat-like paw dangling from the shelf in our child's closet is likely to evoke a different schema, different emotions, and different actions from those evoked by a similar object glimpsed under our hammock in a lean-to in the middle of a Brazilian rain forest. . . . all human behavior must be understood relationally, in relation to "its context" as the expression goes. (pp. 130-131)

What is a context? *A context is a culturally and historically situated place and time, a specific here and now.* It is the unifying link between the analytic categories of macrosociological and microsociological events: The context is the world as realized through interaction and the most immediate frame of reference for mutually engaged actors. "The context may be thought of as a situation and time bounded arena for human activity. It is a unit of culture" (Wentworth, in Cole, 1996, p. 142).

The process of doing interpretation in a cultural-historical framework requires attention to the fit between the local situation within which we have become immersed and the larger picture. A careful analysis is required of the relationship between the local and the larger societal contexts, of the "power/knowledge relations among whatever particular, regional, and contemporary circumstances happen to be present at any given moment" (Fendler & Popkewitz, 1993, p. 24). Some sense, too, is required of our confidence of this relationship. If our focus is socially constructed meaning, then that meaning is shared, at least by those children we study and probably by others like them. Further, that meaning was constructed in contemporary circumstances of which the local context is one example and in which it is located.

We differentiate between the local context, where one conducts one's research, and the larger context, in which the local context is embedded and by which one's research and, ultimately, one's interpretation are framed. A local context is just that, local, right here, right now. It is a physical and social place, a yard or a park or a classroom; it may be even

more localized, a certain work table in a classroom or one climbing structure at a park. Arguing how large a local context can be before it ceases
being local is pointless. The researcher chooses the context, whether a
specific structure in a play area, the play area in the park, or the park
itself. This decision is based on the researcher's interest and resources,
for example, the number of people on a research team and the amount
of time available. We will note that researchers who look too widely risk
losing the chance to look very carefully.

The local context is embedded in many larger nested and overlapping
contexts. The block area is nested within the day care room, which is
nested within the center, which is nested, for example, within the local
day care network, the larger discourse on day care, and a given culture.

More important than the distinction between the local and the larger
context is the relationship between the two. Data records are constructed in and of the local context, but those records cannot be interpreted without reference to their larger milieu. Our emphasis on attending to the specific refers to the process of doing research, to the
systematic observing and listening that constitutes fieldwork as well as
to the broader contexts that comprise the lived experience of our participants. Interpretation must be grounded in the data records constructed in this local process, otherwise it will be thin.

Much interpretive work falls short through failure to connect to the
larger context. Many case studies, in particular, seem to float in a world
of their own. In these works, a researcher conducts a descriptive study
of a single unit, focusing on the individual case (a person, play group,
etc.) in the same way psychological work conceptualizes the individual
person. Where psychological explanations were located within the individual child, the case study locates them within the individual site. No
connection is made beyond the classroom or other walls, no exploration
conducted of the relations among contemporaries, and no links examined concerning community standards and ideals. The case stands
alone, as if in a vacuum. Whatever the benefits of grounded theory (and
we do agree there are benefits), simple uses of it can result in in-
sularity. One cannot explain the here and the now by the here and the
now. Relations among entities in a context and the relations between
data and theory have been underexamined, leaving huge gaps in our
knowledge.

Much of this undercontextualized work relies on the assumption that
individual actions are explainable by an underlying set of beliefs. These

beliefs are contained, formed and framed, within individual heads, untouched by others' ideas, by power relations, or by the cultural-historical forces that shape human thought and action. Although this work is a step beyond the causal analysis of behavior that has dominated much of the research on children, it is small progress to move out of the context-free laboratory to a context-free "natural" setting.

Contexts as Relational

Here and now, place and time, refer to much more than a bounded succession of moments and the intersection of coordinates in space. They are certainly that, but they cannot be reduced to that alone. Our here and now is best thought of as the complex web of personal and temporal interactions that make up everyday life.

A context does not merely contain the child and her actions; contexts are *relational*. They shape and are shaped by individuals, tools, resources, intentions, and ideas in a particular setting, within a particular time. Contexts are not static, to be captured by a series of descriptive variables in a regression equation (Gaskins, Miller, & Corsaro, 1992). Instead, contexts are fluid and dynamic, constantly reconstituting themselves within activity. Contexts are inherently social, reflecting and framing interaction (Wertsch, 1985). Furthermore, contexts are constituted by speakers' and listeners' perceptions (Tsai, 1993). The intentions of actors become part of any context, and those intentions change depending on the actors physically present. The most important facet of any context is the other people who share a particular here and now. Mehan (1980) described the social aspect of context in this way:

> Contexts are not to be equated with the physical surrounding of settings like classrooms, kitchens, and churches; they are constructed by the people present in varying combinations of participants and audience (Erickson & Schultz, 1977; McDermott & Roth, 1978). As McDermott and Roth have put it, contexts are constituted by what people are doing, as well as when and where they are doing it. That is, people in interaction serve as environments for each other. And, ultimately, social contexts consist of mutually ratified and constructed environments. (p. 136)

The emphasis on the social is inherent in the contextual perspective taken here. This social view of children (or any individuals) and context is in contrast to the traditional Western psychological focus on the

private self: The assumption is that "there is some inherently individualistic Self that develops, determined by the universal sense, this
Self is assumed to be ineffable, private" (Bruner, 1986, p. 85). When we
separate consideration of individuals from their contexts (and each
other), we tend to look for all explanations within individuals. Where
else is there to look? A child is having problems in school? It must be the
child. How would it be different if we looked within the context rather
than within the child? How would we define problems and construct
responsibility for action related to children?

Children in Context

If it is important to study people in context, it is particularly important
to study children in context. More often than not, children are placed
into contexts over which they have little control—adults make most
decisions for them. Unlike adults, who can choose to avoid situations
that they find uncomfortable or threatening, children are constantly
challenged to develop competence in settings over which they have very
little control. A child who finds she does not like her kindergarten classroom cannot, like her older sister away at college, "change majors." Furthermore, children rarely are allowed the luxury of refusing participation in research or most other adult-conducted activities; again, adults
are the gatekeepers.

The nature of contemporary children's lives, as they become increasingly institutionalized at school and day care, is such that they are constantly under the watchful eye of adults. Children rarely are given
private places to work and play. Teachers and caregivers are told that
they must be able to see all the children all the time. The boundaries of
children's experiences are patrolled by adults in a way that makes any
researcher-child relationship a strange mix that must be reconciled explicitly within the data collection and analysis process.

This is not to say that children are powerless. Clearly, they resist adult
and other directives (e.g., Skinner, 1989). They are able to invent, within
adult-created contexts, their own subcontexts, which most often remain
invisible to adults but are most visible and salient to children (Corsaro,
1985). Young children, nevertheless, are markedly both more context
dependent and context vulnerable than older children and adults.

Conclusion

Doing research with young children is as complex, rewarding, and messy as living and working with them. It takes a keen eye to their needs, rather than to needs of the research project. It requires attention to the special circumstances that allow children to show us their worlds. In this chapter, we have argued the need for studies that locate children's experience in specific cultural and historical contexts. This approach provides a locally grounded perspective on the experiences of particular individuals that can then be linked to other descriptions. The result of this perspective can be a rich narrative that is at once general and particularistic, broadly focused while thickly descriptive. The interpretive links suggested by the author and the readers must be threaded through the local descriptions of individual children as well as the larger discussions of culture and history.

If interpretive researchers are to take seriously the issue of context, then a number of implications are obvious. First, we need to attend to the larger world of research, including quantitative research. Denzin (personal communication with Daniel Walsh, 1994) described how he was led to his research on Alcoholics Anonymous (AA) by unexplained positive results from quantitative epidemiological studies. Interpretive work filled in the gaps to provide a richer understanding of the process of AA. In addition to using this extant work, we can, as Walsh and colleagues (1993) noted, go beyond it:

> Interpretive research has often been relegated to pilot study status, as though interpretive researchers were merely doing advanced scout work for their positivist colleagues. We argue to the contrary that interpretive inquiry has the potential to allow access to the contextual issues that give meaning to research findings and, in so doing, can provide understandings that allow us to make sense of existing positivist work. (p. 465)

Second, we are going to need to take Theory—that is, theory with a capital T—more seriously. This statement may sound contradictory to our earlier criticism of research aimed at developing grand acultural theory, but our point simply is that one does not go into the field as though one knows nothing about children. Post-Piagetian perspectives (e.g., Inagaki, 1992; Walsh, 1992, 1993), for example, bring to under-

standing children a stress on the importance of culture that is very useful
for interpretive research. For our purposes, activity theory has been particularly helpful as we worked to explore children's lives in context.

We also need to explore the socially constructed positionings that
serve as contexts for children's relations with others. Among the most
important are racial and ethnic identities, gender, and socioeconomic
status. These markers are used by others to frame their interactions with
children in ways that construct who the child is across local contexts.
Thinking about these characteristics as contexts for children's experience could help us understand more about the process of their
growth and development and could move us away from their reification
as determinants of certain outcomes.

Finally, individual research studies need to be seen as part of larger
research programs, both by the individual researcher and by larger
groups of researchers. Connecting individual pieces of interpretive
scholarship to the broader horizon of inquiry is more than the traditional
bow to our intellectual ancestors in a literature review. They must be
linked theoretically, a complex task that requires deep knowledge of the
local context and its data, as well as the terrain of extant research, and
a good grasp of the theories used to frame inquiry. Rather than struggling
to outline the particular contribution of a single slice of work, researchers should highlight how their works add to a growing mosaic of
understanding. We need far more collaborative work, not only with
those we study, as the word *collaborative* has lately come to mean, but
with other researchers. These others include researchers from other disciplines and research methodologies, historians, and sociologists, including our "quantitative" colleagues.

In connecting our work to that of others, we bring the idea of context
full circle. Just as our view of children must be more contextualized, we
recognize that as researchers, we, too, work in context. The rich descriptions that are the hallmark of good interpretive research must be connected to those contexts in which they are embedded—the child within
her setting, the setting within a larger community, the researcher within
her scholarly culture, and ideas within theoretical frameworks. No one
piece should stand alone if we are to hope for a perspective on children
that is as complex as their lives.

In the following chapters, we explore the issue of context as it relates
to research with young children. We look across the research process,

conceptualizing it as a holistic activity. In the rest of Section I, we discuss our notions of research, ethics, theory, and researcher role. In Section II, we examine strategies for generating data and data records. Section III discusses the interpretive process and writing.

2

INTERPRETIVE SCIENCE

No single scientific research method exists. Scientific method encompasses many disparate approaches, as varied as the scientific disciplines themselves. Understanding children well requires combining varied approaches as well as looking for new ones. We begin with a short overview discussion on research, a theory, if you will, of research. The purpose is to situate the approach offered in this book within the larger research context.

Soviet psychologist/physician/neuroscientist Luria (1979) argued for a science that bridges the traditions he referred to as classical and romantic. This need arose as he sought to combine two of his identities, those of research scientist and clinician. As he described it, this synthesis aims to

> view an event from as many perspectives as possible. The eye of science does not probe "a thing," an event isolated from other things or events. Its real object is to see and understand the way a thing or event relates to other things or events. . . . [accomplishing] the classical aim of explaining facts, while not losing the romantic aim of preserving the manifold richness of the subject. (pp. 177-178)

We cannot improve on Luria's insightful eloquence. The goal of working with children should be to explain facts while preserving the

---

AUTHORS' NOTE: Written by Daniel.

manifold richness of their lives. This goal cannot be achieved with a narrowly focused approach.

The research approaches we examine in this book are commonly called qualitative, a term we prefer not to use. A few years back, Erickson proposed the cover term "interpretive" for approaches "alternatively called ethnographic, qualitative, participant observational, case study, symbolic interactionist, phenomenological, constructivist, or interpretive" (1986, p. 119). We, too, favor the term "interpretive." As Erickson noted, it is more inclusive, avoids the nonquantitative connotations that "qualitative" has acquired, and points to the common interest across approaches in "human meaning in social life and in its elucidation and exposition by the researcher" (p. 119).

To think of research as interpretive also reminds one that all research is about interpreting data records and making those interpretations public. We do not find it useful to situate ourselves within the qualitative-versus-quantitative turf battle of the last decade or more. Opposing something inevitably results in defining oneself in oppositional terms—who one is not and what one does not instead of who one is and what one does.

Research in the various sciences has evolved and has gone through many phases. Its goal is the human construction of knowledge based on evidence and argument. Like any human endeavor, it is not beyond morality. Like all else in contemporary life, it and we are moving into a more complicated and less confident "post-everything" era (Erickson, 1992). We are convinced, however, that research is possible and useful, and that finding it out becomes even more important in more complex and less confident times.

We begin by briefly discussing four useful dimensions for conceptualizing research. We caution the reader that the distinctions we make, for example, between face-to-face and distanced research, are not oppositional but instead should be viewed as either end of a continuum. We intend these dimensions to apply to research on human social interaction. Whether they apply, for example, to research in the physical sciences is beyond our expertise.

Proximity

The first dimension is proximity. Here we distinguish between face-to-face and distanced research. The research we describe is basically face-to-face. Studying a particular cluster of children requires face-to-face interaction with them for an extended period of time.

In the research we describe, data records are constructed by the researcher from data that she has collected herself. A more distanced researcher may work on data records that others have collected, for example, data from the NAEP (National Assessment of Educational Progress) or from the SIMS (Second International Mathematics Study). Generally, distanced research requires quantitative analysis and is done at a computer. We are not opposed to distanced research. It can serve an important function.

In the course of fieldwork, one will find that aspects of the data generation process are more face-to-face than others, simply because some children are more accessible than others, or because children are more accessible at certain times and in certain places than others. Any good face-to-face researcher will at times use data that others have collected, for example, census or demographic data, which leads to the first research tip:

- Avoid doing for yourself what others have already done.

Face-to-face research also requires much computer time. We assume that anyone reading this book uses computers at least for word processing, and we encourage readers to use qualitative data analysis packages. People who are not comfortable spending extended periods of time with children, in what are often emotionally and physically demanding circumstances, may want to look into more distanced approaches to doing research.

Duration

The second dimension is duration, or from another perspective, "observation-n" (King et al., 1994). The distinction here is between sampling or "snapshot" research, which looks at many subjects for brief periods one or more times, and field-based research, in which a researcher typically deals with fewer subjects but much more often and for more extended periods. Duration refers to the amount of time actually spent with participants. One might, for example, conduct extended longitudinal research and track individuals from preschool into adulthood (e.g., Schweinhart & Weikart, 1995) and still spend relatively brief periods of time with the subjects, for example, at predetermined intervals, administering questionnaires and conducting interviews.

Another way of looking at this distinction is by addressing the "observation-n" question: How many observations are enough, or, how long does one have to stay in the field? To oversimplify, one can look at many subjects a few times or look at a few subjects many times. The research we describe falls toward the latter end of the continuum.

Description

The third dimension is description. The distinction is between narrative description and measurement description. At the bottom of the qualitative versus quantitative debate is a perceived opposition between these two types of textualization; however, the distinction often is made not between narrative and measurement, but between description and measurement.

Measurement and narrative are both forms of description. For example, a census is a societal description based on measurements. Narrative and measurement are simply two ways researchers describe the world. The good researcher uses the way that makes most sense in the circumstances. It is absurd to argue that one way is essentially preferable to the other, as though the world has a preference for how it is to be described. The researcher faces a multiplicity of complex conceptual structures, many of them superimposed upon or knotted into one another, which are at once strange, irregular, and inexplicit, and which the researcher must contrive somehow first to grasp and then to render (Geertz, 1973, p. 10).

Unfortunately, for some (for many within traditional educational research), measurement is the only way of science. Consider how much research within science in general has been narrative, for example, the amount of time and effort that has gone into classification of plants and animals. Much of the world is not readily measurable, and attempts to make it so have resulted in farfetched operationalizations. As Achen (1977) noted, "To replace the unmeasurable with the unmeaningful is not progress" (p. 806).

A good narrative description is often—to return to an important distinction made in Chapter 1—more accurate than a measurement description, and a good measurement description is often more precise. This does not have to be the case. One can easily imagine inaccurate narratives and imprecise measurements, but in general, the strength of narrative is accuracy, and the strength of measurement is precision. The challenge facing the researcher is to balance the two, because they often entail a trade-off; that is, increased precision often comes at the expense of accuracy, and vice versa. For example, one might attempt to measure children's aggression by counting the number of times they hit each other and come up with very precise measures, assuming the observer is attentive and keeps good records. Such a measure, if it does not distinguish between the aggressive hit and the affectionate playful hit, would be very inaccurate. In fact, what often looks to the adult like aggression between children is not seen that way at all by the children themselves.

Theory

The final dimension involves theory. Is the purpose of the research to build theory or to test theory, or is it somewhere in between?[1] Much of the qualitative-quantitative debate fails to make the distinction between theory building and theory testing; where it does, it gets caught up in arguing which one is better or more important. What is better depends on what one is about and on the state of theory in one's particular area. Building theory in areas where there is no theory or where existing theory is inadequate is very important. Testing theory in areas where a given theory is dominant is likewise important.

One often hears that an important difference between qualitative and quantitative research is that quantitative research begins with hypotheses and qualitative research does not. We argue, instead, that theory-testing research, of whatever kind, begins with expectations or hypotheses—the purpose of theory-testing research is to test the theory, which is very difficult to do without expectations or hypotheses of some kind. If one has a theory, or if one is working within a larger established theoretical framework—for example, Piagetian theory—then generally one should be about testing that theory. To do so requires hypotheses; for example, Piagetian theory predicts that in these circumstances, children this age will act or react this way. One then goes out and tests whether this is indeed the case. The tradition in educational research has been to test hypotheses quantitatively, but that does not have to be the case. Piaget, for example, did not test his hypotheses quantitatively, preferring a more clinical approach to research.

Theory-building research does not begin with hypotheses, at least not in the formal sense. One may well have hunches or guesses, but if one is engaged in building theory, it is because existing theory is inadequate or, to put it another way, because adequate theory does not exist. If one does not have a particular theory or if one is not operating within a specific theoretical framework, then testing hypotheses does not make a lot of sense. A hypothesis should come from a theory, and if one is feeling a little theory-weak, whence the hypothesis? One should be engaged at this point in theory building.

Theory building can, and often should, begin with theory borrowing. One may find oneself with a data record that existing theoretical perspectives do not explain well. For example, Cox (1990a, 1990b) discovered that the theoretical perspective she brought to her study of storybook reading in a kindergarten did not address the conflict she found in her data record, and she sought out a perspective that did.

A curious phenomenon in many disciplines is that theory-testing research is viewed as more important than theory-building work. In other words, if one is not about testing hypotheses, then one is really not doing research. This view is wrong. As Bakan (1967) noted,

> There is nothing wrong with testing hypotheses. It is an important part of the total investigatory enterprise. What I do wish to point out, however, is that by the time the investigatory enterprise has reached the stage of testing hypotheses, most of the important work has been done. (p. 44)

Whether one does face-to-face or distanced, narrative or measurement, or sampling or prolonged research (or anything in between) while trying to build a theory depends on many factors, but it is not useful to argue that one type of research is better for building and another for testing. It all depends on the questions and the context.

Neither end of this dimension, or the previous three, should be seen as being preferred or privileged. The dimensions are not hierarchical. Testing is not superior to building, nor building to testing. Neither testing nor building nor the many points in between are important in themselves. They are important in context; that is, their importance stems from what is needed at a given time and place. We do argue, however, that at this place and time in the study of children, theory building is needed.

SUMMARY

It should be clear that much research on children has been face-to-face as opposed to distanced (face-to-face to the extent that someone was there collecting the test scores); has been of short-term duration, that is, a sampling approach; has used measurement description as opposed to narrative; and has taken the form of theory testing. If one assumes that research should be multidimensional, or at least that the general research program on children should include research from different points along these dimensions, then one must conclude that the view we have of children from the dominant research tradition has been limited.

The research that we talk about in this book can be described best as face-to-face, prolonged, narrative, and theory building. We emphasize this approach because research of this type is a required antidote to the dominant research paradigm and because of our experience as researchers. We are convinced that existing theoretical frameworks for understanding children's interactions are either inadequate or as yet undeveloped; thus, we focus on theory building.

We do not rule out other approaches. No one way of doing research is inherently better than others. The four dimensions should be seen as continuous, and good researchers will move back and forth along the continua. Enhancing face-to-face, prolonged, narrative inquiry with distanced, sampling, and measurement inquiry can strengthen one's work. One can do work that is both face-to-face and distanced, that uses sampling within the context of fieldwork, and that combines narrative and measurement description. One may want to test a theory but not to subject it to the stringent tests appropriate for a well-established theory.

We do not argue that the methods we focus on and describe are better than others. We do argue that they are better for the questions we ask and the contexts we work in, and they are what we do here and now.

To return to the point made at the beginning of the chapter, the goal of finding it out is to be able to explain the facts of contemporary children's lives without losing the "manifold richness" of those lives. The choices of research methods should depend on the context.

In the next chapter, we address the role of theory, both in context and as context.

Note

1. We are indebted to Gary Glen Price for this distinction. We are not sure where he got it.

3

THEORY AS CONTEXT

One is tempted to think that [researchers][1] are often like children playing cowboys; they emulate them in everything but their main work, which is taking care of cows. The main work of scientists is thinking and making discoveries of what was not thought of beforehand. [They] often attempt to "play scientist" by avoiding the main work.

—*David Bakan (1967, p. 44)*

A great deal of interpretive theory in the social sciences is based on thinly described materials. The result has been too much theory and not enough description.

—*Norman Denzin (1989, p. 86)*

In this chapter, we discuss the role and importance of theory. Theory is the context within which researchers work. Researchers build and test theory. They have "extremely extended acquaintances with extremely small matters" (Geertz, 1973, p. 21) to construct explanations that go beyond these small matters.

Researchers go into the field with views about how the world works (explanatory theory). Views about how the world works are very much connected to views about how the world should work (normative theory). Views about how the world should work are connected to views about what is right and wrong (ethical theory). In this chapter, we focus on explanatory theory.

AUTHORS' NOTE: Written by Daniel.

We begin with a general discussion of theory and researcher subjectivity. We then expand an earlier distinction between theory building and theory testing and add a distinction between "big-T" and "little-t" theory. This is followed by a general discussion of theory and children. We conclude with a series of overviews of related theoretical perspectives that we find very useful for studying children.

The Place of Theory

A discomfort that many have with theory is that it is seen as formal and unconnected to real life. The perennial complaint of students in schools of education (where we both labor) is that they get too much theory and not enough practice. In fact, education schools are plagued not by too much theory but by too little. Much of what parades as theory is simply impractical fantasy about how schools should work. Just because something does not work does not make it theory.

A good theory is a coherent narrative that allows one to see some part of the world in a new way. Theory is a map, a guide. It is a wise mentor who says, "You know, if you shift how you're looking at it just a little bit—come try this angle—you'll see it very differently." Theory allows one to see as connected what was unconnected before.

A personal example: When I (Daniel) moved to the University of Illinois from the University of Virginia, I left the Blue Ridge Mountains for the plains of middle Illinois. The area around Urbana-Champaign overwhelmed me with its table-top flatness. Each morning, as I rode my bike into the country south of Urbana, the hopeless flatness of my new home would again impress itself on me. After a few weeks of riding, I learned that the area where I rode was called "Yankee Ridge." My wife and I had a good chuckle about Yankee Ridge. Having lived at the foot of the Blue Ridge Mountains, we could not fathom why anything in middle Illinois would be called a ridge.

About that time, topographical maps I had ordered from the U.S. Geological Survey arrived, and I was startled to see Yankee Ridge clearly visible on the map. The next morning, I went out on my bike, knowing where to look and what to look for, and there it was, right there where it had been for many thousands of years. I could see it. The day before I could not. Now that I have been here more than 7 years, the topography of middle Illinois has become rolling for me, flatter, plainly, than Virginia, or even Beth's Wisconsin, but rolling nevertheless. During the summer, my family and I often go up to the top of Yankee Ridge to watch the sunset. That topographical map served as theory for me. It showed me where to look and what to look for. It gave feature to what had been a featureless landscape of corn and soybean fields. The value of theory is that it allows one to see the previously invisible and to see the previously visible in new ways.

The danger of theory is that it can function like a set of blinders, restricting what one sees and how one sees it. A dominant theory can become hegemonic, dictating not only how to see the world but also what to look at and what not to look at. If one relies completely on a single theoretical perspective, one's inquiry is unlikely to challenge it, for theory not only explains findings but also shapes findings. If, for example, one looks at children from one narrow developmental perspective, one will see only those aspects of children addressed by that perspective.

Researchers operating within hegemonic theoretical perspectives often appear to be working within a hermetically sealed world. Theories have negative as well as positive heuristics (Lakatos, 1977); that is, they not only direct attention, they deflect it. For example, Piagetian theory views young children as egocentric and cognitively limited. As a result, Piagetian researchers not only did not search for evidence to the contrary but also ignored the obvious. Rochel Gelman wrote back in 1979,

> There is so much evidence now coming in about the perspective taking abilities of preschoolers . . . that I find it hard to understand how I or anyone else ever held the belief that preschoolers are egocentric. . . . [T]hey [also] have considerable cognitive abilities. Why, then, has it taken us so long to see them? . . . First, we simply did not look. Indeed, we seemed to choose to ignore facts that were staring us in the face. Consider the case of counting prowess in young children. It is now clear that preschoolers can and do count. . . . I don't remember how many times I saw preschoolers counting in my various experiments before I finally recognized they were indeed able to count, no matter what our theories led us to believe. (p. 901)

Theory, then, is a tool that both supports and constrains research. It provides a perspective on the world, but that perspective can preclude others. Whatever its limitations, however, theory remains a necessary tool, without which research cannot proceed. Like any tool, it should be used wisely. Like any tool, it should be augmented and adjusted when necessary.

All theory is limited; that is, it addresses only a small part of the world. Moving from the local world of fieldwork into the larger world of context often requires theories beyond those used to explain the local. At times, it can be useful to bring in apparently unrelated theory; for example, Beth used Vygotskian theory in her study of readiness (Graue, 1993). Such theories can, in effect, prime the explanatory pump and open up possibilities for building new knowledge in areas where existing theory is inadequate. We argue for a balance between a knowledge of established, well-developed theories and of new, often still-under-construction, theories.

We are troubled by the willingness of some to cut interpretive research adrift from theory. Somehow the notion, "Isn't the whole point that you go out without any theory and kind of let things emerge?" has become part of contemporary research discourse. We would dismiss this as a caricatured misunderstanding except that we frequently hear it from self-described qualitative researchers. The belief that one begins inquiry theory-free is naive empiricism—really very akin to a radical positivism. We state emphatically that studying children in social interaction requires a strong sense of the existing theories on children in social interaction. One cannot address their inadequacies without understanding them.

Grounded Theory

Interpretive research has been strongly influenced by the notion of grounded theory (Glaser, 1967; Glaser & Strauss, 1967; Strauss, 1987). To oversimplify, it refers to the "discovery of theory from data systematically obtained from social research" (Glaser & Strauss, 1967, p. 2). Properly understood, it is an important concept, and it has served as a needed antidote to theory without empirical grounding. Grounded theory does not deny the need for general theory: "The grounded theory style of analysis is based on the premise that theory at various levels of generality is indispensable for deeper knowledge of social phenomena" (Strauss, 1987).

Our view, however, is that the notion has been vulgarized in daily practice into a naive empiricism, as though each researcher goes into the field without theory and there in the amassed data discovers theory, like a jewel hidden in the rubble. Such a view radically individualizes the research process. Theory construction is a social phenomenon. Theory is constructed by the joint efforts of many researchers across many studies. This vulgarized view of grounded theory also restricts the role of interpretive research to theory building—over and over again.

Theory should be empirically grounded, but the strength of that grounding should depend on where one's inquiry lies on the theory-building/theory-testing continuum. A well-established theory, which should be subjected to empirical testing, requires a substantial evidentiary warrant. When one is building a theory, however, one must draw from everywhere—other theories, one's own and others' insights, and empirical evidence. Giving up a potentially productive theory because the evidence is not immediately supportive is unwise. The theory may be inadequate, but it also may be that data generation procedures were weak, data analysis was inadequate, the research site was poorly selected, and so on.

Should theory be grounded? Eventually, it should be well grounded, but theory does not grow on trees, waiting to be plucked by the careful observer. It does not leap out of one's data record. It is constructed, and it has its origins in many places. Theory should be grounded but not stuck.

Subjectivity

One cannot not have theory. Everyone has views about how the world and some of its various parts work. The researcher needs to make these views explicit. Buddy Peshkin has written eloquently about subjectivity and the importance of one's subjectivity in the research process (e.g., 1982, 1988). His discussions on subjectivity focus very much within the researcher, her own personal history, persona, and so on. Exploring one's subjectivity in this way is important, but we argue that more is required, that is, that these views be connected to the larger world of such views.

Obviously, anyone interested in studying children must explore her own views of children and contextualize these culturally and historically. We encourage readers to consider the images of children that they hold dear and to explore the sources of those images. The images one carries are important. The process of finding it out about children begins with these images—what we know and what we think we know about children. Where else could it?

Consider the many metaphors for children that are in the cultural canon: John Locke's tabula rasa, Jean-Jacques Rousseau's noble savage, Friedrich Froebel's flower, Piaget's young scientist. In some Christian traditions, the baptized child who had not yet reached the "age of reason" (typically 7) was seen as embodying the purity and innocence lost by original sin. In Puritan tradition, children were seen in terms of their evil potential; their wills must be bent and tempered. G. Stanley Hall romanticized children as windows onto the voices of human ancestors. Behaviorists saw children as little adults. Piaget saw them as very different from adults. If one goes back across this century and examines the counsel given parents of newborns within this culture, one finds a wide range of recommendations—get them on a feeding schedule, feed them when they are hungry, and so on.

These different views of children are also politically contextualized. The camp whose view of children is in the ascendancy is the camp that controls research and other funding. It is also the camp that will have the most influence on policy and practice. What, for example, the National Association for the Education of Young Children (NAEYC) says about children is of more than just scholarly import. The organization has a sizable stake in its particular view of children, as do we all. A dominant image of children does not simply shape practice with children. The investment in that image promotes practice that develops children in that image.

In exploring subjectivity, then, we emphasize the social nature of research and the researcher as a social self (Bakhtin, 1981). Whatever the researcher discovers about her own personal biases and personal relationships to those with whom she is working, she must also locate herself in the theoretical connections of her field to achieve what Strauss (1987) calls an "informed theoretical sensitivity" (p. 12).

Dominant theories become more than academic explanations. They become reified. They become part of the air a culture breathes, the world it knows, how it thinks, who it is. Bruner (1986) argued that

> theories of human development, once accepted into the prevailing culture, no longer operate simply as descriptions of human nature and its growth.

By their nature, as accepted cultural representations, they, rather, give a
social reality to the processes they seek to explicate and, to a degree, to the
"facts" that they adduce in their support. (p. 134)

He goes on to argue that "the three modern titans of developmental
theory—Freud, Piaget, and Vygotsky—may be constituting the realities
of growth in our culture rather than merely describing them" (p. 136).
Children come into a world and researchers work in a world in which
"stages" and "egos" and "zones of proximal development" have become
cultural realities.

A theme of this book is an emphasis on the between rather than the
within, that is, on linkages and connections. This emphasis refers not
only to the systemic nature of children's social interaction but also to the
systemic nature of the research process. Research is a socially interactive
process. One does not go into the field absent a sense of who children
are, what schools are, what social agencies are, and so on. These perceptions are not merely personal matters. They have been formed in interaction, in one's role as a member of a group that espouses to know something about children, schools, social agencies, and so on.

Beyond, although very connected to, individual subjectivity is shared
subjectivity. Sit, for example, in any Special Interest Group (SIG) meeting at the American Educational Research Association annual meeting
and discover very quickly just how shared perspectives are. Even when
there is disagreement, it is shared disagreement. Asking how "I" see
children in a specific context is not enough. One must also ask how "we"
see children there, and one must ask who are the "we" within whom we
have included our individual "I" and what it means to be included in that
"we." What has one agreed to to become an academic or an early
childhood person or an anthropologist or a feminist and so on? These
are important questions.

Theory and Method

Theory and method are connected, but the temptation to oversimplify
the connection should be avoided. Doing measurement-descriptive research need not doom one to seeing the world only in terms of what can
or cannot be measured any more than doing narrative-descriptive research dooms one to see only that which can be narrated. We remain

sanguine that people can see beyond the margins of the particular research methodology within which they work, despite occasional
evidence to the contrary. Still, how one looks affects what one looks at,
and what one looks at affects how one looks. Both affect how one explains, and how one explains affects what one looks at and how one
looks. Again, the process is not individual. Looking at how I look at what
I look at and how I explain it all is less important than looking at how
"we" do it. Research, like life itself, is a connected endeavor.

Theory Building and Theory Testing

In the following section, we review a distinction made in Chapter 2
and introduce a new distinction. As before, these distinctions are best
understood as being opposite ends of a continuum rather than as
dichotomous.

Research should begin with a question about what is known, both
empirically and theoretically, about what one wishes to study. Others
have been in the field previously, and they have learned about and
thought about the subject. We distinguish between empirical and
theoretical knowledge because it is possible to amass huge amounts of
empirical data and not develop coherent explanations. The Child-Study
movement early in this century is a textbook example (Kliebard, 1986).

Typically one answers the question about what is known by conducting a literature review. The traditional literature review, done before data
generation, makes sense when one is theory testing, that is, when one is
working in an area where there is a well-established theory and when
one's objective is to empirically test the adequacy of that theory. Thus,
back in the heyday of Piagetian theory, a person interested in children's
ability to make inferences would search out what others had discovered
about the topic and then do a study that extended what had been done
previously. Even in this situation, it makes no sense at all to us to stop
reading simply because one has begun data generation. As we show
below, when one is theory building or theory seeking, the literature
review process should be ongoing.

Two general caveats are in order. First, when one is working within
an established theoretical perspective, the temptation can be strong to
look only at research conducted within that theoretical framework—to
keep it in the family. Work challenging the dominant explanation is ignored. Second, when one discovers a coherent narrative running

through a body of research, the temptation can be strong to continue that narrative. The result is a testing process more delicate than it ought be. Efforts to test become instead efforts to confirm.

Finding out what is known in an area where there is no dominant perspective or where the dominant perspective is inadequate is a more complex process. Generally speaking, when one is theory building, the literature review should be ongoing, before, during, and after data generation. Often it is only in the midst of interpretation that one realizes what literature one should be searching. Theory building is much less linear than theory testing, although we believe that theory testing is not and should not be as linear as it often is in practice.

Big-T and Little-t Theory

We find a distinction between upper-case-T (big-T) and lower-case-t (little-t) theory very useful. The distinction is idiosyncratic to us (as far as we know). Big-T theory (Theory) refers to theories that are, or have been, accepted in a field. Big-T theories are familiar. They have been accepted by a critical mass of scholars. They have recognizable names attached—some across disciplines, others within a discipline or a subdiscipline. Big-T theories are public; little-t theories private. Little-t theories (theory) have not achieved acceptance within a field. Many never will. Like earlier distinctions, this too is a continuum, from the well established and well known to the obscure and idiosyncratic.

A short list of big-T theories might include Marxist, Darwinian, Piagetian, grounded, relativity, probability, Vygotskian, social constructionist, Freudian, Bakhtinian, game, number, symbolic interactionist, and so on. In a few minutes, any group of academics could easily generate a very long list of big-T theories.

The influence of a big-T theory can be enormous. As we noted earlier in this chapter, Bruner (1986) argued that big-T theories do not just explain how the world works but also come to constitute what they explain.

Little-t theories also abound, and any group could produce long lists. These lists would, however, be more peculiar to individuals. For example, my uncle's explanation for what is wrong with kids these days may remind you of the explanation one of your relatives favors, but both theories would be little-t. One encounters little-t theories everyday, from friends and neighbors, from Tom after racquetball games, from Jeanie as she cuts one's hair, and from Father Murphy when his sermons begin to wander from the text. Making sense is a universal activity.

Little-t theories should not be dismissed as insignificant. Big-T theories all began as little-t theories. At some point, relativity was no more than a "what if" in the back of Einstein's mind. Darwin kept *On the Origin of Species* in manuscript form for decades (where it stayed little-t) before publishing it and giving it the chance go from little to big. Most of us dream that our little-t theories will become big-T. Recently, Bob Pianta and I (1996) developed the Contextual Systems Model, and we would like very much to see CSM move toward the big-T end of the continuum.

Generally, little-t theories operate within a larger context. My uncle's explanation of what is wrong with kids these day fits somewhere within a larger politically conservative view of the world. The Pianta-Walsh model fits within general systems theory. As researchers attempt to build theory by beginning with a little-t, they must remember that their insights and hunches are contextualized. Hunches do not spring out of thin (or thick) air. They come from somewhere, from experience, one's own or others', from books, from conversations, and from other theories, both big and little t.

Theory and Children

We believe that certain general perspectives are more useful than others for researchers interested in contemporary children. In the discussion below, we address theory useful for understanding the daily interactions of children.

Theory should provide new ways to describe realities that no longer fit the existing explanations. The world that children in this society grow up in today is not the world that those who study them grew up in. Cultural change today is rapid. For example, the first IBM personal computer came out it 1981. It was slow, had 64k on the motherboard, and cost $5,000. Today, one of them sits in my basement, where even my kids will not bother with it.

Culture changes more rapidly than language (Hymes, 1982), which evolves slowly and unpredictably (Rorty, 1989). As a result, today's descriptions are packaged in yesterday's language. It is useful to think of constructing theory as constructing new language. Constructing new language goes beyond making up new terms, something at which academics excel, to finding new ways to talk about something. Good theory produces more than a coherent narrative; it produces a compelling narrative—THAT's what it's like to be a kid today.

For studying children, theory should be dynamic. It should get at process. It should embed children in social practice. Social practice refers to structural elements of society like schooling and child care that do not exist independently of other institutions, most notably economic institutions. For example, child care centers cannot be understood without understanding their role in the larger economy, their relationship to the changing nature of the family, their connection to schooling, and so on.

Finally, theory should be situated, culturally and historically. We argued earlier that at this particular point in history, research on children should be about theory building. Dominant developmental theories are being replaced. Theories that range much wider in their view of development as a social and cultural process are needed—theories that get at the historical child. Theory frozen not so much in time but in timelessness does not serve inquiry well.

The Historical Child

Much of what is known about children comes from efforts to understand the individual child. Ironically, the norm has been to study children in large numbers as a means of understanding individuals. Researchers have been more interested in what individual fifth graders are like than in what fifth grades as social contexts for children are like. Ours is an individually oriented culture with an intellectual tradition that focuses on the "inherently individualistic Self that develops, determined by the universal nature of man, and that it is beyond culture" (Bruner, 1986, p. 85).

Returning to the theme of betweenness, we stress that the goal of research with children should be to understand meaning—what it means, for example, to be in institutional care from an early age, to negotiate the heavily scheduled life of urban middle-class children who move from school to after-school programs to violin to soccer, to live the anxious life of poor children who scurry through urban war zones in which all forms of control have broken down, or to survive the "precariously housed" existence of those children of the poor who teeter on the edge of homelessness. These meanings are shared. These experiences are social.

A movement across the social sciences, drawing on the ideas of Vygotsky, Bruner, and many others, emphasizes people's social nature. As Geertz noted, "Human thought is consummately social—social in its origins, social in its functions, social in its forms, social in its applications" (1973, p. 360). Thus, our emphasis is not on the individual child but on the social child, who is culturally and historically situated in a range of social communities. Our goal is not to look within the child but between children at the interactions and relationships that make up their lives.

As Vygotsky argued, the researcher's quest is not for "the discovery of the eternal child . . . [but for] the historical child" (1934/1987, p. 91). This child is "historical, social, and cultural . . . [and lives] under particular social and historical conditions" (Minick, 1989, p. 162). The historical child exists in real places in real time. She is not a representative sample, somehow timeless and without context.

Getting at what it means to be a kid—my 10-year-old (in 1997) daughter, Scooter, often reminds me, "I'm not a child, I'm a kid"—in today's society requires that we examine how childhood is viewed both by kids and by the larger culture. Societal views of childhood are part of the cultural-historical context within which kids exist. What does it mean to be a kid in a culture with many competing and contradictory views of who kids should be? Childhood is a continual construction. It must be viewed from many angles to be understood and appreciated.

Who Is a Child?

What is childhood? (See Box 1.1.) Both of us teach research methods courses that require fieldwork with children. As students begin to think about their fieldwork, questions about childhood arise: "Are infants children?" "Can we study high school students? Are they still children?" "What about college students? Are they children? What are they?"

Because of our focus on children's interactions, we answer the first question by asking students to study children who are, in fact, interacting. It is increasingly clear that children are able to interact from a very early age. Infant day care places children together from soon after birth. Studies of children can and should begin early. Bruner wrote:

In studying the development of exchange games in infancy . . . I was struck with how quickly and easily a child, once having mastered the manipulation of objects, could enter into a "handing back and forth," handing objects around a circle, exchanging objects for each other. The competence seemed there, as if *ab ovum* [sic]; the performance was what needed some smoothing out. Very young children had something very clearly in mind about what others had in mind, and organized their actions accordingly. I thought of it as the child achieving mastery of one of the precursors of language use: a sense of mutuality in action. (1987, p. 84)

Questions about the end of childhood are more difficult to answer. When does childhood end, and when does it end for whom? How are the ends marked?

Consider the following. In the United States, one can legally buy liquor at the age of 21 and vote and join the military at 18. Typically, one can drive at 16, becomes a "consensual adult" in matters sexual at 17, and can obtain a work permit at 14. The minimum age for marriage varies across states. Insurance companies permit parents to carry children on their insurance policies into their middle twenties if the child is a full-time student.

These legal ages change. A few years back, one could buy liquor in many states at 18. When I was a teenager in Ohio, 18-, 19-, and 20-year-olds could buy "3.2" (alcoholic content) beer, but not regular beer or other alcoholic beverages. The 18-year-olds who died in Vietnam could not vote. In the Middle Ages, the introduction of heavy body armor caused the age of majority (for males) to be moved from 14 to 21— teenagers could not handle the heavy suits of armor. I was recently in Portugal and, noticing vending machines selling beer at the subway stations, asked about the minimum age for purchasing liquor. My host replied that there was none and found it curious that the United States had such a law.

This society has many and varied markers for the end of childhood, some legislated, some not. Our sense is that they reflect an ambiguous underlying cultural view of childhood that is very much dependent on context. Take, for example, three (fictitious) male 19-year-olds who graduate from high school together. One goes to college, lives in the dorm, pledges a fraternity, plays intramural sports, parties on the weekend, and so on. The second attends a community college, gets married and has a pregnant wife, and works nights and weekends at the local Wal-Mart. The third lives at home, works full-time at the local grain elevator, and spends evenings and weekends hanging out with his buddies. Are they all adults? Are one or two still more children than the other(s)?

Less ambiguous is the fact that expressions of societal views of childhood tend to be vague and romantic. Children, are, for example, "the future." When unpacked, these expressions serve as better indicators of the needs of society than of how society actually views children. They are very poor indicators of what kids really think of themselves.

Cultural or societal views are constructs. Once constructs become accepted within a society, they often become reified. Carol Feldman calls the process "ontic dumping"—abstractions become part of culture and take on a reality. Societal views become part of the context within which children live and within which we study them. Consider, for example, readiness, which Beth has spent many years studying (e.g., Graue, 1993). Readiness has become not a way of looking at children and their relation to school but a "thing" that exists within children, that can be measured and established. An idea about childhood has been ontically dumped and has become part of the cultural view of childhood.

It should be clear that as researchers, our access to children is mediated. As enticing as the phrase "through children's eyes" is, we will never see the world through another's, particularly a child's, eyes. Instead, we will see it through multiple layers of experience, theirs and ours, and multiple layers of theory, big-T and little-t. Researchers look less at children directly—or at teachers or politicians or cells—than at socially constructed images of those entities. DNA in a very real sense becomes DNA only when it becomes a building block. Thus, if one views the child as a young scientist, one will tend to see her only when she is acting like a young scientist. The same is true, of course, of any theoretical metaphor.

Theories in Practice

In the following section, we offer brief overviews of theoretical perspectives we have found useful for looking at children. All share an emphasis on the social and the cultural. Our purpose here is simply to prime the reader's theoretical pump.

Social Constructionism[2]

Work from the social constructionist perspective proposes a different way to think about how it is that we come to know things. Ideas about knowledge generation and accumulation are at its foundation; therefore, the assumptions that this work tends to share relate to knowledge. The first assumption is that the accumulation of knowledge, rather than emerging objectively from unbiased observation, is in fact culturally and historically bound. Culture, in terms of the meanings we hold for our experiences, provides a focusing mechanism as we construct knowledge of the world. Our interpretations of what we see and how it relates to other aspects of our experience are framed in terms of the tools we have available, the institutional supports, and the political context in which we act. What it means to know something, what counts as data, and how those data are communicated change over time and from group to group. This proposition is extended to the systematic knowledge-generating practices such as science: Knowledge changes as the tools and ideas we have to probe it evolve over time and across settings. What we know is inextricably bound to when and where we know it: "The objective criteria for identifying such 'behaviors,' 'events,' or 'entities' are shown to be either highly circumscribed by culture, history, or social context or altogether nonexistent" (Gergen, 1985, p. 267).

Second, knowledge, rather than being generated by individuals as they build cognitive models, is seen as a social activity. Knowledge is something that people do together (Gergen, 1985). Geertz (1973) describes the social nature of thought in this way:

> Human thought is consummately social: social in its origins, social in its functions, social in its forms, social in its applications. At base, thinking is a public activity—its natural habitat is the houseyard, the marketplace, and the town square. (p. 360)

From this perspective, knowledge is characterized more as a matter of consensus than verifiability; we agree on what we know rather than uncover a universal reality. Because of its social nature, knowledge maintains communities by providing a shared lexicon that forms the basis of communication and action (Bruffee, 1986). Our conceptions of "what is" hold us together and provide us the currency we need to interact, to make decisions, and to judge the adequacy of our actions and those of others.

The terms we use to depict our understandings of the world are inseparable: knowledge and language are identical from a social constructionist framework. This is a shift from an empiricist notion, in which language comes out of knowledge and physical reality. In its place, the social constructionist proposes that language and knowledge constitute each other: Neither can stand alone. This represents an interpretive approach to the generation of knowledge (Gergen, 1985). The structure of language is tied to what is rendered as knowledge.

The literature on social construction is varied and reflects the foundations of the disciplines in which the work locates itself. Although there is an assumption that social construction means a single thing, it is an amusing example of the construct itself. Social construction is itself socially constructed (Turiel, 1989). The conceptualization is framed by the disciplinary tradition, the language community, and the historical context in which it is used. For the anthropologist, social construction is part and parcel of the academic discipline—it is assumed that meanings vary across cultures because cultures vary. For the psychologist, social construction is a radical turn away from the individualism and empiricism of psychological thought—moving categories to the group level of consideration requires rethinking of the individual characteristic model. For the educator, who works from a hodgepodge of disciplinary traditions, social construction moves attention from individual students to the context in which the student is situated. Unfortunately, no model is provided within education to support that shift.

The thrust of social constructionist thought is to provide broader understandings of commonly used categories or labels by showing discrepancies in their enactment in everyday life. These discrepancies are uncovered through comparison of various kinds: across time, across cases, across settings. In illustrating the differences in conceptualization, the social constructionist pulls attention away from the object/category and focuses on the social processes and resources that provide the foundation for its emerging meaning. Through careful analysis of the underlying assumptions, linguistic markings, and pragmatic implications, common categories are unraveled to illustrate their social nature.

Social constructionist literature can be broadly categorized into two types: theoretical and empirical. The theoretical work deals with the sociology of knowledge in general and the social constructionist perspective in particular. Examination of knowledge generation and use has focused on scientific knowledge as social product (Kuhn, 1970), knowledge as social justification of belief (Rorty, 1979), and the social construction of reality as exemplified in the relationship between sociology of knowledge and the sociology of language (Berger & Luckmann, 1966). This work was the basis of later reviews of social constructionist thought within psychology (Gergen, 1985) and across disciplines (Bruffee, 1986).

The social constructionist prompts us to think of the objects of the world as social accomplishments. "When perceiver and object come together, what is perceived is a function of the interaction between culturally provided categories that the perceiver brings to the interaction and new information about the object that occurs in the interaction" (Mehan, Hertwick, & Meils, 1986, p. 86). This frequently is done without an explicit discussion of the underlying theoretical assumptions that frame their application of the term. The next section proposes a theoretical orientation that is appropriate for exploring socially constructed phenomena, work based on a Vygotskian perspective.

Activity Theory

The goal of interpretive research is to understand the meaning that children construct in their everyday *situated actions*, that is, actions "situated in a cultural setting, and in the mutually interacting intentional states of the participants" (Bruner, 1990, p. 19). Much of the work about children has focused on behavior. A key distinction we would make is between *action* and *behavior*. Action is located within specific cultural and historical practices and time. It is populated by meaning and intentions and is tethered to particular communities and individuals. In contrast, behavior is action stripped of these local characteristics; it is mechanical description without narration. To develop thick descriptions of children's actions, we must go beyond simply detailing what people are doing. Going beyond involves exploring meaning and intention.

A problem that has plagued much research has been the practice of using as one's explanatory factor the very thing that one is trying to explain. Vygotsky (in Kozulin, 1986) was the first to criticize psychology for doing just that—mentalists tried to explain mental activity by mental activity; behaviorists, behavior by behavior. In contrast, Vygotsky argued that psychology should be about explaining human intention by human activity, an idea that later became known as activity theory.[3]

In Vygotsky's activity theory, one begins with "a unit of analysis that includes both the individual and his/her culturally defined environment" (Wertsch, 1979, p. viii). Thus, researchers consider not only the actions of individuals but also the culturally defined context that serves as the origin for these behaviors. This context, called the "activity setting," is seen as

> social institutionally defined settings . . . grounded in a set of assumptions about appropriate roles, goals, and means used by the participants in that setting. . . . [O]ne could say that an activity setting guides the selection of actions and the operational composition of actions, and it determines the functional significance of these actions. (Wertsch, 1985, p. 212)

Individual action is generated out of social interactions and the meanings they create. It is enabled and constrained by the tools and resources (including other individuals) that compose the context. Leont'ev argued forcefully for a perspective on individual action that respected its contextualized nature:

> If we removed human activity from the system of social relationships and social life, it would not exist and would have no structure. With all its varied forms, the human individual's activity is a system in a system of social relations. It does not exist without these relations. . . . It turns out that the activity of separate individuals depends on their place in society, on the conditions that fall to their lot, and on idiosyncratic, individual factors. (1981, p. 47).

For the activity theorist, intention or motive is central. Individuals are motivated to do some things and not others. In much work on children, motivation either has been ignored in favor of developmental bounds or is reduced to external factors such as reward and punishment.

A pair of examples will help to clarify the notion of motive. A kindergarten classroom that Beth observed (Graue, 1993) had a strong emphasis on writing. The teacher, Ms. Carlin, prided herself on the use of what she called writing process, in which children learned to write by writing. In theory, written expression was not limited by knowledge of spelling words; instead, children were encouraged to write their ideas using any notational system they could develop. Over time, children should move into traditional spelling and punctuation as their awareness of print grows. Although she encouraged open expression and invented spelling in a supportive atmosphere, her students focused almost exclusively on spelling words correctly. Attending to surface behavior only, one would conclude that these children were not ready to write. Beth found, however, that the students were using the criteria applied to classroom phonics worksheets to shape their orientation to writing. Rather than being motivated to express themselves in writing, the children wanted to get their writing right, just like the worksheets.

This example illustrates how important it is to carefully look at and listen to young children's actions and ideas. If the teacher's meaning for writing had been taken as that of the children, their meaning would not have been heard or understood. Although there were shared meanings for activities in this classroom, children constructed their own meanings of particular roles and activities in the context of demands and criteria held for different tasks.

This example can be further contextualized by placing it in the larger conflict among the writing process approach to literacy, whole language approaches to reading, and the pervasive efficiency orientation increasingly permeating our schools. One has journals alongside worksheets. This larger contradiction, which affects teachers, parents, and even children, is played out each day in classrooms. Children are caught in the crossfire between these very different theories and practices as adults try to sort out their ideas about how literacy works and how we should measure its development. It is little wonder the children are confused.

A cross-cultural example illustrates how adult motives shape the resources available to children. Gaskins (1990, cited in Gaskins et al., 1992) found that Mayan infants rarely engaged in complex exploratory play because their parents regarded it as unimportant. According to Gaskins, the motivation for encouraging only certain types of play was culturally formed and provided the children with certain types of resources for their development. Here we have a vivid example of local parent-child interactions being culturally and historically contextualized.

Getting at intention and motive is not a simple, straightforward task. As anthropologists are fond of noting, get it indirectly or get very little. Conklin (1954), for example, discovered that the Hanunoo knew the names of 1,400 different plants.[4] He did not learn this all at once by asking people how many plants they could name. Motives are tacit to actors and therefore are not accessible for conscious reflection (Wertsch, 1985). Asking children why they are doing things, explanations they do not give in their normal interactions, is like asking a fish about water. First, you need to explain what water is and remind her that it is there. What the fish then has to say about water may be interesting, but it has as much to do with your question and its setup as it does with the fish's experience with water. To get a sense of motives, it is important to watch children's interactions closely, to listen to children's explanations of their actions, and to be respectful of their voices. It requires the basic methods of interpretive research, plus attention to the connections between the local context and the broader culture and history.

Post-Piagetian Perspectives

This discussion begins with a critique of Piagetian theory, then presents an overview of post-Piagetian perspectives. Both the critique and the overview are brief, and the interested reader is directed to the many authors cited in this section.

Piagetian theory has come under increasing criticism in recent years, particularly for its view of stages and egocentrism, its emphasis on children's incompetence, and its inattention to the cultural and the social.

Stages

The problem with stages as described by Piaget—that is, as all-encompassing, invariant, and universal—is that they have not stood up well under empirical test. Flavell concluded that "human cognitive development is not very 'stage-like,' in the horizontal-structure, high-homogeneity meaning of the term" (1982, p. 17). Gelman and Baillargeon were stronger in their criticism: "[T]here is little evidence to support the idea of major stages in cognitive development of the type described by Piaget" (1983, p. 214). Fischer noted that "unevenness is the rule in development" (1980, p. 510). Echoing Fischer, Gelman and Baillargeon suggested "it could even turn out that there are some cognitive developmental domains wherein there is evidence of stages, and others wherein there is no evidence" (1983, p. 214).

Egocentrism

Piaget himself stopped using the term *egocentrism* in the late 1960s. Unfortunately, many followers did not. In the United States, children are routinely referred to as egocentric. They are not, and so describing them represents a remarkably myopic view of young children. Gelman, quoted earlier, bears repeating here:

> [T]here is so much evidence now coming in about the perspective taking abilities of preschoolers . . . that I find it hard to understand how I or anyone else ever held the belief that preschoolers are egocentric. (1979, p. 901)

Cognitive Competence

Donaldson, in her watershed volume *Children's Minds* (1978), showed convincingly that Piaget underestimated children's cognitive abilities across a number of domains. As many post-Piagetian researchers have shown, children are much more cognitively competent than had been supposed, and older children and adults are much less so.

One is seldom justified in claiming that any individual or group *cannot* do something. What can be concluded is that this individual or this group cannot do this specific task in these circumstances (see Cole, 1996, for excellent examples). As Donaldson argues, Piaget's findings are very stable; that is, children perform Piagetian tasks as Piaget predicted. His claims, or interpretations, however, have not been stable. As has been shown over and over, when tasks logically equivalent to Piaget's are presented to children in meaningful situations, children perform much more competently than predicted by Piaget. Hatano and Inagaki's description is most eloquent:

> [Piaget's] findings will be replicated if we give children novel, nonsignificant problems, and adopt a rigorous criterion for assessing their understanding (for example, stating coherent justifications according to formal logic). What should be emphasized here is that even young children can construct some conceptual knowledge through repeated practice of a procedural skill in a "meaningful" context. (1986, p. 265)

When we give them tasks that are familiar and significant—that make sense to the children—and when we attempt to look carefully at their understanding and adopt sensible criteria for judging their understanding, children appear very competent indeed.

The Cultural and Social

Bruner critiqued the individualism and aculturalism that underlies Western psychology in general and Piaget in particular.

> [The assumption is that] there is some inherently individualistic Self that develops, determined by the universal nature of man, and that it is beyond culture. In some deep sense, this Self is assumed to be ineffable, private. (1986, p. 85)

As Haste commented, from a Piagetian perspective, the young child remains the solitary scientist, "discovering concepts for herself while playing with pebbles on the beach" (1987, p. 170). This focus on the individual has resulted in what Bruner (1986) referred to as "unmediated conceptualism," the assumption that

> the child's growing knowledge of the world is achieved principally by direct encounters with the world rather than mediated through vicarious encounters with it in interacting and negotiating with others. This is the doctrine that the child is going it alone in mastering his knowledge of the world. (p. 85).

Such a view, despite its acceptance, is troublesome. How can it be in this very social world that the child is "going it alone"? Bruner's objections are straightforward: "In the main, we do not construct a reality solely on the basis of private encounters with exemplars of natural states. Most of our approaches to the world are mediated through negotiation with others" (p. 93). As Bruner noted further:

> We need to get away from the image of the child operating entirely on his or her own. I want to look at the development of the child in the context of human interaction. Human knowledge and its acquisition are social—dependent on language, on stored culture, on social modes of transmission. We have not looked at these matters closely enough, given our preoccupation with individual achievement. Now's the time to begin. (quoted in Hall, 1982, p. 63)

Post-Piaget

Hatano and Inagaki (1986) described a post-Piagetian perspective as an attempt at a revival of the Piagetian spirit. Though we have placed greater emphasis on the constraints of eco-social settings and on the domain-specificity of cognitive competence, two of his basic ideas are intact. The first is that human beings have an intrinsic motivation for understanding; the second is that an important part of knowledge acquisition is endogenous, that is, through reflexive abstraction. (p. 265)

This section concludes with a comparison by Inagaki (1992), who differentiated post-Piagetian perspectives from Piagetian ones along three dimensions. First, domain-specific restraints are seen as more significant than domain-general—that is, stage—restraints in the construction of knowledge. Thus, learning and development occur very differently in different areas or domains. Second, the priority of logico-mathematical structures has been abandoned; instead, learning becomes easier as children acquire knowledge relevant to the task at hand. Others have described this as the effect of familiarity—people, including young children, are smarter in familiar situations than in unfamiliar ones, and it is this familiarity or unfamiliarity that will most affect performance. Third, the sociocultural context of development is seen as crucially important.

Systems Theory

The brief discussion of systems theory below is taken from Pianta and Walsh (1996). It gives an overview and introduces some key terms. Other useful descriptions can be found in Ford and Lerner (1992), Boulding (1985), von Bertalanffy (1968), and Sameroff (1983).

General systems theory has a long history in the study of biology and ecology. A system is an organized set of interrelated parts, each of which serves a function in relation to the activity of the whole system. A living or open system is one that exchanges information with the context in which it is embedded and that has self-regulating tendencies (Ford & Ford, 1987). In systems theory, the emphasis is on understanding the actions of parts in relationship to the unit as a whole.

Systems operate at many levels—societies are systems, families are systems, classrooms are systems, group homes are systems, and a child is a system, as is the brain and as are certain behaviors. Systems have subordinate and superordinate relations to one another, with units at the superordinate level having some degree of control or constraint over the activity of the subordinate units. A primary purpose of a system is to regulate the activity of its subordinate units with respect to a particular goal or function. Thus, a classroom system constrains the actions of teachers and students with respect to the goals of the school.

Co-Action

Co-action refers to the premise that the activity of a given system, for example, an after-school program, is not independent. It relies on activity elsewhere, and it affects the activity of other systems. For example, the after-school program is affected by the school where it is located, and it affects the activity of the families of children in the program. This web of systems acts together, and this co-action is organized; that is, it is not random. Thus, to some degree the co-action is patterned and predictable, and there are more or less complex ways in which the organization is present (Greenspan, 1989; Sameroff, 1983).

Unit of Analysis

The unit of analysis is the whole. Behaviors of superordinate systems are used to explain the behavior of subordinate systems. The focus of attention and analysis is at a level higher than the one in which the initial question is framed. For example, to understand the behavior of a child in a group home, one must know something about the home itself, the social services system of which it is a part, and so on. Explanation of individual or small group behaviors requires understanding how that activity relates to the purpose of the larger system.

Differentiation and Integration

Differentiation refers to the fact that over time, in response to internal and external pressures, one of the ways in which systems adapt is by differentiation of subunits. That is, units within the system take on different roles so that the system as a whole can function. Conversely, integration refers to the fact that for the system as a whole to maintain its integrity and identity, differentiated subunits must also be integrated with one another to accomplish the primary function of the system. For example, a school that increases the number of specialists who deal with children with diverse needs becomes increasingly differentiated. A school that instead increases staff in response to demands but brings in more teachers—that is, generalists—becomes more integrated.

Differentiation and integration allow systems to behave efficiently. Systems that are both differentiated and integrated have a much wider variety of ways to adapt to pressure than those in which units are redundant and not connected. An overdifferentiated system is unable to act as a whole; an example is an organization with many specialists who are unable or unwilling to communicate with one another. An overintegrated system is unable to respond to change; for example, a school may increase staff because of an influx of non-English-speaking students, but none of the new faculty members have skills necessary to work with those students.

Systems theory has many similarities to the post-Piagetian perspectives described above. Many of those working in the post-Piagetian tradition take a systemic approach to development. The emphasis on the whole and on connections within and across systems can be very useful as one seeks to understand children in context.

Conclusion

We have attempted in this chapter to explore the relevance of theory to the research process. Theory is the context within which researchers work. It can allow one to see a part of the world in new ways, ways which would not have been considered previously. It also can be a blind spot that prevents one from seeing the obvious, as well as the not-so-obvious. The challenge is to use theory, and not to be used by it.

In the next section, Peggy Miller examines how she has used theory in her work. Her blending of a focus on socialization and an interest in narrative provides a great example of the utility of theory in interpretive inquiry.

Some Personal Reflections
on the Role of Theory in My Work

Peggy J. Miller
University of Illinois at Urbana-Champaign

The big problem that has always interested me is the problem of socialization—how children come to orient themselves within the meaning systems of their culture, how they come to operate in terms of shared beliefs, values, and frameworks for interpreting experience. I've been especially interested in the role that language plays in this process. Caregivers rely heavily on language as they wittingly or unwittingly pass on cultural traditions to the next generation. In learning language, children gain entry to shared meaning systems and access to the tools needed to re-create and transform those systems. Because of the way in which human action has been partitioned for study—culture and society belong to anthropology and sociology, children to psychology and education—it has been difficult to forge a truly integrated conception of socialization, one that slights neither culture nor children. So, one story that I could tell is a quest story, a story about seeking theoretical perspectives that transcend disciplinary division and unite children with contexts.

To take up that story line, however, would be misleading given the task at hand: to offer to novice researchers an example of one researcher's experience. It would be misleading because I had only the vaguest sense of this problem when I began doing research and no clear idea of which theories would be relevant. I did have some strong pretheoretical commitments. I was fascinated by language. I loved to observe, and I believed in the importance of observing children as they interacted with significant others in their ordinary environments. I had some dim apprehension of the holistic nature of lived experience. I believed that developmental psychology and educational practice should be based on research with children from the full variety of social classes and cultural backgrounds.

These commitments did not find especially fertile soil in my graduate program in developmental psychology. When I began doing child language research in graduate school, Chomsky and Piaget were the prevailing theorists. From Chomsky, I learned that language is an innate faculty of the human mind, that all natural languages are highly complex and systematic, and that young children learn language with amazing ease and rapidity even though the speech that they hear is inadequate to the task. From Piaget, I learned that children are active sense-makers who first construct an understanding of the world and then encode that understanding in language. Both of these theorists continue to inform the way I think about children and language—I would not want to get along without them. Neither, however, was especially resonant with my configuration of interests. So, ironically, one of the first (and most abiding) roles that theory has played in my work is to make me aware of the limitations of theory, of the interesting questions that get left out or trivialized. Neither Chomsky nor Piaget had anything to say about the ways in which language is actually used by living people to conduct their everyday affairs. Neither was interested in understanding how the contexts and meanings of language learning varied within and across cultures because both thought that such differences made no difference.

What turned out to be much more productive for me was the insight that I learned from my mentor, Lois Bloom, namely that meaning can be understood only in context. In her landmark study of children's early grammatical development (Bloom, 1970), she devised a method for inferring the meanings of young children's early sentences by examining what they said in relation to what they and their companions were doing at that time in that setting. Although my own work has moved beyond the immediate context to include multiple embedded contexts in an attempt to understand cultural meanings more fully, much of the discipline of my "craft" as a researcher is carryover from my mentor's practice.

This is apparent, for example, in a recent study of narrative practices in middle-class Taiwanese and middle-class European American families. In this project, my students and I studied early socialization through the prism of personal storytelling, a type of narrative discourse in which people re-create past experiences from their own lives (Miller, Fung, & Mintz, 1996). We wanted to understand the kinds of interpretive frameworks that were used in narrating young children's past experiences in these two cultural cases. Which of the children's past experiences were talked about? How were these past experiences interpreted? Our approach was to observe the children talking, listening, and doing in the course of everyday domestic life. We observed them and their families for extended periods of time, recording our observations on audio- and videotapes. We reconstructed in writing what the child said and did in relation to what other people said and did, preserving the temporal sequence of the interactive flow. We checked and rechecked for accuracy.

We then worked from these transcripts to try to understand the storytelling that we saw. We began with the expectation, derived from pilot work, that the Taiwanese families would be more didactic than the European American families in their storytelling practices. With this idea in mind, and with intuitions that developed in the course of the study, we scanned and rescanned the transcripts. We tried to relate what we saw to what we knew about the family and about the caregivers' beliefs and values. Gradually, a set of categories emerged as the outcome of repeated passes through the transcripts and repeated revisions of tentative categories (Bloom, 1974). At some point, we began to feel satisfied that we had captured some regularities in the meanings that the children and caregivers constructed. We saw, for example, that the Taiwanese families were much more likely than their European American counterparts to invoke rules and rule violations when narrating young children's experiences and to structure stories so as to establish the child's transgression as the point of the story. By contrast, the European American families seemed to use personal storytelling as a medium of entertainment and affirmation. We know that there is much more to personal storytelling for the Taiwanese families and for the European American families than this contrast would suggest; that's where our next analysis will begin. In other words, this "result" will give way to another analysis, and, we hope, to a deeper interpretation.

You may be wondering, where is the theory in all of this? What began as a reflection on theory has become a description of method. This exactly parallels my own experience. A theoretical insight about meaning was very closely tied to an approach to studying meaning. Adopting that approach expanded my vision so that I could notice things when I observed that I otherwise would not have seen. Those other things included pretend play, teasing, personal storytelling, and other types of everyday talk. Trying to understand these types of everyday talk led me to Vygotskian theory and to practice theories of language. Vygotskian theory provided a model of socialization that incorporated everyday discourse in a principled way, and practice theories of language offered a corrective to the Vygotskian emphasis on scaffolded interactions. They said, in effect, not to simply look for interactions in which a more experienced storyteller helps an eager and able learner to tell his own story; pay attention to all the ways in which children participate in personal storytelling, such as by overhearing other people's stories or by resisting another person's rendition of one's own experience. The point that I want to stress is that theory and observation have worked hand in hand for me: Theories have enlarged my vision of what to observe, and observations have sent me in search of theories to understand what I see.

Also worth noting is the continuity of the commitments that I brought to research in the first place—commitments to observation, language, everyday contexts, and inclusiveness. These run steadily through my autobiography as a researcher. I still believe that we cannot hope to understand how children become members of a society without watching and listening to children from diverse cultural backgrounds as they go about their daily lives. At present, the theory that is most useful to me is a theory of cultural practices that borrows heavily from Vygotsky and from other practice theories (Goodnow, Miller, & Kessel, 1995; Miller et al., 1996). From the standpoint of practice theory, children create meaning by participating with others in culturally organized routine practices. To understand this process requires careful documentation of which practices are available to children and how they and their companions participate. When the practice—for example, storytelling—is taken as the unit of analysis, it becomes possible to document how children and caregivers negotiate meanings moment by moment and how their mutual participation changes along with the practice. This perspective thus affords greater insight into the actual dynamics of socialization. It also permits a more holistic understanding of the child. When the object of study is the child-participating-in-storytelling, it becomes possible to keep the whole child in view and to see that narrators and listeners are engaged as acting, thinking, feeling, and valuing persons.

There is much more that could be said about the advantages of this theoretical perspective for understanding socialization, but this is not the place for that argument. My point, instead, is this: From my current vantage point, a practice theory of socialization is appealing, at least in part, because it honors my basic commitments and provides an updated and more powerful rationale for a methodological approach that has become second nature to me. Again, there is an intimate relationship between theory and methods, with the influence flowing both ways: Theory steers one to a particular kind of empirical work, and a particular kind of empirical work steers one to compatible theories.

In conclusion, let me make two final comments. Although I have often found myself out of step with prevailing scientific theories, I have rarely encountered a theory of development or socialization that was not useful in some way. This is another way of saying that because every theory has its limitations, one is always better off having several theories at hand in the interest of clear vision. For example, although Chomsky's theory of language was irrelevant in many ways to my interest in how children learn to use language, his emphasis on the species-wide capacity to learn language and his insistence that every natural language is highly complex and systematic led me to doubt widespread claims, apparently supported by research, that poor and minority children were linguistically deprived. Piaget's image of the child as an active constructor of meanings served as a much needed corrective to deterministic or "transmission" theories of socialization. Although I have never written a paper from a psychoanalytic perspective, insights from that tradition have informed my work from time to time. For example, from a psychoanalytic perspective, it is easy to see that one of the parts of practice theory that is woefully underdeveloped is that having to do with the motivational and emotional dimensions of practice, how people become invested in certain practices and how certain kinds of affective stances get created.

Finally, there is still another role that theory has played in my work, a role that stems from the recognition that it is not just social scientists who have theories about the way the world works. I have been interested in folk theories that are implicit in and motivate people's everyday practices. The importance of everyday theories has arisen for me most powerfully when I have observed caregiving practices that were initially incomprehensible to me or struck me as dubious. In other words, these were practices that did not fit within my theories, folk or scientific. For example, when I studied families from the white, working-class community of South Baltimore, I was surprised to see that mothers routinely teased their 2-year-old daughters into speaking up and talking back, even going so far as to goad them into putting up their fists. These mothers also talked about violent death, wife beatings, and child abuse in front of their young children. These practices became intelligible to me only after I listened to the mothers' life histories and their beliefs and values about childrearing. Their own life experiences had taught them that their daughters would grow up in a harsh world and that they would be remiss as parents if they did not "toughen" their daughters and equip them with the skills they would need to survive (Miller & Sperry, 1987). Implicit in these practices is a model about the way the world works, about the nature of children, and about the best ways to raise a strong and mentally healthy child. Clearly, these kinds of theories have to be taken into account if we are to understand socialization more fully.

References

Bloom, L. (1970). *Language development: Form and function in emerging grammars.* Cambridge, MA: MIT Press.

Bloom, L. (1974). The accountability of evidence in studies of child language: Comment on "Everyday preschool interpersonal speech usage: Methodological, developmental, and sociolinguistic studies" by F. F. Schacter, K. Kirschner, B. Klips, M. Friedricks, & K. Sanders. *Monographs of the Society for Research in Child Development, 19*(156).

Goodnow, J. J., Miller, P. J., & Kessel, J. (1995). *Cultural practices as contexts for development.* San Francisco: Jossey-Bass.

Miller, P. J., Fung, H., & Mintz, J. (1996). Self-construction through narrative practices: A Chinese and American comparison of early socialization. *Ethos, 24,* 1-44.

Miller, P. J., & Sperry, L. L. (1987). The socialization of anger and aggression. *Merrill-Palmer Quarterly, 33,* 1-31.

Notes

1. Bakan was talking specifically about psychologists. We have extended this to refer to researchers in general.

2. From Graue (1993).

3. Kozulin (1986) has shown that later Russian psychologists fell into this very trap that Vygotsky criticized by explaining activity by activity.

4. We first came across this example in Spradley (1979).

4

ETHICS: BEING FAIR

Our discussion of ethics in research will be brief. Many excellent resources are available (see Box 4.1). Two books are particularly useful. Joan Sieber's (1992) *Planning Ethically Responsible Research: A Guide for Students and Internal Review Boards* is extensive and detailed. Barbara Stanley and Joan Sieber's edited volume (1992), *Social Research on Children and Adolescents: Ethical Issues*, addresses specific ethical issues encountered by researchers working with children.

Augustine wrote, "Love and do what you will." Our treatment of ethics will, like Augustine, concentrate on the big picture, not on love but on respect. To act ethically is to act the way one acts toward people whom one respects. Bruce Jackson used "Being Fair" as the title for his chapter on ethics in *Fieldwork* (1987). His discussion ends with a variation on the golden rule.

> When you're in doubt about whether an action on your part is ethical or not, a good starting place is to put yourself in the subject's position and consider how you would feel if you learned what that friendly person was really up to. If you'd be annoyed and offended that you were made a sample in a study you didn't want to be part of . . ., don't do those things to others. If you'd feel betrayed because things you said in confidence were made part of a public report, then don't betray confidences—or at least tell people

AUTHORS' NOTE: Written by Daniel.

Box 4.1

Resources

Fine, G. A., & Sandstrom, K. L. (1988). *Knowing children: Participant observation with children*. Newbury Park, CA: Sage. Discussions of ethical issues in sections on preschoolers, preadolescents, and adolescents.

Jackson, B. (1987). Being fair. In *Fieldwork*. Urbana: University of Illinois Press.

Reece, R. D., & Siegel, H. (1986). *Studying people: A primer in the ethics of social research*. Macon, GA: Mercer University Press.

Sieber, Joan E. (1992). *Planning ethically responsible research: A guide for students and internal review boards*. Newbury Park, CA: Sage.

Stanley, B., & Sieber, J. E. (Eds). (1992). *Social research on children and adolescents: Ethical issues*. Newbury Park, CA: Sage.

World Wide Web

Poynter Center for the Study of Ethics. http://www.indiana.edu/poynter/index.html

University of Wales-Bangor. http://www.psych.bangor.ac.uk/deptpsych/ethics/humanresearch.html

University of Wisconsin. http://justzaam.stat.wisc.edu/other/ethics

---

who think they can trust you that you can't keep secrets. Hemingway once defined the good as "what you feel good after." Think how you'll feel later—perhaps how you'll feel if you ever see that person again. If the answer is "not so good," then don't do it. (pp. 278-279)

Ethical behavior is really about attitude—the attitude that one brings into the field and that one brings to one's interpretation. Entering other people's lives is intrusive. It requires permission, permission that goes beyond the kind that comes from consent forms. It is the permission that permeates any respectful relationship between people.

In everyday life, people continually negotiate this permission with others, but adults seldom do it with children. In relationships between adults and children, adults are most often the knowledge holders, the permission granters, and the rule setters. In research with children,

children are the knowledge holders, the permission granters, and the rule setters—for adults. Research with children turns part of the world upside down. The adult researcher who goes to another adult and asks that person to be her teacher is doing something she has done many times before—adults teach other adults all the time. In our culture, children do not teach adults. They may manipulate adults, but they typically do so within a context where the adult is putatively in charge. The researcher who works with children must carefully consider what it means to work in this upside-down world.

She must also learn to live with the reality that she will always be an outsider in that world, and that is how it should be. The researcher who believes that she is being completely accepted is living in the same state of tenuously constructed reality as the teacher who claims to know everything that occurs in his room or the parent who claims the same with her children. No one has total knowledge of another—at best, one approximates. What Geertz said of adults is particularly true of children:

> We cannot live other people's lives, and it is a piece of bad faith to try. We can but listen to what . . . they say about their lives. . . . Whatever sense we have of how things stand with someone else's inner life, we gain through their expressions, not through some magical intrusion into their consciousness. It's all a matter of scratching surfaces. (1986, p. 373)

In Chapter 6, we describe the posture of the researcher as a humble one. One enters the field as though on one's knees, requesting permission to be there. This posture is not merely an entry ploy but a posture that one maintains throughout the entire research. We also list three basic assumptions underlying fieldwork—the kids are smart, they make sense, and they want to have a good life.[1] A humble researcher who respects the kids who host her as smart, sensible, and desirous of a good life will be ethical in her relationship with them.

To enter into research with children with these attitudes and assumptions requires a relationship very different from the traditional relationship between researcher and researched. It is not enough to say that one is treating children the way good researchers have always treated adults. It is not that easy. One cannot simply treat children like adults. They are not adults. One must treat them like children, but in a way that adults normally do not treat children. Therein lies the challenge.

We conclude with a few comments on responsibility, discomfort, and identity.

Responsibility

Researchers entering children's worlds for the first time are often troubled by what may happen if they give up their responsibilities as adults. Fine and Sandstrom (1988) present interesting discussions on the researcher faced with the challenge of responsibility, most often for one of two reasons—a child is in danger of being injured, or children are involved in some sort of illegal or otherwise culpable activity.

Danger of Injury

It is one thing to assert that one would not stand by while a child is being injured, another to make the decision in the field. One of the reasons kids often avoid adults is because of different views of what constitutes dangerous activity. Nor do adults agree among themselves. I have, for example, encountered adults who consider me irresponsible for permitting my daughter to play ice hockey (with boys).

The fact is that what constitutes dangerous behavior depends very much on who is making the judgment, and when. As a culture, we no longer accept rough-and-tumble play in most institutional contexts, yet when I was a child, rough-and-tumble play was common on school playgrounds. Not everyone is happy that it has disappeared. Anthony Pellegrini has long argued for the importance of rough-and-tumble activity (e.g., 1987, 1988) for children's development. Fighting, of course, has become completely unacceptable in schools in this culture. In *Preschool in Three Cultures* (Tobin, Wu, & Davidson, 1989), a Japanese principal explains to Joe Tobin and his colleagues that it is important for children to learn to fight in preschool because they have no siblings at home from whom they can learn.

I find that most often discussions about intervening to prevent injury are unrealistic. Even in a situation where serious injury appears imminent—for example, a child is about to strike another with a sharp object—unless one is right there, paying attention to the right kids (that is, the child on the right with the shovel in the air instead of the child on the left filling the bucket), and unless one has the reflexes and speed of a world-class athlete (which neither of us possesses), stopping the action is unlikely. In the hypothetical world of class discussions, one can dart across the playground and grab the shovel before it strikes a child's skull. In the real world of the playground, getting up and running across a playground takes a little longer than it takes Martin or Mary to reach over and whack a playmate.

Wrongdoing

As for kids involved in wrongdoing, again, who is deciding what constitutes wrongdoing? At what level of wrongdoing is one going to intervene? When children are whispering at nap time? Telling dirty jokes in the corner of the playground? Stealing candy bars from the corner store?

It does seem pointless to me to work for many months or more writing proposals, acquiring funding, and gaining entry and permissions, then to get nervous because kids are "doing things." Did you expect otherwise? Kids do stuff. If they didn't do things that adults don't like, adults wouldn't spend so much time monitoring them. In fact, kids often do stuff to keep adults at a distance—stay away from the climbing structure unless you want to hear fart jokes.

Unless one is only going to study virtuous children in pristine contexts, one is going to see kids doing things of which one may not approve. There may be a point at which one must personally draw the line, in which case one should probably not be studying this particular group of kids, or at least not in this particular context—one does not have to accompany the members of the soccer team on a Friday night trip to the local necking spot to study kids in sports. If one knows anything about a group, which one should, before entering the group, there already should be some sense of what these particular kids do. Bruce Jackson (1987), who worked not with children but with many marginal adults—for example, men on death row—made the following observation.

> You don't have to agree with everything you hear or approve of everything you see when you're doing fieldwork. Like the work done by doctors or lawyers or ministers or accountants, . . . fieldwork involves a suspension of moral evaluation while you're on the job. The fieldworker's task isn't to decide whether or not people should be doing what they do, it's to find out what they do and what it means. . . . If in literature we follow Coleridge's dictum about suspending disbelief, in fieldwork we suspend moral judgment. We don't usually pretend we agree with things with which we don't

agree, but neither do we argue points we might in other circumstances argue or contemn behaviors we might in other circumstances contemn. The point of fieldwork is to learn what people do or think; changing or judging what they do and think is a different task entirely. But if our learning requires us to pretend to believe things we don't believe or say things we don't want to say, we should examine the moral price the present fieldwork is exacting and ask if the trade is really worth the gain. (pp. 266-267)

Discomfort

Being in the field will at times make one uncomfortable—they are telling me things I don't want to hear and showing me things I don't want to see. So too will the process of writing—I'm not sure I want to write this. We caution, however, that being ethical is not the same thing as being comfortable, and being unethical is not the same thing as being uncomfortable. Too often what begin as discussions of research ethics turn into discussions of the discomfort produced by writing less than flattering prose about someone to whom one feels indebted. Unless one restricts fieldwork to very competent saints and heroes, such discomfort is inevitable.

Being ethical is not being fawning. It is one thing to decide to respect another's privacy; it is another to write a dishonest narrative because of fears of causing someone discomfort, although often the discomfort is more one's own than that of the person about whom one writes.

One must respect others' privacy. One must carefully attend to issues of anonymity and confidentiality. If there are areas into which one would rather not go, then one should not go into those areas. "Remember: The first ethical decision you make in research is whether to collect certain kinds of information at all" (Bernard, 1988, p. 216). One has a debt to one's readers, and to oneself, as well as to those with whom one has worked.

Other Ideas on Comfort

Balancing your perceived responsibilities among various groups is one of the biggest issues you will face. It's always been amazing to me (Beth) that people have such strong alliances to a blind body of science or research. Vicious depictions have been crafted by researchers who argue that they are honor bound to share their view of reality with the world, as if their portrait of someone else's misfortune will change lives. Dishonesty is undertaken in data generation and writing so that researchers can get the "real story." Methodological and theoretical issues supersede personal concerns, as if they are separable. Three dimensions of the research act—the interpersonal, methodological, and theoretical—are parts of a whole that play off one another and must be thought of as united.

One question you must address is how much your participants will shape the final form of your work: Will they be invited to read fieldnotes? Will they be invited to amend them? Will they participate in analysis? Will they read or listen to final drafts of reports? The answers to these questions are not simply developmental (rated X, adults only), nor methodological (forbidden or suggested to enhance study validity), nor ethical (of course, participants should/should not see what you're writing about them). They are complex combinations of the interpersonal, methodological, and theoretical. It is never simple and rarely obvious.

One thing my mother taught me is the rule that you don't have to say everything you think. Eventually, I came to understand that as discretion. The concept has been a good one to use when thinking about research. I have transformed it slightly to say, "You don't have to tell everything you know." This rule has come in handy a number of times when I have tried to make decisions about whether to include information that is sensitive to those with whom I work. Typically, it is an example that illustrates a point that I am trying to make—an illustration of relations among individuals or of cultural practices. What seems trivial to me has taken on great import among participants who have asked me not to share the information. The funny thing is that the request not to write about something often has been an example of even more interesting cultural and social rules.[2]

Identity

We end this brief discussion of ethics with a few words on identity as a researcher. Doing research is a highly structured, self-conscious activity. One chooses to do it and, based on it, advances or fails to advance as an academic. Discussions of values in science often ignore the value of the research to the person doing it. It is in the researcher's self-interest to do research. It also should be in the interests of others. Doing research, however, is what researchers do and what they get rewarded for.

> In each case, all you can do (and what you must do) is assess the potential human costs and the potential benefits—to you, personally, and to humanity—through the accumulation of knowledge. Don't hide from the fact that you are interested in your own glory, your own career, your own advancement. It's a safe bet that your colleagues are interested in theirs. (Bernard, 1988, pp. 117-118)

It is not wrong to be self-interested. It is unwise to act as though one is not. The fact that we like what we are doing and that we may actually do some good by doing it does not change the fact that it is in our interest to do it and to do it well. Being ethical requires honesty, to ourselves as well as to others. Robin Lynn Leavitt shows how thorny those ethical issues can be in her discussion of her work with day care providers in the next section.

Webs of Trust and Deception[3]

Robin Lynn Leavitt
Illinois Wesleyan University

How did I find myself researching the lives of our youngest children and their caregivers in infant day care centers? My immersion into the lives of the infants and toddlers and their caregivers emerged over about a 7- to 10-year period. It began, significantly, not as a research project, but with the supervision of university undergraduate practicum students in child psychology. My fieldwork, then, was part of my everyday life; it emerged over time and was not a systematically planned excursion into the world of others. I believe that this ambiguous beginning, from which I gathered the stories for a damning critique of infant-toddler day care (Leavitt, 1994), set the stage for many of the messy ethical dilemmas I encountered. I am not convinced, however, that had I entered the field up front as a researcher, the dilemmas I describe here would have been totally avoided.

Each week, I spent several hours in the field at local day care programs. I was in these programs to observe, support, and evaluate my students, but the activities of the entire classroom were available to me as an integral part of those observations. I saw the day care setting as *public*. To this day, I am conflicted by the possibility that I exploited this situation. The research project emerged as I asked questions about the experiences my students and I encountered, and as I played these experiences against personal beliefs about child caregiving and my graduate education encounter with a variety of philosophical and sociological literature.

What was my first priority? To whom was I most responsible? The students? What would help them learn and grow most? My students experienced the conflict of the contradictions between their university education and real-world activities. How could I support their emerging competencies as caregivers and be responsive to their observations and concerns about working in these day care programs?

What was my responsibility to the caregivers? I didn't approach any agreement of informed consent until years later, when I realized I had the makings of a research project and engaged student assistants in independent studies as observers. Although the caregivers may have been aware of my dual role as researcher/supervisor, they still had little idea of the content of my fieldnotes. The caregivers opened their classrooms to me, unsuspecting of the sense I would make of them. My guilt: that caregivers feel betrayed by the stories I now tell.

And the children? Did I always, as I stated in justifying my critical narrative, consider paramount my responsibility to these other innocents, wholly dependent on adults to meet their physical and emotional needs? Has my work made their voices (or only mine) heard? Has it changed their daily experiences of care?

I vacillated in my stance according to every situation, never completely developing a coherent rationale for any action. The situations below illustrate the conflicts I had negotiating role boundaries at the day care center. They illustrate my concern with respect to my responsibility to the children—an experience I believe common to many participant-observer researchers.

I was observing in the infant room when Rory's mother dropped him off for the day. Rory (17 months) cried as his mother left the room. His crying escalated as he pressed his face to the window in the door. Occasionally, he turned around to look at the two caregivers, who ignored him. Rory's face and eyes were red from the intensity of his distress. While I debated about intervening, a caregiver went and stood over Rory and com-

manded him to calm down. Rory momentarily stopped crying and looked
at the caregiver, I believe in anticipation that she would attend to him.
The caregiver simply stared at him, and he resumed his crying. She told
him again to calm down. Rory continued to cry. The caregiver then
walked away, saying, "Someone take me out of here!" After several
minutes, the center director, having noticed the scene through the windows, entered the room and picked up and held Rory. He quieted immediately. The director stayed with Rory and after a few minutes was able
to interest him in some toys. Still teary-eyed and whimpering, he gradually
responded to her initiations.

The scene with Rory was very painful for me to observe. I was
paralyzed by conflict. Should I have intervened at the moment I observed the caregivers ignoring Rory's distress? A minute or two's
delay might be justified by allowing Rory the opportunity to calm
himself in his own way, as we hope infants will learn to do. The caregivers seemed concerned only that Rory stop crying (his screaming
was hard for all of us to listen to), and not with his felt emotions. This
was a classroom where I did not know the new caregivers well; I was
hesitant to step in and take over by responding to Rory. In the end,
the center director tended to the situation. What if she hadn't? What
was my responsibility to Rory, in the short and long terms? What was
my relationship with the caregivers, my role in that setting? What
were my boundaries as practicum supervisor or researcher (neither
was a well-defined role in the first place)?

Always, it seemed that both the students and I needed to get
along—for our own benefit, as well as on behalf of any future students to be placed in these programs. Establishing cordial relations
with local caregivers in child care programs had been an ongoing
process since I moved to the community and, as a young graduate
student, spent some time working as a caregiver in a local program.
The university was dependent on these programs for practicum sites.
What I realize now is that this interest in maintaining a relationship
with caregivers may have been interpreted on their part as acceptance and agreement with their practices. Indeed, the act of placing students in their rooms may have been reasonably interpreted as
condoning caregiver practices, and thus a deception on my part—
a false premise to my participation and tacit contract with these
caregivers.

Fieldnotes from another day illustrate how my stance vacillated. I
had a long-standing relationship with the caregivers at one center,
having visited over a number of years. My visits generally were informal and relaxed; caregivers regularly engaged me in conversation,

and I felt free to interact with the children. The following describes a recurring dilemma:

> As I entered the infant room, 12-month-old Clarke toddled over to me crying, tears streaming down his face. The caregiver, Nan, was a few feet away, standing, watching over the other five children playing on the carpet. I knelt to talk to Clarke. He reached out his arms to me, still crying. Hoping to both soothe Clarke, *and* model my idea of responsive caregiving for the practicum student, I said to Clarke, "I think you need a hug," and held him. He quieted and clung to me. This was our first meeting—I was a stranger to Clarke. As I held Clarke, Nan matter-of-factly told me he had been crying all morning. She explained that recently he had been at his grandmother's house, where, Nan believed, his grandmother held him all the time. She suggested that this was why he wanted to be held now (implying it was not a legitimate need). She told me she was not going to hold Clarke all day like his grandmother does. (Was she criticizing me for interfering? Was she feeling defensive before an expert?) Continuing to hold Clarke, I simply and inadequately replied, "Oh, I see." (What did I see? That Nan couldn't take the perspective of this toddler? That she couldn't individualize care for Clarke and care for the other children simultaneously? That she had better insight into Clarke's behavior and needs than I, a sometime visitor?) When I left the center an hour later, I put Clarke down, and he began to cry vehemently again, despite my efforts to comfort him. (Now what had I done? By engaging in my own caregiving, had I made the situation worse for both Clarke and Nan, who now had to contend with his renewed crying?) I left feeling wholly unsatisfied and guilty. But I had gotten some good data.

When I eventually wrote up this incident for publication, the caregiver was criticized for emotionally distancing herself from the children. At the time, why didn't I engage Nan in a discussion about the differences in our beliefs? For one reason, I felt it would be disruptive to our relationship, such as it was—a surface but cordial relationship. I was concerned about entering her space as the ivory tower expert, putting her on the defensive and risking our future relationship, that is, her willingness to take practicum students. The reader may wonder why it was so important to maintain this site, given the problematic caregiving. Simply, there were too few sites locally to place students. The faculty in our program agreed, as problematic as these sites were, that students needed to learn to negotiate the real world of early childhood programs. In addition, I'm not sure I had the diplomatic skills to acknowledge the very real challenges of Nan's daily job and engage her in reflection about how to meet them responsively. I didn't know how to bridge the communication distance arising from our different life experiences. I didn't want further discomfort. It was, frankly, easier to take up the issues in the student practicum seminar, behind the caregivers' backs. I rationalized this as helping students negotiate their practicum sites.

The incidents with Rory, Clarke, and Nan begin by telling the tale of the researcher's conflict with respect to children and the boundaries of intervention faced by participant-observers. Yet, before the tale is complete, I see it also as the story of my role negotiation with the caregivers. When I visited these programs, I frequently talked and played with the children. As often, caregivers would engage me in conversation, sometimes about themselves, their lives, their coworkers, and the children and their parents. Most often, I took the role of a neutral listener, only nodding and acknowledging. Occasionally, caregivers would seek my opinion regarding some child care practice. These were not what I would call teachable moments. It seemed that caregivers' questions were more often attempts to have their opinions and practices verified.

For example, one day, at another center, Shirley asked me what I thought about picking up crying babies. I began my response by acknowledging how difficult it is when three or four babies are crying at once and another needs to be fed and yet another needs to be changed and another is about to topple while another is pulling the hair of a nearby infant. I went on to say that I believe in responding, whenever possible, to babies' distress, picking them up as circumstances permitted. I added that, in fact, research shows that responding to babies' cries actually lessens their crying. This said, Shirley responded, "I'd have to be holding babies all day long." I acknowledged that it certainly must seem that way sometimes, thinking to myself, isn't this her job? Shirley went on to assert that holding babies all day long spoils them. Given that students and other caregivers were in the room, the dictates of good manners, and the desire to get along, I decided not to pursue the issue. At the time, I was sure that Shirley really (mistakenly) believed what she said, a common enough belief; now I wonder if her comment wasn't a defensive or face-saving reaction to her inability to meet the demands of multiple crying babies, given the institutional constraints of the child care setting. In the end, I was useless in effecting any change in her understandings or practices on behalf of the infants. And once again, I had data for my research critique.

The stories I have told do not, for the most part, include the caregivers' perspectives, their stories, or their voices. It is not that I believe obtaining their stories would change my critique. I always held the power over the data and their interpretation. My decision to write on behalf of the children put me in opposition to their caregivers. Ultimately, I decided against what might be acceptable to these caregivers (although other caregivers have since resonated to my accounts) in favor of the need for a wider audience to hear the story as I wished to tell it. Yet who is more able to change the lives of the children? I am haunted by wondering if indeed the caregivers should have been my primary audience. I feel compelled, but frustrated and perplexed, by the ethical responsibility to engage caregivers in a fully honest conversation. I am confronted by the challenge of how to engage in dialogue with individuals who see the world through very different lenses.

In my most secret moments of guilt, I consider it my good fortune that my academic appointment ended before the publication of my study, and that I was forced to relocate, though only 50 miles away. I still struggle with my role in the field and the dilemma of how to re-engage caregivers in an honest dialogue about their daily work. How can I now work with them, if they have encountered my published account? Can I show them my fieldnotes and ask, see here, how do you explain this? It was disturbing enough to have a faculty colleague tell me her opinion that I damaged family child care in the area by the accounts emerging from a previous study. Not only are caregivers' perspectives lacking in my interpretations; to the extent that they are theoretically grounded and engage the language of academicians, they are not accessible to caregivers. Although I do not believe we could have worked out a shared interpretation of the fieldnotes, multiple interpretations might have emerged had I been braver, more willing to risk the relationships and access to centers I had established. This would have been more fair not only to the caregivers but also to my readers.

This brief account of the ethical issues emerging during the course of the research project, including the interpretation and publication of data, reflects three overlapping dilemmas. First, *multiple roles competed* for primacy while I was at the field site. I was practicum supervisor, researcher, and child advocate. Second, although my clinical and research purposes (overt and concealed) both required access to the field, these multiple roles made *informed consent* particularly problematic. What should I have told the caregivers about my purposes—initially and ongoing—keeping in mind whether I would still have been able to place practicum students and gather good data? This question was not neatly resolvable, not only because of my conflicting roles but also because of the emerging nature and focus of the project (inherent in and inescapable in interpretive research).

The third dilemma is integrally linked to my inability to achieve a hybrid identity that met my own needs and those of the children and caregivers. *Who is the research for?* The children, on whose behalf I write; the caregivers, who control access and mediate the children's experiences; myself, who must publish or perish; or the public, whom I hope to move? At this time, I still believe my first responsibility was to the children, to tell the stories of their daily experiences, even if at the caregivers' expense. The fact is that the children's experiences were constructed in relation to the caregivers. This is a complexity I attempted to address sympathetically, but my account objectifies the caregivers as a strategy to give primacy to the children's experiences. (The children have names in the published fieldnotes, the caregivers do not.)

My involvement with these ethical dilemmas continues today, 5 years after discontinuing to visit the field sites. Some of my floundering undoubtedly is due to the fact that I was learning and studying research methods and their philosophical groundings as I went along, although even the most experienced and expert researchers are similarly troubled. Moreover, most methodology discussions treat the researcher-researched relationship as *dyadic*, inadequately addressing the competing interests in research projects with multiple participants. My response to these dilemmas therefore seems less theoretically and more practically driven, despite my commitment to critical and feminist research principles, with some regrettable consequences. My research was not just *about* children, but *for* them, which seems to mean it was not for their caregivers. All the same, I maintain that none of my doubts invalidates the credibility of the stories I have told. I am still committed to the truths therein and the need to share them on behalf of the children. I only hope that I haven't closed myself off from the ongoing stories of others as I continue to research the lives of children and their caregivers.

Notes

1. We are indebted to Ray McDermott for these ideas.

2. I would love to be able to give more concrete illustrations, but it doesn't seem appropriate to use examples of examples I haven't used because I was asked in other situations not to share them. Yes, even I am confused, but I don't feel like I am being unethical, just unclear.

3. This paper was supported by an Illinois Wesleyan University Fellows Summer Research Grant.

5

RESEARCHER ROLE
AS CONTEXT

Much of my work in classrooms, as a researcher, has put me in the role of teacher aide. As a former kindergarten teacher, I knew that I would not be able to sit in the back of the classroom taking notes—I was itching to interact with children. A number of issues shaped this decision. I felt that the kinds of understandings I wanted to develop about children and their interactions with teachers might best be shaped by working within a teacher's instructional program. If I listened carefully to how teachers developed curriculum and ideas about children while watching and listening to those children, I might see how a classroom culture was lived by participants. I also felt that I had skills as a teacher that could be beneficial in a classroom and that taking this role might provide some badly needed reciprocity for my teacher-participants. Finally, I think it fulfilled my need to interact with children in a way in which I am familiar. I took this role in a number of settings, across several studies. I thought I was pretty good at it. . . .

But First, Do No Harm: What Not to Do
in Field Research With Children

Matthew was the kind of kid who has always been close to my heart. He often seemed to work on a side road to the classroom show, joining in

AUTHORS' NOTE: Written by Beth.

on the action but often going off on a tangent that took him to a different product or conclusion. Mrs. Harris, the first-grade teacher with whom I was working, more frequently found Matthew to be exasperating than challenging. She valued good workers who followed directions, an important skill in first grade. Matthew was placed in the low reading group, a label that did not bode well for his educational future in a school where being above average was more important than anything else.

I found myself wanting to find ways to help Mrs. Harris see what a creative, intelligent, and curious person Matthew was. I caught glimpses of Matthew stretching classroom activities farther than any of his classmates. I was presented with an opportunity one day during whole class mathematics instruction. The class was working on representing story problems with background pictures and markers. That day, they were doing stories about frogs in a pond. "Three frogs were playing in the sun in the muddy muddy pond. Four more frogs came to play. How many frogs are there all together?" This had been going on for 10 minutes or so, and the children were moving their little chips around mats that showed a pond complete with lily pads.

Walking around the room, I was to watch and help anyone who needed assistance. I spied Matthew looking down at his lap, zipping his fingers along a number line that he had taken out of his desk. He was using the number line instead of moving the chips on and off the mat. I thought that it was a more sophisticated approach to the problem and showed that he was transferring understanding from one medium to another. Maybe this would be the chance to show Matthew in a new light. During a break in the action, I whispered to Mrs. Harris that she might be interested in what Matthew was doing. I waited, hoping that this was a teachable moment for the teacher. How arrogant! Mrs. Harris walked over to Matthew and snatched the number line out of his hands. She told him sternly but quietly that they were working with the markers now and that she did not appreciate him digging around in his desk. She flung the number line on her desk and began work on the next problem. Matthew did not even look up. He gathered his markers and moved them in accord with "Eight frogs were sleeping in the sun. A splashing fish woke up 4 of them and they hopped away. How many frogs were left?"

I later apologized to Matthew and Mrs. Harris. Why? I had violated one of the main rules of being a good teacher aide, that of working within the teacher's system. The context in which I was working, as support staff in Mrs. Harris's classroom, dictated certain rules for inter-action. I had been in this classroom long enough to know that Mrs. Harris needed order in her classroom and following direction was part of keeping order. I had heightened Matthew's status as someone who worked on the fringe by calling Mrs. Harris' attention to his divergent thinking. On the playground, I told Matthew that I was sorry that I had gotten him in trouble with Mrs. Harris and asked him what I should do next time. He very wisely told me that I should remind him to get back to work; that way, he would not get in trouble. Why wasn't I smart enough to figure that out? Mrs. Harris said about the same thing, that Matthew needed help staying with their activities and that I could be a big boost for him in that area.

Relationship and Role as a Context

Our interest in context extends not only to thinking about children within specific historical, social, and political contexts, but also to con-ceptualizing the researcher and her work within context. This context includes not only the physical aspect of doing fieldwork but also condi-tions brought to the project such as personal history, perspectives on research and the topic of the project, and methodological choices made within the project.

We will approach the issues in this chapter from the assumption that understanding comes out of ways of seeing, knowing, and relating. What we can know is inherently linked to how and why we look, as well as how we interact with those around us. For this reason, we will look closely at how researchers come to their work, shaping their actions and interpretations in ways that are not merely a matter of technique.

Distinction Between Collecting and Generating Data

In many descriptions of the research act, the process of amassing in-formation is described as data collection. This notion can be seen along a continuum that describes a way of looking at the world. At one end of this continuum is the view that researchers collect preformed data and then make valid inferences from these pieces of evidence. The key to this kind of work is to have valid and reliable measures so that the repre-sentation of reality is as accurate as possible (within an identifiable margin of error). In addition, there is a concern for the replicability of the research—if methodology is discussed in sufficient detail, other researchers could come to the original conclusions (King et al., 1994). From this perspective, researchers are interchangeable parts in the data collection machine, and our main concerns would be calibrating any researcher/instrument so that he provides unbiased estimates of the phenomenon of interest.

At the other end of the continuum is a much more interactive/generative view of data. The act of research is conceived as nested contexts, including the researcher's perspectives on research, theory, and, in this case, children; the role negotiated with/by the participants; and the relationships that ensue over time. From these contexts, data are generated in a local way that represents their complex and dialectical relations. Data are not "out there" to be collected by objective researchers. Instead, they come out of the researcher's interactions in a local setting, through relationships with participants, and out of interpretations of what is important to the questions of interest. Data to one researcher are noise to another. The key to generating valuable data is to link them interpretively to relevant audiences so that they can understand the data's meaning. It is this position that we will explore in this book.

- The goal of research frames its nature.

As a starting point, the reasons for doing research are framed by disciplinary traditions, funding opportunities, career pressures, fashion, and serendipity, among other things. Individuals are propelled to set up research projects for a variety of reasons that focus attention, define variables, and set up opportunities for seeing things. Research questions situate the researcher in particular ways so that only certain things can be perceived and interpreted. It often seems to be assumed that reality is defined by the results of a given study—we know things because they have the support of empirical research. It might be more sensible to suggest that all that evidence supports is the coherence of the theoretical and empirical history it seeks to validate. It reflects *how* the researcher looks as much as it reflects *what* was seen.

Another way to look at this is that constructs used to organize and theorize research provide contexts that are just as important to the researcher's way of knowing as the physical and social context in which the child lives. These constructs, such as peer relationships, gender, readiness, language competence, and identity, all shape how the researcher sees children and their roles within research.

Barrie Thorne (1993) gives a wonderful example of this in *Gender Play*. Reviewing work on gender differences, she notes that when studies focus on mean differences in behavior, they often fail to attend to the variance within a group, the overlap across groups, and the contextual nature of activity (pp. 57-58). Attention to one time-honored way of knowing (group differences) in research precludes understanding from other perspectives and sets up high likelihoods that particular findings will come to light. For example, if the goal of a project is to explore the trajectory of development, it is difficult to perceive things that are not developmentally oriented. If behavior is seen to be age- rather than context-dependent, it is unlikely that context will be attended to in a way that is very complex.

Researcher perspective situates work in quite particular ways. This is even more personal than theoretical frameworks or disciplinary traditions—it includes personal experience, memory, identity, and our tacit hopes for children and their place in society. Ann Oakley (1994) situates her discussion of this issue within the notion that we have all experienced childhood but that we filter our understandings of it through our adult meanings of the phenomenon:

> Childhood is not only something to be studied, it is something we all hold within us: a set of memories, a collection of ideas. . . . Our own childhoods were lived by us and are variously remembered, though usually not in a linear way. Memories are filtered through the lens of how we have learnt as adults to think of childhood. In studying children, therefore, there is a sense in which we are likely to be studying the child within ourselves. (p. 28)

As researchers, we bring to our work metaphors, images, and hopes for what we think the world is and should be like. With children, these images seem particularly powerful as they shape our views both of our past and of the children in our empirical present. "Adults' perceptions of children are inevitably context-bound, partial and disputed, influenced by their time and place" (Alderson, 1994, p. 49). We see the children in our work through prisms of our memory, romantic images of the ideal child (parent, or teacher), and hopeful emotions for the future.

The particular package of characteristics and experience that we call ourselves are powerful contexts for our inquiry. Barrie Thorne describes how her gender identity and experience were integral parts of her knowing about gender play. She felt closer to the girls because she had been one of them, playing the same gender-typed interactions. The empathy she felt also worked in some ways to obscure her understandings of social relations. She felt she could interpret boys' interactions more clearly because she was more detached. In addition, many of the constructs used to analyze interaction have come more out of the lives of males than of females (1993, p. 26). She used her knowledge of what she called "tugs of memory" to try to revise her field strategies. She attempted to see children's experiences from multiple perspectives—through their varied positions in the social hierarchy of the classroom and through the prism of her memory as a child in the middle of a social system.

- Only certain roles are available
  within a given perspective.

Researcher role could be seen as a combination of the boundaries for interactions developed in the professional community and the individual researcher's expression it (what Eisenhart & Graue [1990] have called role and role identity). The literature on research has developed an array of roles that represent epistemological positions about relations between adults and children and how to uncover cover participants' perspectives. Spradley's notion of participant observer (1979), with its gradations of participation, Corsaro's reactive role (1985), and Mandell's least adult role (1988) all represent ways of thinking about how a researcher needs to position herself in the field. The choice of role should be a theoretically driven decision, at least in part, because it is related to the kinds of understandings the researcher hopes to generate. The role negotiated by a researcher makes some things more prominent in data generation than others, thereby constituting reality in quite specific ways.

If a researcher believes interaction with children will alter child activity and therefore invalidate observations, it is highly unlikely that a participant observer role would be taken. If a researcher presumes that the only way that one can hope to understand children's perspectives is to be a part of their world, the types of roles taken can vary immensely. They include an interactive adult who retains the power and privileges adults typically hold, to what Mandell calls the least adult role, which minimizes adult intervention in child interactions and activity.

An example of how roles shape data and understanding can be seen in my work as a teacher aide. I found that the depth of my fieldnotes varied immensely depending on the time of the day I was narrating. My notes were quite detailed during teacher-directed periods, when I did not have a task—for example, during calendar time in most classrooms. The combination of having my hands free and the routine nature of this period made it easy to get many verbatim quotes and record the script of these classroom interactions. At other times, such as when I was in charge of a learning center and was participating with children in as-signed activities, my notes had a more telegraphic quality, capturing the general essence of interactions. In addition, I was unable to attend to the action at other centers other than to note disruptions or the overall tenor of the group. Does that mean that the notes of group time were more valuable? Not necessarily. The nature of what may have seemed to be the thinner notes was complemented by what Ottenberg (1990) has called *headnotes*, defined as understandings that are not written down but that are carried within the researcher's frame of reference. The under-standings that came out of my interactions with children within instruc-tional settings would not have been available to me if I had been a passive participant.

Because interpretive research comes out of interactions among people, role construction is an ongoing process. Needs of participants shift over time as conditions change, physical demands shift, and relationships build, rupture, and are repaired. Role negotiation occurs repeatedly over the course of a study.

The researcher is not the only person making decisions about position and role. Participants also make and remake these decisions as they come to know more about the situation and realize benefits and difficulties that were not initially apparent. For example, in the fieldwork that was the basis of *Ready for What?* (1993), the role assigned to me in each of three kindergartens was similar, but there were local variations. Al-though I had presented myself in what I thought was the same way, par-ticipants constructed my role to complement the needs of the settings and the strengths they perceived I could offer. At Fulton, I was defined as a paraprofessional with less status than the teacher and was expected to do support work in an efficient and timely manner. At Norwood, I was an expert from the university who was consulted about best educational practices. At Rochester, I was an uninformed but interested outsider who needed to learn about bilingual education in addition to learning about this particular program. The role in that setting felt much like being a student teacher who was learning from everyone in the school. Do these variations in role mean my understandings in each setting were different? Absolutely. But that should be expected because the expectations and interactions in each of these contexts were not the same. Methodologically, the issue centers on knowing about the differences and understanding how they shape the development of data and interpretation.

Nancy Mandell, who initially wanted to be seen as a least adult in all situations, claimed that her role was not specified unidimensionally in all contexts. Instead, she concluded that over time, children and adults expected different things from her depending on the immediate situation—sometimes teachers needed an extra pair of hands to do what Mandell called "dirty work."[1] Taking on those duties did not damage her status with children. She interpreted what she saw as teachers and children with boundaries for behavior that allowed her to meet the needs of both her research project and her participants.

In *Crafting Selves*, Dorrine Kondo (1990) described how her understandings of Japanese identity came out of ongoing negotiation with her participants. It was a dynamic process that represented the shifting power relations and her emerging construction of self:

> At stake in my narrative of emerging order are the constantly contested and shifting boundaries of my identity and the identities of my Japanese relatives, friends, and acquaintances. We participated in each other's lives and sought to make sense of one another. In that attempt to understand, power inevitably came into play as we tried to force each other into appropriately comprehensible categories. This nexus of power and meaning was also creative, the crucible within which we forged our relationship. In turn, our negotiated understandings of one another enabled me to shape the particular problematic that now animates my research. (p. 10)

In a provocative essay, William Hart (1994) criticizes technical approaches to knowing children that focus all attention on methodological tools for gathering information. He contrasts child study method, which highlights the science of child observation, with deep relationships with children that build understanding at the level of personal interaction:

The call to study children—"so as to understand your own child better"—is a pretense that you can get such understanding on the cheap, without you having to do anything about yourself and your own relationship with the child. . . . If you can't see in what way the obstacles to understanding children lie within ourselves and are first and foremost PERSONAL, you are apt to think of them as being TECHNICAL—and therefore to look to a technical solution to get you off the hook. But then the whole direction of child study is away from the kinds of understanding children which we have as particular men and women, towards the kinds of understanding which we have by courtesy of technique. It doesn't seek to build on your or my personal knowledge of children but to replace it with something else. (pp. 13-14).

Hart's caution is an important one, and one that we come up against each time we teach courses in qualitative methods of studying children. Students often ask us about the "right way" to do this kind of research, and we meet much frustration when we cannot give them a recipe for the perfect study. The singular focus on methodology—on proper observation techniques, valid fieldnotes, unbiased interview questions, and reliable coding—is seductive. It allows researchers to lull themselves into thinking that they can get it right by being a technician rather than a caring person who has responsibilities to her participants. As with everything else, the question of whether something is good methodologically will be met with the gloriously fuzzy answer, "It depends—on the context." The personal dimension of being a researcher should not be overlooked or underestimated if you hope to keep your work in context.

- The type of relationship that might develop is
  constrained by the role negotiated.

Interactions with participants, whether they are adults or children, are framed in part by the tacit role enacted by the researcher. The types of interactions and the kinds of emotional bonds forged are linked in subtle but substantial ways to the roles undertaken in a study. For example, one-shot, scripted interview protocols do not provide the opportunity to explore a child's perspective in depth at either a single point in time or across time. There is no time to develop the understanding that emerges from ongoing give and take.

Aligning oneself with an authority figure—as an aide or other caregiver—sets up particular expectations for interactions. If children expect that you intervene in disputes and stop behavior that is against the rules, they will be less likely to do those things in your presence. Some researchers have suggested that it is necessary to suspend the power differences between children and researchers, especially if the work is focused on peer culture.

The arguments for and against this stance are framed in terms of perspectives on the nature of the differences between adults and children. Are they physical realities, or are they merely socially constructed categories that are malleable if we hope to change relations? Are the maturational differences between adults and children, with an assumption of increasing sophistication and complexity, permeable or inseparable boundaries?

We believe that the heart of these arguments is the meaning of these differences—that they need to take into account the meanings of differences in power between adults and children. These differences certainly should be minimized if we hope to have respectful, complex, and responsive accounts of children's experiences. Our assumptions of immaturity and our underestimations of children's abilities have not furthered our understandings of them, but pretending that they do not exist in the hope of getting the juiciest data possible may not be the best approach either.

Adults are never *full* participants in the lives of those whom they research. This border is even more impermeable with children: Adults cannot put aside all markers of difference and become full participants in the lives of children. As a researcher, you are there for a particular purpose, and you will leave when that purpose has been accomplished. You dip in and out of life at will, for primarily empirical reasons. Your life is *not* the same as theirs. A good example is that adults can choose to take on a child role, choosing to disregard the expectations of adults in social situations and taking cues instead from children. Children cannot make the equivalent role switch, and probably not for the developmental reasons that would usually be cited in psychological research. In most contexts in contemporary society, the role of adult is not available to children, and therefore the power available to adults to select a role a position is quite different from that of children.

The boundaries between children and adults are much more elastic than many researchers seem to think. Children are capable of sharing their experiences with adults, and adults are capable of understanding those experiences, to an important extent, if they make wise choices about their work and relations with children. The notion of elasticity is an important one. Although total separation between adult and child worlds is not desirable, there are salient limits to the degree to which we can access children's lives and worlds. It is just as disrespectful to figure that children will not notice these boundaries if we are skillful field-workers as to assume that these boundaries are developmentally and irrevocably imposed.

Interactions Between Children's Contexts and Researcher Knowing

The child's context constitutes reality in a dynamic and dualistic manner. It shapes the opportunities and expectations for interaction experienced by the child. Who a child is is different on the school bus from in reading group and is different still at the kitchen table. The parameters for behavior, the level and type of interaction between adults and children, and the amount of freedom the child has to define her own activity are contextually generated and negotiated. Berry Mayall (1994) elaborates on this point in her discussion of the differences between adults and children:

> The critical and distinctive characteristics of the subgroup children's interactions with both other people and with daily settings depend not so much on their absolute powerlessness vis-à-vis adults, but on the precise nature of the power relationship between the children and the adults in any given setting. Thus I want to suggest that the level of their powerlessness varies according to how the adults in the specific social settings conceptualize children and childhood. Childhood, it is argued here, is not experienced as one set of relationships; rather its character in time and place is modified by adult understandings in those times and places of what children are, and what adult relationships with children are proper. (p. 116)

This brings up a second critical point. How a researcher knows a child is also a contextual entity. It is defined in complementary parts by how adults in the setting define children and their activity (parents, teachers, caregivers, etc.) and by how the researcher conceptualizes and comes to know the child. Without attention to how this dance of meaning is played out in a locally specific manner, data generated about children are brittle and lifeless. A researcher must nest her understanding in multiple contexts, purposefully trying to learn from where her knowing comes.

A personal example might clarify this point. I recently spent 7 weeks in Munich with my then 22-month-old son, Sam. We spent much of our time on playgrounds populated by other children and their mothers and caregivers. After a few visits, I began to think that German children did not seem to fight much over possessions—there was some shouting of "Mein," but things seemed to flow relatively smoothly. I easily could have come to the conclusion that the stages of development were different in Germany, with less egocentrism and possessiveness than in the United States. I also noticed that I was frequently the only adult playing with a child on the playground—the rest sat on benches and talked, read, or relaxed alone. Children managed their activity on their own for the most part unless there was some kind of danger.

How did these observations intersect, and how did my knowing have a particular situated quality? First, I seriously doubt that I would have had the opportunity to develop the mini-theories if I had not been the mother of a child in need of recreation. My son gave me the opportunity to be on the Spielplatz. Further, because he was constructed by me as a certain kind of child—a U.S. almost-2-year-old (with all the emotional volatility built in)—I had certain expectations of how he and I should be. I should play with him and make sure that he did not take other people's things. I should reinforce sharing by reminding him to share when other people wanted to use his things (but he should not use theirs—rather curious). I brought these cultural assumptions as a mother to a new context and found that they did not work—that my behavior restricted his interactions with others and provoked many power struggles. I slowly learned that things brought to the Spielplatz became materials for group use that were gathered up and brought home by the bringers at the end of the visit. I also learned to sit and watch as Sam wandered around the playground. These knowings had a reflective quality because I was also an educational researcher who has done work on how parents learn their role and was also thinking about issues of studying children. My knowing came out of a specific confluence of time, space, and experience that shaped what I attended to and how I interpreted things.

Reciprocity in Work With Children

Building on the discussion on ethics in the previous chapter, the idea of researcher role includes relational aspects that make us answerable to our participants. What are our responsibilities in work with children? At the most basic level, we have a responsibility to be ethical in our dealings with them. We should do our best to ensure that no harm comes of our interactions with them (not an aspect of my interaction with Matthew). Beyond that, what do we owe children who participate in our research? To what extent do we do research *for* children, advancing our participants' knowledge of their social positions? Some have suggested that researching children is done more for our academic selves than for those with whom we work (Oakley, 1994). Can we extend the values of perspectives such as critical ethnography to groups of people who have different rights and understandings than we do? Can a researcher really do collaborative work with young children? Berry Mayall (1994) suggests some possibilities and constraints in her discussion of equalizing the power relations with children:

> Although the researcher's relationship with the researched in general is conducted with more power on the researcher's side, both during data collection and in the analysis and use of data, it is possible to redress that balance somewhat, through enabling data-collection methods and through including the researched in the later analysis and presentation phases. Women's research with and for women has provided examples. But whatever data-collection method is used, from pure ethnography to structured questionnaires, power lies with the researcher to interpret what she sees and hears. These issues are much more problematic where children are the researched. However much one may involve children in considering data, the presentation of it is likely to require analyses and interpretations, at least for some purposes, which do demand different knowledge than that generally available to children, in order to explicate children's social status and structural positioning. So there is an important respect in which research cannot be wholly for the children researched, even where the researcher puts aside her own career (writing academic papers). (pp. 11-12)

In many ways, these questions come to the same resolution as that on which questions of participation seemed to converge—that the boundaries between adult and child experience are elastic but not boundlessly so. The agendas of adults and children are different (particularly those of academics interested in children and the children themselves): Their needs for information and the actions they can take concerning this information are defined by their social status and positions. That insight does not mean, however, that we have no responsibility to our participants. It calls for consideration of other forms of reciprocity than baking cookies for a classroom of children with whom you have worked or taking individuals out to a movie. We must consider how a particular context constitutes a specific set of needs and expectations as well as how it provides us with ways that we can try to both help children's voices be heard by the greater community and help children learn about themselves. As with all good interpretive work, it might require periodically that we put the needs of participants ahead of our own. We must keep in mind that collaboration should be beneficial for both ourselves and our participants; otherwise, it is not true collaboration.

SUMMARY

In this chapter, we have tried to heighten attention to the nested manner in which we conduct research. We have pointed out how researchers bring experience, theory, and method to their work in ways that shape what they can see. Furthermore, we have discussed the array of roles that can be taken in qualitative work with children, relating it to the perspective taken in a particular project. We have examined the connections between relations developed with children and the kinds of interpretations that can be generated, and we have explored the possibilities for collaboration in our work with children. These issues come alive in the next section, with David Fernie and Rebecca Kantor's discussion of their long-term group research in a campus child care center.

Our Reflection on a Collaborative Research Experience

David E. Fernie
Rebecca Kantor
The Ohio State University

Beginning in 1987, we have been researching and writing about daily life in a single preschool setting. Our collaborative preschool ethnography used numerous linked analyses, shaped and conducted within our research team, to reveal how aspects of a "lifeworld" were created in this setting. In our writings, we typically have emphasized the formal descriptions of our methods and findings related to aspects of school culture and peer culture within this setting; here, we focus on the more personal and social aspects of this work. Specifically, we have been asked to reflect on how we have managed to create a long-term research collaboration—the conditions that created and then supported such collaboration, as well as the challenges and issues we have faced.

When we met in 1985, we had in common that we were two untenured assistant professors of early childhood education (but in two different departments at Ohio State). In the Family Relations and Human Development Department of the College of Human Ecology, Rebecca had both the typical assistant professor responsibilities (including creating a tenureable research record) and, for a professor, the unusual part-time lead teacher responsibilities in the department's laboratory school, the A. Sophie Rogers Laboratory for Child and Family Studies. This professor/practitioner configuration was the department's strategy both to introduce more constructivist-oriented programming and to create a more visible research program in the lab. The lab school had its own dual identity—the traditional tension between the goal of quality programming and the need to meet experimental conditions as a research site.

Within the Educational Theory and Practice Department in the College of Education, David (and Elisa Klein, a colleague who began the ethnography with us but moved to another university) faced another set of diverse and separate responsibilities, including conducting research, teaching, and supervising and mentoring undergraduate and graduate students at the largest land grant institution in the country. In addition, Ohio State's location and high status in the Columbus community intensified the press we felt for public service and involvement in local educational programs and reform efforts. At this early point in our history, our major concern was how to meet these multiple demands and create a professional life with integrity and a degree of sanity. It is also important to our history that we had both recently relocated to Columbus and were both new parents, each with a 2-year-old boy.

Our early conversations revealed our mutual strong interest in understanding preschool classrooms like those we had experienced as teachers. Each of us, trained in early childhood's prevailing tradition of individually oriented child development knowledge, previously had conducted research that took us away from the messiness and excitement of classroom life to conduct more controlled clinical interview, structured observational, and task-oriented research, typical of the time. Another part of our common ground, then, was a mutual dissatisfaction with doing those kinds of research and a search for a method that would allow us to understand and describe the classroom as a social setting. This symmetry in our professional and personal lives, though serendipitous, was very significant. Looking back, we see that being "in the same place at the same time" was key to our creation of a long-term, co-equal version of collaboration.

The next significant turn in our history was the chance meeting of two people who became our mentors throughout this project—Judith Green and Bill Corsaro. Judith, a leader in educational ethnography with a focus on classroom discourse, was also on the Ohio State faculty. She was instrumental in creating a community of scholars on campus who were interested in issues of language and culture, and she invited us into that group. We spent long, animated hours in discussion with Judith and others, discovering the potential of a sociocultural-ethnographic perspective on classroom life. Judith's generous mentorship, critical initially in helping us to shift to a new paradigm, continued (and continues) throughout the project in many ways.

As part of her campus leadership in qualitative inquiry, Judith arranged for childhood sociologist Bill Corsaro to conduct a 3-day research retreat for the College of Education faculty (which Rebecca also attended). Fortuitously, this opportunity to hear an exciting, in-depth description of an early childhood ethnography coincided with our own emergent plans to launch a similar venture. Beginning with interactions at this retreat, we struck up a relationship with Bill that we continued to rely on over the years of the project.

Bill and Judith presented two models of professional success in conducting long-term educational ethnography, countering negative messages we were receiving from others. Some well-meaning colleagues had counseled us against beginning an ethnographic project because of the long lead time before the project would yield publications. Other colleagues expressed the prejudice, common at that time, that qualitative inquiry was not rigorous or meaningful research. As untenured professors, we worried about the relative scarcity of outlets publishing educational ethnography 10 years ago. Bill and Judith's encouragement, their generosity, their example, and their excitement about their own work all were critical in helping us to override our concerns and anxieties and to decide to launch a new, long-term research project.

Simultaneously with our transition to a new mode of inquiry, Rebecca and the other teachers in the lab school were conducting curricular inquiry within the lab school classrooms and working on how to improve their mentoring of undergraduate preschool teachers. At the time, they were articulating their classroom philosophy and practice in a formal curriculum document to share with their undergraduate practicum students. As part of documenting the curriculum, the teachers were struggling to find the perspective and language to better capture and make visible to students the more social aspects of a curriculum—what happens "between the heads" as opposed to "within the heads" of children and teachers as they engage in curricular experience. In retrospect, both the researchers and the teachers were searching for the framework that we now call "social constructionism." A basic premise of social constructionism is that people construct meanings in face-to-face interactions that are situated in specific cultural contexts; thus, "knowledge is not something people possess somewhere in their heads, but rather, something people do together" (Gergen, 1985, p. 270). This perspective holds many meanings for us because we find it useful in describing both how children come to understand their worlds and how researchers in collaboration come to understand children.

Practically, the dual expectation that Rebecca would conduct significant research and at the same time lead the development of the lab school made studying this classroom logical, as did the natural access that we would have to the setting. Retrospectively, however, we can see the additional advantages of the correspondence between the lab school goals and ethnographic research methods. The words "evolving," "inductive," and "transformative" apply to the inquiry processes of both interpretive researchers and teachers reflecting on practice. The search for patterns within everyday life, a central feature of ethnographic research, nicely met the lab teachers' need to "get a handle" on the complexity of classroom life. Over time, we have come to think of ethnography more as research related to practice than as research translated into practice. We also are convinced that the social negotiation of knowledge is synergistic; that is, the total yield is more than the sum of individual contributions. This makes the interpretation of all participants more broadly and critically informed (although we should acknowledge the possibility of "folie à group"—a consensus of misinterpretation).

So far, we have emphasized the complex of influences, events, people, and demands within which our professional lives and activities were situated as we began our program of research. From there, however, we began proactively to create strategies to create greater coherence in our professional lives and to move our collaborative research agenda forward. Our personal response has been to create a whole out of diverse activities through the integration of teaching, research, and service—with our research collaboration and the venue of the lab school at its center.

An early integrative strategy, one we came to rely on (and still use), was to design co-led graduate seminars around topics related to the ethnography. The first of such seminars was a vehicle to explore ethnography as theory and methodology; later, we examined new literatures (e.g., social competence and social development) to frame and inform the topical analyses being conducted by research team members. These co-taught seminars satisfied our need to immerse ourselves in new literatures, to construct knowledge with and alongside our students, and to bring our teaching and research agendas together.

There was a good flow between these seminars and the development of our research team. Many of the seminar participants were, or became, members of the research team, and the seminars helped to establish new roles that carried over into the research project—less hierarchical relationships that differed from the traditional combination of lead professors charting the whole of a research project and junior doctoral researchers conducting subsidiary analyses.

Over time, our collaborative research team has included a dynamic mix of classroom teachers, honors undergraduate students, and master's and doctoral students, with new students joining, completing pieces within the research project, and moving on to other aspects of their careers. Establishing a group for conducting programmatic research is common (and was familiar to Dave, who had worked at Project Zero during and after his doctoral training), but it was how the group proceeded that was new and interesting to us.

The ways in which the research group proceeded were socially created and emergent over time. The research group met each week to work on various aspects of the research—conceptualizing topics, analyzing data, and critiquing and contributing written text to manuscripts and presentations. Although individuals often took the lead in pursuing individual topics, we worked extensively with students, and students worked collaboratively with each other and with teachers in the lab to develop research strategies inductively, to code and triangulate data, and to develop and articulate interpretations of data.

These day-to-day social processes were essential to the creation of a group identity, the development of shared knowledge, and the design and conduct of linked analyses. By "linked," we mean that each new analysis was provoked by understandings gained in previous analyses and that each new analysis both informed and was informed by interpretations we made in other analyses. The commitment to collaborative inquiry did more than create a different social network for the research: It provided a social structure that made the in-depth study and a shared understanding of this setting possible. This was a really exciting time in our research careers—sharing our ideas and insights, learning how to collaborate and write together, helping each other puzzle through issues in interpretation and method, being part of a team, presenting our work to colleagues at the American Educational Research Association (AERA) and other meetings, and moving the work and our understanding of the setting forward.

Despite this satisfaction and excitement, working in an intensive group context in a university culture raised a number of problematic issues that were challenging to resolve (beyond your garden variety interpersonal misunderstandings, miscommunications, and personality differences). One fundamental issue that played out in various ways concerned the "ownership" of knowledge that was created within the research team. Although individuals certainly initiated ideas or interpretive insights within our project, these ideas and insights were always built on prior group thinking and dialogue and then further shaped by group process. Ultimately, it became difficult and even unreasonable to trace credit for an idea to any individual, or conversely, for any individual to take sole credit for an idea. Group ownership of ideas takes some getting used to in our society, where individual accomplishments are lauded all through the educational process. This is especially true in a university context, where the strength and originality of our ideas are at the core of our academic identities. So, who "owns" intellectual ideas when their invention is explicitly recognized as communal?

To cite another significant and ongoing dynamic, the students often came with the traditional expectation that they would locate an original dissertation topic and conduct a discrete analysis. In contrast, we had been learning that all of our topics for analyses had to be germane and salient to life in that particular classroom. So, although students could bring their own broad interests to the project (e.g., literacy, gender, or friendship issues), they had to be flexible enough to situate their examination within the larger ethnography and to allow topics and questions to emerge inductively. To their credit, students developed the patience to inform themselves about what the group already knew and the vision to see how an intensive group process could benefit a traditional, individually constructed product such as a dissertation.

The embedded and interrelated nature of these linked analyses raised further issues related to student and faculty roles. For example, we had to develop an unconventional style of advisement as faculty members: Regardless of who served as a student's official adviser, both of us worked extensively with each other's advisees, much beyond the time investment and resulting credit a university assigns to the role of dissertation committee member. Although students presumably benefited from our close involvement, it also reduced their ability to be independent, a status already difficult to achieve within the structure of professor/graduate student relationships.

Given our press to achieve tenure, authorship issues were thorny for us, especially at the beginning of the project. Originally, we had planned simply to rotate authorship position among the professors (reflecting the shared endeavor), but with graduate students assuming first authorship on their distinct analyses. This invariably turned out to be too simplistic a formula. For example, as each of us approached tenure, university dossier requirements, such as noting the percentage of contribution to each article, worried us and showed that the university was not yet ready or able (despite its rhetoric) to accept and support collaborative work. At that time, we negotiated authorship order of impending publications to fit our respective tenure clocks.

All the above issues emerged within our collaborative ethnography because, in general, the conventions of traditional inquiry seemed not to apply. The various "solutions" to these issues, of course, had to be found within existing relationships, to use ongoing social negotiation processes, and to be situated within our own context. We suspect that other readers and contributors to this volume who are working collaboratively will resonate with our points, especially if they are also working in new paradigms or nontraditional topics. They too will have found new ways of doing things within their particular contexts.

What, then, have we learned about collaboration in general that is useful to share here? To answer this question, we find ourselves returning to our enduring, combined images of development and social construction. Some processes and some issues in collaborating turn out to be developmental; that is, they emerge at a point in time, are salient for the time, and then are worked through cognitively and socially to a new place. For example, early on, we struggled more than we do now to create manuscripts, spending a great deal of time negotiating written text while trying to accommodate each other's writing habits and styles. Over time, this tension has diminished as we have developed some group ways of writing and a shared language for communicating our insights, and as we have accommodated to each other's styles of writing. Other processes and issues, such as the ownership and authorship dynamics we have described, are periodic and recurring. Over time, we have been convinced that these issues are not permanently resolved by invoking enduring procedural rules, but instead addressed for the moment through their social construction in dialogue and negotiation.

For all of us involved in the ethnography, integrating the research process with teaching and program development in the lab school has been transformative—that is, it has forever changed what we see, think about, and can describe in this and any classroom. What we did not anticipate was the parallel and more personal transformation we would experience in becoming collaborative researchers. We feel fortunate that our partnership continues to be productive, as we realize that many others fade away or end over conflicts that people are unable to resolve. Interestingly, we feel that we now have a mature inquiry process in place and are searching for the right topic domain within which to apply it. Additionally, we face a new university-related issue—the press to bring in significant external grant money, which is hard to come by for any qualitative project. These emergent issues will have to be explored as a social process, too. What feels different this time is our confidence that group collaboration can be a satisfying, viable, and even advantageous way of conducting research and that continuing challenges can be met through dialogue, negotiation, and group social action.

Reference

Gergen, K. J. (1985). The social constructionist movement in modern psychology. *American Psychologist, 40*(3), 266-275.

Note

1. This label has a flavor to it that seems distasteful and includes physical caregiving such as wiping noses, wiping up tables, and diapering.

6

GENERATING DATA

Kurt, hang around with people who are smarter than you. In your case, that should be easy.

—*Kurt Vonnegut's father*

Think about research with kids as a disciplined and systematic form of hanging around with kids who are smarter about their world than you are. This chapter addresses what to do while hanging around.

As noted earlier, we prefer *generating* data to the more common *collecting* data. Data are not out there, waiting, like tomatoes on a vine, to be picked. Acquiring data is a very active, creative, improvisational process. Data must be generated before they can be collected. If research is the process of soaking and poking, we emphasize the poking over the soaking, or better, first poke and then soak. The researcher is not a fly on the wall or a frog in the pocket. The researcher is there. She cannot be otherwise. She is in the mix.

AUTHORS' NOTE: Written by Daniel.

Before Entering the Field

Questions

Data generation begins with questions. The questions may be as general as "What is going on here?" to the more specific "What do these kids know about what, when, where, how, why, and with whom in order for them to be able to do what they do together?" to specific theory-testing questions such as "If physical aggression is a sign of friendship among preadolescent boys, will I in fact see more aggression between boys who identify themselves as friends than between boys who do not?"

The notion that one goes into the field without questions and there waits for questions to emerge like flowers in the spring is foolish. Research is not a random endeavor. One has reasons for choosing to do fieldwork in a day care setting instead of in a turnip field. Specifically, one has interests that pertain to children and not to turnips. Questions may change once fieldwork has begun. In fact, one may develop new questions entirely. New questions, however, build on old questions. Questions prime the pump of inquiry. You will develop good questions in the field in direct relation to the quality of the questions you bring in with you. Going into the field without questions is like going to the dance without your dancing shoes. The dances aren't in the shoes, but at least they get you on the floor. If you want to waste a lot of good time, yours and everyone else's, go into the field question-free.

Prior Knowledge

The same is true about the curious belief that the ideal is to go into the field without any prior knowledge to avoid being biased. Ignorance does not inoculate against bias. Knowledge is important. The more one knows about what is known about the part of the world being explored, the better. Reviewing the literature is critical. The knowledge gained in the review becomes part of one's subjectivity (discussed in Chapter 3) and should, like all knowledge, be treated critically. What is known may well be wrong and certainly is incomplete, but purposely not gathering information before going into the field is unwise. Little, in fact, may be known or understood. The lack of knowledge and understanding may well be the reason one has chosen a particular area for research, but there is a difference between the unknown and the ignored.

Plans

The detail of research plans depends to a large extent on how much is known beforehand. In theory-building research, very little may be known, in which case Bakan's advice is apt:

> For the fact of the matter is that good research into the unknown cannot be well designed, in the usual sense of the term. Truly good research means that one allows the investigation to be guided by the experiences of the investigation. And this cannot be predicted. If it can be predicted, then there is little information to be gathered from the research; and considerably less reason to do the research. (1967, p. xiv)

Even if venturing into the unknown, a researcher can and should make general plans, knowing that plans, like questions, likely will change. At the very least, a preliminary timetable should be constructed—when fieldwork will begin, when it will end, how many hours a day will be spent in the field, how many days a week, how those hours and those days will be varied, how much time each day will be devoted to data record construction, and so on.

Formulating questions, reviewing the literature, and making plans are all important pre-fieldwork activities. They do not end when fieldwork begins.

Methods

> All there is to thinking [research] is seeing something noticeable which makes you see something you weren't noticing which makes you see something that isn't even visible. (Paul, in Maclean, 1976, p. 92)

Finding it out requires inquiry that gets below the surface of human interaction. In the scene excerpted above from Norman Maclean's novella *A River Runs Through It,* two brothers are fishing on the Blackfoot River in Montana. Both are accomplished fly fishermen, but one is a master. The non-master asks the other, Paul, how he knew fish were in a certain spot in the river. Paul's reply is quoted above. Getting at the invisible through the visible is what research is all about.

Like Paul, we see the research process as having three levels: (a) the everyday observable, (b) rich description, and (c) theorized explanation, that is, getting at the invisible or unobservable.

The *everyday observable* refers to that which is immediately visible, what anyone walking into a site would see. Anyone who has done interpretive research goes through an initial period when all one sees is the obvious. The first few weeks can be frustrating—"I've been here for x number of hours and I don't know any more than I did 30 minutes after I arrived the first day."

The understanding developed at this level is the kind developed within day-to-day experience—the uncritical knowledge of daily life. Its attributes are its experiential quality and lack of both systematic observation and reflection. Not all people, for example, watching a youth soccer practice would see the same things—perspective shapes attention in particular ways. The individuals watching that practice would, however, likely share recollections of events in overlapping ways so that they could describe things to one another and recognize them as similar—even if they disagreed about the value of what the coach was doing. A lot of life is lived at this level. From viewing the world at this surface level, one reflexively draws conclusions about how the world works. If one is of a mind to "make it up," a few observations at this first level are all that is needed.

Rich description comes as the result of careful, systematic, and disciplined observing. *Careful* refers to the level of attentiveness; *systematic*, to the planned nature of the observation; and *disciplined*, to the self-critical nature of the process.

The researcher who hangs in there during the first period of seeing the obvious and carefully records what she sees eventually begins to notice other things, things that have been there all along but were not so obvious. This is the second level. The second level is visible, but only to the careful observer. It comes as one extends one's acquaintances with the extremely small matters in which one is immersed. To return to the fishing example, that day was not the first that Paul had been on the Blackfoot River.

Rich description differentiates interpretive research from understanding developed from lived experience. The systematic nature of rich description includes, among many other activities, an explicit focus, sampling decisions that attempt to see a phenomenon from various perspectives, cross-checking hunches that develop from a variety of data sources (commonly known as triangulation), counting, looking for patterns and anomalies, and developing themes. Rich description comes from paying close attention to *something in particular* and paying attention to it over a period of time. It has both scientific and artistic aspects in that it is disciplined in the amassing of data while at the same time evocative of human life in all its quirkiness.

Theoretical explanations go below the surface, to the invisible, to an understanding of what the mundane social life of human interactions means. "The task of science is precisely to discover reality which is not immediately in evidence" (Bakan, 1967, p. 144). Theoretical explanations broaden the scope of rich descriptions, connecting observations and developing ideas about a setting that explain why things happen the way they do. Theory provides a framework for understanding description. It makes descriptions less local, moving them to *instances of something* rather than isolated observations. It also gives the researcher what Denzin (1994) calls a *public persona*, a position that readers can use to read the interpretation. Finally, theoretical explanations capitalize on knowledge of the social, historical, political, and cultural dimensions of the local setting to situate actions and interactions in contexts that give them meaning.

The process of getting to the invisible begins with the generation of data. Data generation requires refined skills in the three basic data generation strategies—interviewing, observing, and artifact collection. Our view is that there is an indefinite number of ways to generate data, but each is a variation on these three genres. The challenge is to view the three basic generic strategies as broadly as possible. There are, for example, many ways to interview.

A series of boxes in this chapter lists resources for gaining expertise in data generation strategies, beginning with Box 6.1, listing general resources. Generally in the methodological literature, more attention has been paid to interviewing and observing than artifact collection. The resource lists reflect this bias.

Research is and should be a creative process, and generating data on children challenges one to be very creative. Once in the field with children, one must continually find new and different ways to listen to and observe children, and to collect physical traces of their lives. Our discussion illustrates a few of the possible variations. Once one realizes, for example, that interviews can be conducted without asking questions, as did Tobin and colleagues with their use of videotapes (1989), other possibilities begin to emerge.

Studying children is a different and more problematic endeavor from studying adults, and studying young children is even more so. Physical,

---

Box 6.1
Overviews

Bernard, H. R. (1988). *Research methods in cultural anthropology.* Beverly Hills, CA: Sage.

Delamont, S. (1992). *Fieldwork in educational settings: Methods, pitfalls, and perspectives.* London: Falmer.

Denzin, N. K. (1989). *Interpretive interactionism.* Newbury Park, CA: Sage.

Denzin, N. K., & Lincoln, Y. S. (Eds.). (1994). *Handbook of qualitative research.* Thousand Oaks, CA: Sage.

Erickson, F. (1986). Qualitative methods in research on teaching. In M. C. Wittrock (Ed.), *Handbook of research on teaching* (3rd ed., pp. 119-161). New York: Macmillan. (Also available in Linn, R., & Erickson, F. (1990). *Quantitative methods/qualitative methods.* New York: Macmillan.)

Glesne, C., & Peshkin, A. (1992). *Becoming qualitative researchers: An introduction.* White Plains, NY: Longman.

Jackson, B. (1987). *Fieldwork.* Urbana: University of Illinois Press. Particularly useful on technology, although slightly dated.

Peshkin, A. (1988). Understanding complexity: A gift of qualitative inquiry. *Anthropology and Education Quarterly, 19,* 416-424.

Sanjek, R. (Ed.). (1990). *Fieldnotes: The makings of anthropology.* Ithaca, NY: Cornell University Press.

Webb, E., Campbell, D. T., Schwartz, R. D., & Sechrest, L. (1966). *Unobtrusive measures: Nonreactive research in the social sciences.* Chicago: Rand McNally.

---

social, cognitive, and political distances between the adult and child make their relationship very different from adult relationships. A participant observer can never become a child. He remains a very definite and readily identifiable "other."

Researchers, unless working "under cover"—which raises serious ethical issues—remain "others" in whatever group studied. The degree of "otherness," however, is relative, depending on cultural, gender, and other distances. In most cases, adults working with other adults are able to decrease the distance between researcher and subject by finding salient areas of commonality. For example, many people doing research on teachers were once teachers themselves. Although the distance between adult and child is less absolute than gender (generally), because we all were once children ourselves, the distance is also ambiguous, for children are often *physically* close but *socially* distant.

> While there is some disagreement among scholars as to how easy it is for adults to gain access to the world of children (Wacksler, 1986), the assumptions and values of these two social categories [adults and children] inevitably differ. . . . Like the white researcher in black society, the male researcher studying women, or the ethnologist observing a distant tribal culture, the adult participant observer who attempts to understand a children's culture cannot pass unnoticed as a member of that group. (Fine & Sandstrom, 1988, pp. 10-13)

Gaining Entry

A friend related the story of asking his nephew, a freshman at a prestigious university, whether college was hard. The young man laughed, "College is easy. Getting into college is hard."

The same is true of fieldwork. Fieldwork, once begun, can be easy. Getting into the field can be hard. Getting into the field with children can be very hard. Gatekeepers, people who are responsible for groups of children, are understandably protective of them and are not always comfortable having an outsider view their children and their interactions with them. Certain places and certain groups of children are more accessible than others. Schools are more accessible than group homes or shelters for the homeless or support groups for unwed teenage mothers. Gatekeepers' desires to protect the privacy of their charges are understandable and laudable, but there are groups of kids about whom society knows little and about whom it needs to develop understanding.

Access also can be difficult because of gatekeepers' prior unpleasant experience with researchers. Bruce Jackson (1987) tells troubling stories of people refusing to talk to him and others because of the dishonesty of earlier researchers. Buddy Peshkin (personal communication, 1995) described how important it was for his gaining entry into American Indian communities in New Mexico that he was not an anthropologist. Because of previous experiences with anthropologists, these communities no longer welcomed them.

Researchers at major universities often discover that gaining entry into institutions in the immediate vicinity can be difficult for a different reason. Even when gatekeepers have not had bad experiences with re-

---

Box 6.2
Gaining Entry

1. "First of all, there is no reason to select a site that is difficult to enter when equally good sites are available that are easy to enter" (Bernard, 1988, p. 160).

2. "Go into the field with plenty of written documentation about yourself and your project. You need one or more letters of introduction from your university, your funding agency, or your client if you are doing contract research" (Bernard, 1988, pp. 160-161).

3. Identify the gatekeepers—the official ones and the daily ones. Make sure you understand how and what you will be negotiating with each.

4. Be honest, be brief, and be humble. The objective is to gain entry, not to impress. Establish who it is you are gaining entry for, that is, who you are in this work.

5. Find ways to make yourself useful. Volunteer to stuff envelopes, do bulletin boards, clean up, and so on. It not only helps gain entry but also gets you quickly and deeply into the daily life of the context.

6. Once in, gaining permission from parents and others is ongoing. A multiple-stage approach works best: First, introduce yourself and give a general description; later, add more detail. Give people a chance to check you out and hear from kids about you before asking permission for specific activities, such as interviewing or videotaping. Don't do them until you have permission.

---

searchers, they often feel like they have "been researched to death." One teacher I know at a university laboratory school has been a central figure in three different dissertations.

- It can be well worth the drive to put some distance between one's research site and a major research university.

We make one final point about gatekeepers of young children. The gatekeeper whom one must first deal with and upon whom one is dependent for initial entry is most often an administrator and removed from the children with whom one will be working. The director of a youth club, for example, may most often be in his office or out fund-raising. The gatekeepers with whom one must work each day—the teachers, counselors, group leaders, and so on—normally are not in a position to give entry permission, although they can often officially deny permission. Even if they cannot, they can most certainly unofficially deny entry by being uncooperative.

Obtaining permission from the first gatekeeper ordinarily is a one-time, either-or procedure. Once entry has been gained, assuming original agreements are maintained, permission does not have to be continually negotiated. An administrator may have a change of mind, but as a rule, once in, one remains in and may rarely see the initial gatekeeper again.

Gaining entry with the daily gatekeepers, the adults who actually work with the children, is a daily process that usually gets easier but never stops. This process is ongoing and requires daily negotiation.

Positioning

The subject of building rapport with subjects gets much attention in most treatises on qualitative research. Building rapport can be hard work. People who do prolonged face-to-face research should be skilled at getting along with people, even people who are not easy to get along with. Our discussion takes a different tack and concentrates on the notion of positioning; that is, how does one place oneself in the field in relationship to the people there? We make two main points. The first has to do with attitude, the second with relationships.

Being a Learner

The researcher goes into the field as a learner. If she already knew what the kids "there" knew, she would not be there. The researcher is saying to the kids, "I want to learn from you. Will you be my teachers?" We do not exaggerate when we say that the researcher should see herself as on her knees, continually asking permission to be there. Her presence depends on the permission of those who are "there," whose "there" it is. Three basic assumptions should underlie the researcher's attitude toward the children she is studying:

1. *All kids are smart.* They know how to get along in the world they inhabit. They know what works there, what does not work. The only way to get as smart as they are about their world is to learn from them.
2. *All kids makes sense.* What may appear from the outside to be dysfunctional activity, from the inside, to those involved, makes sense.

The only way to understand how these actions makes sense is to listen and observe very carefully.

3. *All kids want to have a good life.* What may appear from the outside to be self-destructive or other-destructive, from the inside has a purpose—the attainment of a good life.

These three assumptions and basic positioning[1] should be a researcher's faithful companions in the field. They make gaining others' perspectives possible, and they require the researcher to abandon attitudinal baggage that interferes with data generating.

We are not espousing a moral relativism, but as Jackson has noted, "The fieldworker's task isn't to decide whether or not people *should* be doing what they do, it's to find out what they do and what it means" (1987, p. 266). One can seek to understand why it makes sense to an oversized 12-year-old to bully his smaller peers without condoning his behavior. Unquestionably, the desires of some for a good life have wreaked havoc on others; nevertheless, one can respect basic human capabilities without necessarily respecting the particular ways to which they are put to use. Finding out, as Geertz put it, "What the devil people think they are up to" (1983, p. 58) requires attending very carefully to them and respecting their abilities.

One should consider carefully one's attitude toward and possible relationships with a specific group before engaging in research with it. If one knows in advance that working with certain groups of kids (for example, adolescents who engage in promiscuous and unprotected sexual behavior) is going to be very difficult—"How can I keep reminding myself that these kids are smart when everything they do is so stupid?"— then think carefully about actually doing the research. At the same time, if societal knowledge of kids is highly correlated with ease of access and degree of comfort, then what is known, or thought to be known, about kids is going to be limited to middle- and upper-middle-class kids in very public contexts, for example, schools, camps, and little leagues.

Relationships

George Spindler tells,[2] more eloquently and accurately than we, the story of an anthropologist traveling with a nomadic band of aboriginal Australians. He was having no success building rapport with the band. No matter how hard he tried and what he did, he was ignored and kept on the edge of the group's daily life. The only person who approached him was an apparently marginal older woman who had little interaction with others in the group and who constantly begged for candy and cigarettes. (To understand the story, one must know that Australian aboriginal groups have extremely complex kinship systems with more than 200 kinship terms.) Finally, one day, in frustration, the anthropologist lost his temper and yelled at the old woman, "You old mother, go away and stop bothering me!" At that point, everyone in the band came running up to him smiling and saying, "If she's your mother, then you're my . . ."

The story has a hint of the apocryphal to it, but it contains an important truth about human relationships with important implications for research. It is very difficult to relate to another person unless that person can be positioned within one's larger "kinship" system. For me to know who you are, I have to have an analog for you within my experience. All interactions are mediated. People do not interact directly, but through cultural definitions, expectations, roles, and so on.

A very important question, then, for the researcher to ask and answer is, "Who will I be in my relationship to these kids and these adults?" That role will develop and be negotiated, but an important first activity for the researcher is to teach people who she is and who she is not. In Chapter 5, Beth described taking on the role of a teacher's aide. It allowed her to be comfortable in the classroom. As important, it gave her an identity in the classroom that was familiar to both kids and adults. It made interaction possible.

Teachers, caregivers, parents, kids, and so on will give a new person in their environment the most readily accessible identity. Most university types who come into classrooms come in to supervise or to evaluate. Enter another university type, and the identity is there waiting for her. The identity is not a useful one for a researcher. I once was introduced to a group of teachers by a central office administrator as an "evaluator" rather than an ethnographer (I suspect purposefully), and it took me months before I could begin to gain their trust.

The challenge is to decide who one will be, to make sure that that persona is accessible to the kids and adults one will be working with and that one can be that persona, and then to teach people who one is—all this in the context of being a learner. If people have difficulty accepting a university person as a learner, it should come as no surprise.

Improvising

Miles Davis often commented to band members, "You need to know your horn, know the chords, know all the tunes. Then you forget about all that, and just play" (Sanjek, 1990, p. 411).[3] The same is true of doing fieldwork. Generating data requires constant improvisation, but improvisation requires all the skills.

Learning how to observe and how to interview means beginning with the basics and learning them and then practicing them until one can do them without thinking, then just doing fieldwork.

Improvisation presupposes a plan. Data generation needs to be systematic—there should be a plan that allows one to conclude that one has had a good thorough look. Clearly, there are times when plans need to be changed, but these changes should remain within the broad parameters of the plan. If not, the plan itself should be reevaluated. Improvisation is grounded—but not stuck.

Triangulating

Using only one research strategy—for example, only observation, or worse, only one kind of observation—introduces bias into the data record. A good data record contains views "from as many perspectives as possible" (Luria, 1979, p. 177). Triangulation is commonly stressed in treatments of qualitative research, but it is important to understand exactly what it means and what function it serves.

Looking from many different angles and in many different ways provides a more complete description of the part of the social world being investigated. Denzin (1978) suggested three ways of triangulating: (a) using many data sources across time, space, and persons; (b) using different investigators; and (c) using multiple methods. The researcher working alone may not be able to use other investigators, but making use of multiple data sources and methods is vital to data generation.

The danger of not looking in many ways is that human beings are pattern and narrative constructors. They will construct coherent narratives to explain the world from whatever data are available. They will construct patterns and explanations even when faced with chaos and randomness, for example, from computer-generated random forms. Researchers have to monitor themselves constantly as they seek to understand interactions. Triangulation provides an important way of doing this.

"Being there," that is, in the field, is necessary, but it is not sufficient. While there, one must explore various ways to generate data. It is a big world out there, and the little parts of it chosen for study are extremely multifaceted and complex. Getting to understand them requires that one look carefully at them in many ways. Watching and taking notes is important, but there is more to life, even life as a researcher.

Ting's (1992) study of preschool children's interactions provides a good example of multiple ways of generating data. From the beginning, she took the simple but important step of sitting in a different place each day to observe. She observed at various times during the day. She did further observations with extensive videotaping, leaving the camera running on different areas of the room for 30-minute periods each day and also videotaping from a second-floor observation booth. She invented ways of putting information from videos on paper. She conducted many informal interviews with children. With instruments she constructed in the field, she also conducted more formal interviews. Employing Corsaro's (1985) "reactive" strategy (discussed later in this chapter), she was invited into children's play in many areas of the classroom. She also interviewed teachers and collected the notes and other printed material that went home with children each day. The result was a data record that allowed one to view the day care and specific children she targeted in great detail and from multiple perspectives. When, for example, she argued that Teddy is a "child on the edge," she was able to demonstrate his positioning very convincingly with different kinds of evidence.

Triangulation extends beyond the field. Often ignored is the importance of interaction with others, not only with other researchers in team efforts but also with other researchers who are working in related efforts (see Wasser & Bresler, 1996). The discussion on doing a literature review in Chapter 3 emphasized that in theory-building research, the review of literature should be ongoing. Answering questions about what is known, however, requires more than reading; it requires talking with other scholars. Of particular importance to researchers whose data generation activities are focused on "extremely extended acquaintance with extremely small matters" (Geertz, 1973, p. 21) is building relationships with archival and big-picture folks—historians, philosophers, sociologists, and so on. Learning anything truly useful is going to require extensive digging by many people in many different places using a wide array of tools and perspectives. Good research comes from much thought between many heads.

Observing

Disciplined and systematic observation is a skill, one that can be learned. Good observers see things that others do not. To return to the line from Norman Maclean, "All there is to thinking is seeing something noticeable which makes you see something you weren't noticing which makes you see something that isn't even visible," observing is about beginning with the noticeable, that which the casual observer sees, and then going beyond that to that which you weren't noticing, that which the casual observer misses.

- Write it down.

The first step is to record what is observed. Unrecorded observations are not data. A lot of fieldwork consists of writing things down. How one takes fieldnotes is an individual matter. Beth prefers to use a steno pad. She finds the divided page very useful for devising systems for recording, for example, describing the teacher on the left and the children on the right. I type much faster and more legibly than I write and prefer to use a notebook computer. At times, however, a computer is intrusive, and I use a small notebook—preferring a small three-ring binder with dividers. Both of us have found that at times even a notebook is obtrusive, and we must record in memory until we can find time and place to record in a more secure place.

Knowing shorthand is an invaluable research tool, one that neither of us possesses. Most people who find their way into graduate school avoided business classes. Inevitably, fieldworkers invent idiosyncratic shorthands, using many abbreviations, leaving out vowels, and so on. When I type fieldnotes, I never hit the shift key or use punctuation. Instead, I hit the space bar twice between sentences or thoughts (it works for me; it may not for you). One advantage of using a notebook computer for fieldnotes is that expanding the fieldnotes later is faster than having to begin with handwritten notes.

Concrete Particulars

The goal of observation is to record the "concrete particulars" (Erickson, 1986) of everyday life. One problem with many observation records is that they are generic and lack detail. The very things that one tends to miss in everyday interactions are the stuff of records—detailed descrip-

---

Box 6.3
Observing

Adler, P. A., & Adler, P. (1994). Observational techniques. In N. K. Denzin
& Y. S. Lincoln (Eds.), *Handbook of qualitative research* (pp. 377-392).
Thousand Oaks, CA: Sage.
Bernard, H. R. (1988). Participant observation. In *Research methods in
cultural anthropology*. Beverly Hills, CA: Sage.
Fine, G. A., & Sandstrom, K. L. (1988). *Knowing children: Participant ob-
servation with minors*. Newbury Park, CA: Sage.
Spradley, J. P. (1980). *Participant observation*. New York: Holt, Rinehart
& Winston.
Wolcott, H. F. (1981). Confessions of a "trained" observer. In T. S. Pop-
kewitz & B. R. Tabachnick (Eds.), *The study of schooling: Field based
methodologies in educational research and evaluation* (pp. 247-263).
New York: Praeger.

---

tions of clothing, hair, lunch boxes, expressions, posture, ages, gender,
what kids look like, what they say, and what they do. These are some of
the concrete details of kids' daily lives. It is these concrete particulars
that those who make it up fail to attend to or to see the importance of.
Concrete particulars are the only way to the meaning that kids are constructing in their everyday *situated actions*, that is, actions "situated in a
cultural setting, and in the mutually interacting intentional states of the
participants" (Bruner, 1990, p. 19).

Harry Wolcott (1981) tells the story of Nathaniel Shaler, who, in the
late 1800s at the age of 18, began a tutorial in the lab of Louis Agassiz,
an eminent biologist-naturalist.

[Shaler] was directed to sit at a small table with a rusty tin pan on it. Agassiz
placed before him a small fish, directing him only to "study it" without
damaging the specimen and to confine his attention to the specimen itself,
rather than consulting printed sources or conversing with other individuals
in the laboratory.

After about an hour, Shaler . . . had completed his examination and was
ready to proceed to a more challenging task. . . . To his mounting distress,
however, Shaler realized that Agassiz . . . had no immediate intention of
returning to question him. Not that day, not the next, not for a week. And
so Shaler committed himself anew to the task of observation—and in due

course felt he had learned a hundred times more than in his cursory initial inspection. . . . [O]n the seventh day . . . Agassiz approached and inquired, "Well?" His question unleashed an hour-long explication, while Agassiz sat on the edge of the table and puffed a cigar. Suddenly, he interrupted with the statement, "That is not right," and walked abruptly away.

Fortunately, Shaler interpreted Agassiz's behavior as a test of whether he could do hard, continuous work without constant direction. He returned to his observation task afresh, discarding his original set of notes and working up detailed new ones from some ten hours a day for another week. And at the end of that time . . . he had results that astonished himself and apparently satisfied Agassiz, for although there were no words of praise, Agassiz subsequently placed before him a new and more complicated task and told him to see what he could make of it. That task took two months. (pp. 248-249)

Our point is not that everyone should spend many weeks getting very acquainted with a dead fish, but that most of life passes the casual observer by. By necessity, one views surroundings very selectively. To do otherwise would result in being overwhelmed by the surrounding sensory stimuli. The good observer becomes overwhelmed. Entering the field, one is most often struck by the ordinariness of it all. Like the dead fish, what is there is obviously there and readily described. Careful observation, however, leads one to the second level, to the visible but previously unnoticed, which can be overwhelming. The challenge becomes not to find something to record but to find how to record it all. At this point, one must become selective in one's observation. Also at this point, one is becoming a skilled observer.

The Observational Continuum

Observation generally is described along a continuum from detached observation (for example, taking notes from behind a one-way mirror or a screen in an observation booth) to full participant observation (for example, working as a counselor). Each point along the continuum presents advantages and challenges. The person in the observation booth is able to take notes without being distracted by children asking for help or curious about what he is doing. He does not have to worry about the effect he will have on others if he focuses on one child or one group. He may well stay healthier than he would if out in the mix, being coughed on. At the same time, he is removed from the children, most often unable to hear clearly what they are saying. He cannot ask questions or interact.

Observation booths provide clearer views of some parts of the room than others. In fact, some parts of the room may be unobservable.

Full participation makes taking fieldnotes problematic. One must rely on short reminder notes as well as "headnotes" (Ottenberg, 1990), what one knows from having been there but has not yet been able to write down, and then attempt to expand these from memory as the opportunity arises, retreating periodically to an out-of-the-way spot. George Spindler related being in one school where the only place he could go to write notes was the lavatory. Given the limitations of memory, writing good notes is a challenge. A participant observer, however, is "there," not behind a screen or glass, rubbing up against the children, able to hear what is being said, interacting, and sharing, to some extent, in their experiences.

Researchers have tried different ways to be participant observers. Corsaro's "reactive strategy" has proved to be a useful way for an adult researcher to participate in a "least adult" way. Looking for ways not to act like an adult, he noticed that "adults primarily initiate contacts with children: that is, they were primarily *active* rather than *reactive*" (1985, p. 28). He found, for example, that adults began conversations with children without expecting to become engaged in extended interaction. Adults also tended to stay in certain areas while avoiding others. "Adults seldom entered the playhouses, outside sandpiles, climbing bars, or climbing house" (p. 28). His strategy became one not of acting like a child but rather of not acting like an adult.

Different Perspectives

A research plan that allows one to observe from as many different perspectives as possible is important, but it also may make it difficult to take on a specified participant role. How one finds all the perspectives, all the angles from which to view a site, is not something that can be detailed here. Each room, playground, group home, park, or skating rink presents different challenges. These challenges are situated and will have to be met by the researcher who is there. One colleague, who was studying an adult education class, found that the only place from which he could adequately video the room was perched precariously atop the door.

What can be said is that much planning is required, for example, spending a weekend in an empty classroom, experimenting with camera angles and placements and searching for places to mount a microphone (Ting, 1992). William Corsaro (1985) described how he spent an extended period studying children's records and observing the children from an observation booth before he entered the classroom. One of the first things to do in any site is to explore and to discover what can be seen from different vantage points. These vantage points are not only physical but also the roles one assumes. One should also consider what cannot be seen from these positions.

Sometimes taking a different vantage point may be as simple as moving to another part of the setting. Human beings are creatures of habit. Going into a strange place with all the adjustments required makes finding some kind of routine very attractive. Finding a place that provides some comfort and possibly some identity—a corner of a classroom or a seat on the bus—can help one get through the initial phase of being a stranger, but full observing requires one to move.

Two brief stories illustrate the difference a slight change in perspective can make. Some years back, I (Daniel) found myself observing a first-year fourth-grade teacher in a rural Virginia school. I sat in the back of the room and out of habit took in my surroundings. Some things jumped out at me almost immediately. The first was that this did not appear to be a happy room. Neither teacher nor children gave any indication of wanting to be there. The second was that the teacher did not move. She stood in front of her desk, exactly in the middle, during the entire lesson—as I recall, it was history—never budging from that spot. The final thing that stood out, more than the first two, was how cluttered and disorganized the classroom was. It almost looked abandoned. I counted eight dead plants, all in pots, but quite dead.

After the lesson, the teacher and her class went out to recess. Out of curiosity, I went to the front of the empty classroom and stood where she had moored herself. From that spot, because of the clutter, the way the bookcases were arranged—although I am not sure arrangement is the right word—none of the dead plants was visible. I moved a little to the right, and a couple came into view. I moved to the left, and a couple more did. I moved back to the middle, and they all disappeared. I had been wondering why she did not do something about the dead plants. She already had.

A second example: A few years ago, two students taking my child study class opted to study children in school lunchrooms. Three times a week, they visited the lunchroom of a large elementary school and sat along the wall and watched. At times, they tried to talk to children, but the volume of the noise made that impossible. They became increasingly frustrated, and each week they came to the seminar saying that they were seeing nothing and that they were wasting their time—school lunchrooms were unbearably noisy and chaotic, kids ate hurriedly and threw out a lot of food, and that was it. I urged them to stick it out and keep observing.

One week, they entered the seminar room with grand smiles. Everyone, of course, wanted to know what had happened. "We stood up," they said. They explained that they had been reluctant to stand because they wanted to remain unobtrusive and they did not want to be identified with the lunchroom monitors who patrolled the room. Finally, in frustration, one of the women stood up and looked down at the table nearest her. At that moment, the lunchroom changed from chaos to clusters of socially constructed relationships. As she looked down, she saw a group of four young girls talking and eating. More important, she saw that the four trays were identical—the hamburger half eaten, a scoop taken out of the middle of the mashed potatoes, the cupcake gone, the wrapper rolled up, and milk poured in that section of the tray about an eighth of an inch deep. She looked at the next table and saw another cluster of kids, each with identically organized trays, different from the first group's. At the next table, she found another cluster, and so on.

At that moment the lunchroom changed. They had moved to the second level. They saw groups of kids who found ways to identify with one another by how they ate their lunches, or better, by how they organized their trays. Eating lunch was not simply eating, it was a complex social affair. In some ways, this is an obvious finding. Eating often is a ritualized event, but it took standing up and moving around to see it.

Taking different perspectives refers, of course, to more than simply changing physical locations. It refers to the whole process of data generation. Sometimes, though, simply moving around is a good start.

Using Video

Video can be useful for recording observations. A video record of an event allows it to be observed many times and is particularly useful for microlevel analysis. The use of video has become increasingly popular, to the point that beginning researchers may feel that they cannot do research without video. Like any research tool, video has strengths and weaknesses. Deciding whether or when to use it should be based on the same criteria used for making decisions about any research tool.

A few of the limitations of using video deserve discussion. The first is that video records can be very inaccessible because of the time required to view them. Even the most detailed written record of a 30-minute session at a basketball camp takes much less than 30 minutes to read, and it can be spread out on a table and viewed as a whole. It can be written on and plastered with Post-it notes. A 30-minute video of that same session takes 30 minutes to view. It cannot be seen as a whole or worked on directly. Multiply that 30 minutes by a few sessions a day across weeks and months, and one is soon staring at hundreds of hours of videotape on the shelf. In the next chapter, we talk about how to make video more accessible. If you plan to use video, be aware of the time factor.

A second limitation is the "being-there" illusion. Watching video can give the viewer a false sense of experiencing what she is viewing, of actually being there. Unless one actually was there when the video was taken, one was, quite simply, not there. John D'Amato describes the importance of experiencing the taped episode as the here and now, but doing so requires knowledge of the kids who are taped that goes beyond the particular video record. To "be there" in the tape, one must have been there originally. One must have headnotes. D'Amato wrote of a tape segment that became the basis for his monumental dissertation (1986):

> Here's something to think about: My account of this [video-recorded] lesson is rich because I spent a lot of time looking at the tape and I knew a lot about the kids. But you know what? The first time I looked at it, I thought, "This was it? What did they get so excited about?" I mean . . . the tape seemed not too much. The fullness of the moment lies in the sensuality of the experience of the here-and-now. That feeling is missing when you're looking at a tape or a transcript because your ongoing experience is not of the here-and-now of the interactional record but of your own context. Making the record come alive is a creative act. It requires engaging the document as if it were the here-and-now, building up a stream of thought within the record itself. (personal communication, 1986)

The challenge with video, as with any research tool, is to find creative ways of employing it. Ting used video to record children's locations (for more detail, see her essay following Chapter 7). She began, from an observation booth, recording locations by hand at 5-minute intervals, using maps of the classroom. She found this method clumsy, as it took her more than a minute to record all the children, and often children moved before she finished. She also found the method inadequate for differentiating between children who were actually playing in a place and children who were wandering and happened to be at spot x when the 5-minute signal went off. She then tried taking photographs but found that she had to take three or four to cover the entire classroom and that she often could not identify the children from the photographs. She then turned to video, panning the room every 5 minutes. The video allowed her to identify whether children were moving or stationary, the children were readily identifiable, and she could pan the entire classroom in a few seconds. (Readers wondering why she simply did not video the entire 1-hour free-play period are referred back to the first limitation above.)

Ting also had success using an unattended camera to record activities in specific areas of the room, for example, the block center. She remarked that children seemed less conscious of the video camera when she was not standing near it. If she was holding the camera, children often stopped what they were doing to perform for it, but if it was on an unattended tripod, they ignored it. She set the camera up before free play, trained on one activity area, and let it run unattended. She also hooked up a PZM microphone (discussed later in this chapter) to the camera and mounted it unobtrusively in that area. The result was a relatively unobtrusive recording of children's play.

One cautionary note: It is easy to conclude after gaining some acceptance that children "don't even notice I'm here." One brief episode convinced Ting that neither researcher nor camera ever become invisible. During the middle of one free-play session, three boys suddenly turned toward the camera. One pulled his pants down and waved his penis at the camera. They then returned to their play as though nothing had happened. The episode took less than 5 seconds, but the message was clear: We know that you're watching—so watch this!

Asher and Gabriel (1993) were able to examine children's social interactions on playgrounds by using a video camera with a zoom lens and a wireless microphone.

The components of the wireless transmission system worn by the child included a small, lavaliere microphone (Sony ECM-44), and a pocket trans

mitter (Samson TH-1 Belt Pack). The microphone was attached to the col-
lar of the child's clothing, and the transmitter was contained in a small
padded pouch on a belt fastened around the child's waist. . . . [W]ith our
audio transmission equipment the observer could be as much as 300 feet
away from the child. . . . (p. 198)

The wireless microphone allowed them to record conversations that
adults seldom hear. They described their methodology as "ideally suited
for capturing the hidden world of children's conversations in settings
such as the playground or lunchroom" (p. 202).

Video recording also presents troubling ethical issues. It produces a
record that is not easily disguised by assigning fictitious names to people
and places. It also produces a record that is problematic in other ways:

Contemporary social science's ravenous appetite to see in and through
people, our insatiable "panopticism" (Foucault, 1978) produces in the objects of our gaze a self-awareness and self-consciousness that inevitably
changes notions of who they are and how they should behave. Videotaping
focuses, magnifies, distorts, and prolongs this effect. (Tobin & Davidson,
1990, p. 276)

Interviewing

Children know more than they know they know. They surely know
more about what they know than the researcher does. The purpose of
interviews is to get them to talk about what they know.

The typical sit-down research interview is difficult to conduct with
children. The younger the children are, the more difficult it is. They
most likely have not had any experience with this particular form of
interaction. They may not find sitting and answering an adult's questions
an attractive activity—"Would you rather stay here and answer my clumsy
questions or go have fun with your friends?"

An interview is a unique speech act (Mishler, 1986), very different in
form and purpose from ordinary conversation. One expects adults to be
familiar with the interview. Even if they never have been interviewed
themselves, given the many television "interview" shows, they have most
likely seen an interview.

Children's experiences can be very different. They may not have had
much experience conversing with adults. The experience they have had
may have been very ritualistic—for example, classroom question and
answer routines. They may be accustomed to adults whose approach to

---

Box 6.4

Interviewing

Anderson, K., & Jack, D.C. (1991). Learning to listen: Interview techniques and analysis. In S. B. Gluck & D. Patai (Eds.), *Women's words: The feminist practice of oral history* (pp. 11-26). New York: Routledge.

Briggs, C. L. (1986). *Learning how to ask: A sociolinguistic appraisal of the role of the interview in social science research.* Cambridge, UK: Cambridge University Press.

Fujita, M., & Sano, T. (1988). Children at American and Japanese day-care centers: Ethnography and reflective cross-cultural interviewing. In H. Trueba & C. Delgado-Gaitan (Eds.), *School and society: Learning content through culture* (pp. 73-97). New York: Praeger.

Hatch, J. A. (1990). Young children as informants in classroom studies. *Early Childhood Research Quarterly, 5,* 251-264.

Jackson, B. (1987). Interviewing. In *Fieldwork.* Urbana: University of Illinois Press.

Kvale, S. (1996). *InterViews: An introduction to qualitative research interviewing.* Thousand Oaks, CA: Sage.

Mishler, E. G. (1986). *Research interviewing: Context and narrative.* Cambridge, MA: Harvard University Press.

Parker, W. C. (1984). Interviewing children: Problems and promise. *Journal of Negro Education, 53,* 18-28.

Spradley, J. P. (1979). *The ethnographic interview.* New York: Holt, Rinehart & Winston.

Tammivaara, J., & Enright, D. S. (1986). On eliciting information: Dialogues with child informants. *Anthropology and Education Quarterly, 17,* 218-238.

---

talking to children involves changing their tone of voice and assuming a curious version of "kid-talk." They have come to expect that when adults ask them questions, either the adult already knows the answer, as in "What color is this?" or they are in trouble, as in, "What were you thinking about when you threw the ball through the window?" Few children have had the experience of being approached by an adult who wants them, the kids, to teach her, the adult, about their lives.

The first step, then, in interviewing children is negotiating the process—what it is all about and how one does it. Depending on the children and the context, this initial negotiation phase may be very time-consuming. Expect the first real interview session to be a long time in coming. Expect to have to be very creative in finding ways to interview.

Research in general is an indirect and repetitious process, interviewing especially so. Most of what kids know, they know implicitly. Knowledge is not filed away in kids' heads in answer form waiting for the stimulus of the perfect question to release it. No researcher has ever found out what it means to be a soccer player or a foster child or a pompon girl or a teenage mother by asking directly, "What does it mean to be a . . .?" Harold Conklin, an anthropologist, gave researchers a choice—get information indirectly or get garbage. Conklin himself eventually discovered that the Hanunoo of the Philippines could identify almost 1,400 kinds of plants. He did not learn this by asking people to name all the plants they knew. He learned it indirectly as the result of very attentive and patient persistence (1954, in Spradley, 1979, p. 124). Be attentive. Be patient. Be persistent.

In the following section, we give specific suggestions for interviewing children.

Pair or small-group interviews. An extremely useful strategy, first suggested to us by D'Amato, is to interview children in pairs or triads. D'Amato (1986) and Baturka and Walsh (1991) used this strategy most effectively with kindergarten, first-, and second-grade children. Kids are more relaxed when with a friend than alone with an adult. They help each other with their answers. They also keep one another on track and truthful. D'Amato described how, when one would begin to embellish a tale, the other would respond, "You lie! You lie!" (personal communication, 1986).

Baturka found that the richest parts of the interviews came from the discussion between the children as they talked to each other about her questions, rather than from their direct answers, which often appeared to be attempts to give the "right" answer. In their discussions, the children modified the questions to ones they liked more and then answered their questions. Spradley's counsel that *"both the questions and answers must be discovered from informants"* (1979, p. 84) is worth remembering. Interviewing kids in pairs and triads leads to discussions that identify better questions.

Props. With young children, it is useful to bring props—objects—to the interview. Children's attention can be sustained more easily when they have something concrete to focus on. For example, pictures of the children in a classroom can be very useful for getting at children's understandings of classroom social interactions. One might array the photos on the table, then pick out the photo of Mary and ask, "If Mary was working at the art table, what other children would come and work with her?" Be aware that small details, like picture size, are important. Discovering that pictures will not all fit on the table one is using will make for an awkward interview session. Laminating paper props makes sense.

Hypothetical questions. Well-formed hypothetical questions allow young children to turn the interview into pretend play, an activity they are more familiar with and more competent in than interviewing. Hypothetical questions allow older children the freedom to move from looking for a "right" answer. "Suppose I was a little kid and I was coming to this camp for the first time and I ran and hid in the bushes because I didn't know what to do or where to go, and suppose you found me. What would you tell me so I wouldn't be so scared and so I would come out of the bushes?"

Third-person questions. An easy way to make questions less threatening to kids and to allow them some leeway in how they answer is to ask questions about kids in general in their context. The interviewer makes it clear that she is not trying to delve into the child's privacy. She is also communicating that she sees the child as an expert on this particular subject, for example, kids' ways in a group home. Questions about "what kids do," as opposed to "what you do," permit a respondent to answer honestly without having to implicate himself. "Sometimes kids sneak out at night and go hang out in the park. One of the kids stole a key, so they can get back in without waking the staff."

Video as questions. Some researchers have had success using videotape as an interview tool. George and Louise Spindler (1987) made pioneering contributions to the use of visual images as "evocative stimuli" and "reflective interviewing tools" in their comparative study of German and American views of elementary education. Their students, Fujita and Sano, used videotape in a similar way in their comparisons (1988) of Japanese and American nursery schools. Joe Tobin, David Wu, and Dana Davidson showed videotapes of typical days in Chinese, Japanese, and

American preschools to children, staff, and parents in each culture to stimulate a cross-cultural, "multivocal" ethnographic text (Tobin et al., 1989). In her study of group-time in a preschool classroom, Hong (1995) showed small groups of children video excerpts from group-time and asked the children to explain to her what was going on. The children's responses often were richly informative.

Obviously, one is not limited to using video as the question or stimulus. Low-tech objects like photographs can also work well.

Conversations as interviews. In the field, interviews often will be short and on the fly. Much of what is learned will be from short conversations throughout the day. The trick here is to be very attentive and to find ways to record what is being said during these brief interactions. Colleagues who have worked with preadolescents and adolescents describe kids who become very formal or clam up during an interview, even when one tries to make the process as informal as possible, but who love to just sit and talk to anyone who will listen. One must adapt to the context. As the old saying advises, "Dance with who brung you."

Timing. Interviewing kids when more interesting activities are available to them is not a good strategy. What child wants to sit down and answer dumb questions when she could be playing with friends on the climbing structure? Timing is important. Interviewing kids in "down" times, perhaps during "quiet time" or at the end of the day in an after-school program when kids are tired and more interested in sitting and talking quietly than in running around, works well. Baturka (Baturka & Walsh, 1991) was able to get permission to take kids out of class to interview. She discovered that 20 minutes out of class complete with secret snacks appealed to children. Interviewing children who do not like to sleep during nap time can work—if one can get permission or sneak it in. These are just examples. The point is to find times when sitting and talking is appealing to children, or at least as appealing as the alternatives.

Recording Interviews

Although recording interviews on audio- or videotape is common, recording by hand with a pen or a pencil in a notebook, as "retro" as it may sound, can be a more productive option and definitely is a skill that should be developed. Tape recorders affect what is being said and how it is being said. With young children, one may soon end up playing the game of listening to children talk into the tape recorder and playing back what they say. One may learn what young kids think is funny but little else. Writing down what children say communicates to them that one is taking them very seriously.

My experience is that even after rapport has been established and people appear comfortable, there still is hesitation about talking freely into a recorder. I am convinced that this is the case with adults. I am less sure about kids, but I am reluctant to conclude that they are unaware of the recorder and that the presence of the recorder has no effect. Arguments that children do not care about being recorded strike me as a combination of two claims: "Children are so innocent" and "They don't even know I am there." I do not buy either one. Kids are not that innocent, and they are very aware.

With adults, a ritual often gets established wherein the informant periodically asks that the tape recorder be turned off before answering a question. I have never had anyone object to my writing down something they said, even when I have asked them to repeat it, but something about saying it into a recorder makes people reluctant. I have used audio- and videotaping extensively, and even with a tape recorder on the floor and an unobtrusive external microphone on the end of the table, I always have been mindful of the respondent's awareness of the recorder. People, including children, will say things when the recorder is turned off that they will not say when it is running.

I have used video for recording interviews with both children and adults. I like the result. Viewing a video brings me back into the interview in a way that audio does not. Video records children's facial expressions, both while they are talking and while another child is talking, and often the expressions are more informative than what is said. I find that the visual image helps me decipher unclear responses more easily than if I were listening to an audiotape. The main disadvantage to using a video recorder is that it is very obtrusive. Using video requires the interviewer to position people and to consider light and shadows. A video recorder cannot be put out of sight the way an audio recorder can. The only camcorders I have used have been large and require substantial tripods. Newer, smaller machines with smaller tripods should be less obtrusive.

Digital video recorders, although in 1997 still very expensive, are quite small (5″ by 3½″ by 2″) and may make video recording interviews much more practical.

Recording in general is problematic in other ways. We discuss three. First, dependence on a recorder can lead one to be less attentive—"It's okay if I miss something being said because I have it on tape." Bruce Jackson warned,

> Almost every fieldworker I know who has done a lot of taped interviews has had the experience of realizing he or she had no idea of what was said in the past minute of five minutes. . . . If I know the tape is doing the remembering (far better than I could), I relax. I might think about the nail that seems to be working its way through my boot. I might think about the rest of the day's work. I might think of what he just reminded me of. I can . . . oh, damn: he's looking at me and waiting for an answer. An answer to what? You can feel pretty stupid when you're interviewing someone and you have to ask, "What was that you just said?" And the feeling is justified. (1987, p. 100)

Taking notes by hand or on a notebook computer forces an interviewer to attend to what someone is saying. Spradley (1979) urges interviewers to continually express their ignorance of and their interest in what people are saying. His advice is important. The *sine qua non* of a good interviewer is total attention to a kid and what he is saying. A good interviewer must first be a good listener. She cannot let a recorder do the listening for her.

Second, the recorder can become a distraction for the interviewer who is not completely familiar with and comfortable using it. Once the interview begins, one's total focus should be on the interview, not on the machine—"Did I remember to turn it on? Did I push *record*? Did I put the mike jack in the earphone socket? Is the recording level set right? Are the batteries dead?"

If children already find a recorder a diverting novelty, directing their attention to it by constantly fiddling with it will make it even more distracting. Practice using the machine before going into the field. Practice until it becomes automatic. Always check the batteries *before* going into the field, both in the recorder and in the microphone. Carry extra batteries. If you are a worrisome individual, consider using two recorders, but realize that this precaution may actually cause more worry. Once in the field, establish a routine that ensures that the recorder is working and that begins the interview. Sandy Ives describes his routine.

> When I am ready to begin the interview, I pick up the mike and say something like, "Well, let's get started." Then I speak directly into the mike, not looking at the informant at all, while I say, "This is Friday, September 29, 1980, and I am up in Argyle, Maine in the home of [Now I look at the informant] Ernest Kennedy, and we're going to be talking about the days when he was a river-driver. My name is Sandy Ives and this is tape 80.3." Then I put the mike back in its place, sit back and relax, and continue, "O.K., now that's taken care of. Now. . . ." That is to say, I involve myself with the machine to begin with, then I involve the informant, and the interview is suddenly underway. I try to do it all in an offhand, diffident way. At the same time, I have made it unmistakably clear that the interview has begun. (in Jackson, 1987, p. 89)

Having completed the preliminaries, begin the interview, concentrating all your attention on the interview. Get a mike with a long cord. Put the recorder off to the side or, better, on the floor out of sight. Never interrupt an interview to check the recorder. And take notes. Despite all your precautions, the machine may fail you.

Third, be aware that speech recorded in the field is often unclear, even with a good microphone. Words often are inaudible. Children spend much of their lives in relatively noisy places. Noise that is not noticed during an interview can become annoyingly loud on the tape. At times, it appears that everything gets recorded except what is being said—the toilet flushing down the hall, someone tapping the table with a pencil. You often will find yourself leaning forward in your chair while transcribing, trying to get physically closer to the sound coming through earphones.

External microphones are a necessity. The internal microphone on even the best recorder is limited in its sensitivity to prevent it from recording the internal noise of the machine. We recommend PZM microphones (both Crown and Radio Shack make them). They are very sensitive. They are omnidirectional; that is, they do not have to be aimed at the speaker. A PZM is unobtrusive. It is flat and does not look like a microphone. Children will not be tempted to press their lips against a PZM, imitating the singers they see on MTV.

It should be clear that there are trade-offs involved in how one records interviews, and taping is not always better. Jackson (1987) gives the following advice: "Use whatever machines will help you, but remember who's the boss: don't let the machines let you get lazy" (p. 102).

- Get the best recorder and the best external microphone you can afford.

Truth and Interviews

What is truth? A common concern is whether kids are telling the truth. "What if they lie to me, and I believe them?" Undoubtedly, people lie in interviews, on questionnaires, and on any other information-gathering instrument. To what extent is this an issue?

Interviews are not confessions. In fact, they are about more than getting "facts." Most interesting questions have no single true answer. Ask a graduate student, "Do you like grad school?" Ask a friend, "Do you like your boyfriend or girlfriend?" "Do you like being married?" "Do you like your kids?" A thoughtful answer to any stimulating question will contain many "it depends" and "compared to's," and it is going to vary day to day. Further, if confronted with a truly novel question, one may take a while to come up with a good answer, and chances are the next day one will think of another, seemingly better answer.

Even fabricated answers can assist the search for meaning. Kids fabricate their answers within a given social context and within a given range of possible answers. They will follow a pattern for fabrications. The story being told has a function as well as an element of truth even if details are not true. Every fiction is a variation on something. Exaggerations are part of the story about being a kid.

A lie also may be true at a deeper level. For example, a kid may say she doesn't like the food in the school cafeteria when in fact she does (admittedly, this may be a farfetched example). She does so because she is giving the group-defined true answer; that is, part of our identity as kids is that we don't like cafeteria food, and I'm a kid and therefore I don't like the food, whether I personally do or not.

Finally, the interviewing process is iterative, that is, lots of short interviews over a prolonged period of time. Interviews are done in conjunction with observation and artifact gathering that is also prolonged. Any single answer in an interview is situated within a much larger data record, allowing the researcher to make judgments about the believability of what who said when. There is a reason for "being there."

Instruments

Most discussions of qualitative research give short shrift to instruments. They emphasize that the researcher is the primary instrument, but understanding what it means to be an instrument requires a thorough understanding of what an instrument is. One way to do this is to think about using instruments. The instrumentality of the researcher will be discussed in Chapter 8. Here we focus on the use of instruments in the field.

Interpretive researchers do and should use instruments in the field. An instrument is a research tool constructed to assist in the generation of a certain kind of data in a systematic way. The creative use of instruments is particularly appropriate when doing research with young children because of the inherent limitations of interviewing and because of the constraints of distance discussed earlier.

When instruments are discussed, the standard instruction is that they should be constructed in the field. Emphasis both on the researcher as instrument and on the construction of instruments in the field is a reaction to a rather narrow view of research that long dominated some disciplines, particularly educational psychology and, through them, schools of education. In research located at the testing end of the theory continuum, the snapshot end of the duration continuum, and the measurement end of the description continuum, developing instruments (most often tests and observation forms) and subjecting them to strenuous examination of validity and reliability has merit. The research we do is located at other points along the continua. We have no interest in defining ourselves as researchers by reacting to others' narrow perspectives. Life is too short.

Instruments, whether developed in the field or modified from instruments that others have used, are important tools for generating data and important ways of ensuring that the data generation process includes multiple perspectives. Instruments are things. They are used to assist in systematic description—whether measurement or narrative. A good instrument makes a particular kind of systematic description easier. Earlier in the chapter, Ting's use of video to track children's movement during free play was described. Someone studying gender interactions in mixed-gender sports might develop an instrument that allows for accurate recording of how many times boys pass to girls and vice versa during a

soccer game. There are times when it is useful to get very specific information, information not obtainable from general descriptive fieldnotes.

Instruments can be as simple as maps of a site that allow one to track
children's movements. We mentioned earlier using children's pictures
during interviews. As research questions are refined and changed during
fieldwork, so should instruments change. It is crucial that one maintain
a record of both what modifications are made and when they were made
to avoid drawing unsupported conclusions or making senseless comparisons later.

Many instruments will be constructed in the field, but emphasizing
that aspect of instruments alone ignores the shared nature of the research
endeavor. A researcher entering a preschool room in a day care center is
not the first researcher to do so: Preschool rooms in general have been
entered many times; perhaps that room in particular has been entered by
a researcher if it is near a university. Why should she make up from
scratch everything that she will do, as though no one else ever has been
interested in the questions she has? Other people may well have constructed very useful instruments. One inevitably will find that borrowed
instruments work better after some modification, but the person who
originally developed them probably did so only after much experimen-
tation and modification.

Going into the field without knowledge of possibly useful instruments
is as pointless as going in without questions. It is important to know what
others in similar situations have done and to borrow and build on what
they have done. Research is social. The individual does not start from
scratch. He works within a larger and ongoing context.

- Don't invent what someone else already has invented. Chances are
  she did it better anyway.

We made the distinction earlier (Chapters 1 and 2) between accuracy
and precision. The strength of instruments is their precision. The danger
of precision is that it often is confused with accuracy. An instrument that
is designed to describe aggression levels on playgrounds but that does
not distinguish between playful hits and aggressive hits is not accurate.
An instrument designed to record the number of times that boys pass to
girls in the course of a soccer game may, for the sake of example, miss
the fact that boys do not pass to girls when their team has a scoring

opportunity. Keeping the precision/accuracy trade-off in mind when constructing instruments is critical.

Artifact Gathering

Artifact gathering is seldom given the attention it deserves. Our treatment will be shorter than the discussions of observing and interviewing, not because it is less important but because it is less problematic. Artifact collection is a critical aspect of the research process.

Artifacts, like all other data, must be generated; that is, the process of accumulating them is a very active and creative one. When early anthropologists traveled to far corners of the world to study exotic cultures, they often returned with items from those cultures—clothing, utensils, religious objects, and so on, the stuff of natural history museums. A native him- or herself might also be brought back and displayed. Items often were brought back that should not have been, for example, sacred items, which later generations have attempted to reclaim.

Early ethnographies were exhaustively descriptive, and displays of artifacts were part of the description. It must be remembered that early in the history of anthropology, visual recording was limited to drawings and, later, large, clumsy, and primitive cameras.

In today's academic world, a display of artifacts from a day care center or a youth hockey league or a girl scout camp would have little currency and audience. Unlike objects from a tribe in the mountains of New Guinea or the deserts of Australia, these artifacts would not be seen, at least at first glance, as exotic—the stuff of museums. Much of children's lives is hidden, however, and artifacts from that hidden life can illuminate it.

Consider for a moment the items contained in my daughter's hockey bag. I use this as an example because I suspect that many readers are not familiar with hockey bags and their contents. Most readers would be surprised at how big they are. Scooter's is 35" by 16" by 16," with two side pockets and two end pockets, along with lots of zippers and a heavy shoulder strap. The bag has an unmistakable locker-room aroma to it, particularly when initially opened. The pants come out first. Most people have seen hockey pants, but most would be surprised at how big and heavy they are. When Scooter began playing at the age of 6, the total weight of her equipment was about a quarter of her body weight. Next come shoulder pads, about what one would expect. Socks, gloves, shin pads, neck protector, and skates follow, again what one would expect. But what's this? It looks like a garter belt, heavier and more utilitarian than those displayed in the lingerie department but unquestionably a garter belt. Upon reflection, it makes sense. How else do hockey players keep those heavy socks up? Many readers probably never considered that Mario Lemieux wears a garter belt. Here's a little plastic container with a piece of wax inside. It turns out that many hockey players wax the tape on the blade of their stick—it holds the puck a little better, and because it seals the tape from moisture, the tape lasts longer. Next come two rolls of tape, one black and one clear. The black roll is for the stick. She wraps the clear tape around her socks to keep her shin guards in place. A few items are left at the bottom of the bag—extra laces, a mouth guard, some pucks, a pair of sweat socks, elbow pads, and a large—about 5 inches in diameter—ball of clear tape. What is this all about? Well, sit in the locker room after a practice or a game and watch most of the kids carefully roll the tape off their socks onto their tape ball as they see who can have the biggest tape ball at the end of the season. Watch the parents grumbling, "Sheesh, just take the tape off and get dressed so we can go home." Watch the kids nod and continue to painstakingly build their tape balls. A researcher who wanted to take a reader inside the world of youth hockey would do well to take the reader inside the bags that kids lug in and out of the rink.

In a world where kids are killed on urban streets for their jackets and their shoes, when the pressure on children to have a certain kind of jacket or shoe—inevitably a very expensive kind—is immense, the daily artifacts of life are central to any narrative that attempts to get at the meanings that children construct in their lives.

Some General Thoughts

As should be clear by now, artifacts can be more than pieces of paper, for example, children's work in a classroom or the weekly newsletter of the Boys and Girls Club. Artifacts do not have to be physically collected. Scooter may let you look in her hockey bag, but she is not going to let you have it. What is in that bag can be drawn, photographed, videotaped, recorded, or photocopied, as can the locker rooms she changes in and the rinks she plays on. Maps of rooms, of playgrounds, and of video arcades can be artifacts. Color photocopying makes it possible to keep true records of material that once had to be kept in black and white. Color photocopies from slides make it economical to put large color photographs into the data record.

Not enough attention has been paid in interpretive research to the use of what Eugene Webb and colleagues (Webb, Campbell, Schwartz, & Sechrest, 1966) called "physical trace" measures, ways of generating data by attending to the ways that human interaction leaves its mark on the environment. They described the "erosion" of tiles around exhibits at the Museum of Science and Industry in Chicago: The vinyl tiles around the hatching chicks needed to be replaced every 6 weeks, whereas the tiles around other exhibits lasted for years. Bernard (1988) refers to "behavior trace" studies, for example, studies of graffiti in public toilets (Sechrest & Flores, 1969) and of used-up (as opposed to smashed-up) cars in junkyards (Gould & Potter, 1984).

All things being equal (which they often are not), popular parts of a playground should show more wear and tear than unpopular parts. Swing seats become worn and the ground beneath the swings dug out. Favored toys get worn from constant handling. Preferred clothing fades with repeated washings. Containers of favored paint colors show up more often in the garbage. In fact, one of the best-known behavior trace studies, the "Garbage Project," has been carried out since 1973 by William Rathje and colleagues at the University of Arizona. They have been investigating consumer behavior patterns by sorting and analyzing garbage (see Bernard [1988, pp. 291 ff.] for more extensive description).

Getting at trace measures requires creativity and attention to details. Going through the garbage at the end of the day in a day care center may not sound appealing, but it may in fact provide important information about the actions and interactions of the people at the site. Volume of tissue may give an indication of the prevalence of colds; volume of discarded food, a clue to children's food preferences. As in all data generation, collecting unobtrusive measures can be problematic and present challenges. It may be the case, for example, that at the height of the flu season the trash cans are emptied more often, severely biasing observations made only at the end of the day. The challenge is to find the ways human action and interaction leave their mark on the environment and to find ways to describe those marks accurately.

We conclude with a brief comment on artifacts and confidentiality. Maintaining confidentiality with artifacts requires special care. The Boys and Girls Club newsletter contains names, photographs have faces, and so on. Names can be blocked out, as can faces, but the fact remains that there are many road maps back to the research site. The researcher must take care not to identify them.

Bias and Efficiency

Bias and efficiency challenge all researchers. Bias is systematic error in description. Efficiency refers to maximizing the information gathered in data generation.

Bias

Two earlier discussions, on triangulation (this chapter) and subjectivity (Chapter 3), explicitly addressed bias. In the discussion on triangulation, we wrote, "Using only one research strategy—for example, only observation, or worse, only one kind of observation—introduces bias into the data record." Bias can be introduced in many ways in data generation. A researcher observing a playground at the same time each day may conclude that the playground is used primarily by toddlers and their mothers when, in fact, at other times of the day the playground may be filled with older children. A researcher who interviews only those children recommended by a camp counselor may conclude that all the children at camp are happy and well adjusted when some kids at the camp may hate being there.

In the discussion on subjectivity, we wrote,

> Whatever the researcher discovers about her own personal biases and personal relationships to those with whom she is working, she must also locate herself in the theoretical connections of her field to achieve what Strauss (1987) calls an "informed theoretical sensitivity" (p. 12).

Bias can be introduced into the data record by attitudes and beliefs brought into the field. One cannot be free of attitudes and beliefs. Who one is affects how one sees the world. The trick is to develop a strong sense of that identity and how it affects one as a researcher in the specific contexts within which one is working. Bias cannot be removed. It can be identified and its effects explicitly monitored.

Efficiency

Absent unlimited time and money, a researcher must consider carefully the efficiency of data generating procedures. Asher and Gabriel (1993) moved their research on schoolchildren's social interactions to the playground after discovering that they were seeing very little social interaction in the classroom. The data being generated in the classroom were not worth the time and effort. By looking only at interactions on the playground, they biased their observations but made them much more efficient. They also were very aware of the direction and extent of the bias—the interactions on the playground were more frequent and less constrained by adult supervision than the interactions in the classroom.

There often is a trade-off between bias and efficiency. A representative sample of informants may contain individuals who are not good interview subjects. Good interview subjects may not be representative of the group being studied. Unbiased but extremely inefficient procedures do not generate much data. Extremely biased but efficient procedures may generate large amounts of uninterpretable data. The art of data generation is striking a balance. The integrity of data generation is communicating to oneself and to one's audience the limitations of the data record.

Not all description error is systematic. A person can be a poor fieldworker and generate very superficial data that are not so much biased as useless. Consider the researcher in the playground example above who addresses the observation bias issue but who never looks carefully enough to discover that many of the women with toddlers are not mothers but nannies.

Conclusion

Anthropologist Charles Frake responded to the author of an article on his work in this way:

> You go overboard about my skills as an ethnographer. It is likely to make others who are as good or better than I am mad. . . . I only claim to worry more about how to do it than most. I worry a lot. (in McDermott, 1982, p. 328)

Good researchers should worry a lot. As human beings, we are easily fooled by appearances—ask any journeyman magician. We are remarkably adept at fooling ourselves. We need to worry when we are generating data. If we are fooling ourselves, eventually we will be fooling others. The only research sin is arrogance, particularly arrogance of method—the arrogance that one's method puts one above worry. No method does.

Data generation is a collection of many skills. Acquiring any skill requires practice, at times much practice. A good researcher has generated data x number of times. She has worried about her data generating strategies y number of times. Both x and y are very large numbers.

Notes

1. Again, we are indebted to Ray McDermott for these ideas.
2. I (Daniel) heard the story in a graduate seminar at the University of Wisconsin-Madison in the fall of 1981.
3. We found this in Eisenhart (1995).

7

CONSTRUCTING A DATA RECORD

Our experience is that beginning researchers gain data generation skills rapidly. Learning to transform data into a workable
data record occurs more slowly.

Generating data is challenging, but fieldwork, "being there," soon
becomes enjoyable, exciting, even addictive. *There* is often a hospitable
place. I certainly find it more enjoyable than being here in my office.
Anthropologists George and Louise Spindler admit to having "fallen ill,
been cold, wet, and insect bitten, suffered from having to struggle along
in someone else's language, been rejected by the very people we wanted
to know, harassed by children when we wanted to work with their
elders . . ." (1970, p. 300), but nevertheless, they proudly report, "We
have never had a truly bad time in the field . . ." (p. 300).

In comparison, constructing a data record is drudgery—tedious,
demanding work often done late into the night. The temptation to focus
on fieldwork at the expense of constructing a data record can be strong.
One easily can convince oneself, as I have done and have sorely
regretted, that, given limited time, generating data is more important

---

AUTHORS' NOTE: Written by Daniel.

that working on a data record, which can be put off for a few days or weeks or months.

Messy and cryptic fieldnotes worked on and expanded soon after they were taken become windows onto one's field experience. Scribbles remain legible, and the briefest notes brim with meaning. Weeks or even days later, the fieldnotes begin to wilt. The handwriting becomes difficult to read; the notes, meaningless—why did I write this? They no longer return one to the experience recorded. The immediacy has faded. Data records should be constructed as soon as possible. George Spindler used to tell his graduate students (one of whom was me) not to sleep between data generation and data record construction. By the time you wake up in the morning, he told us, something will be lost.

- Data records deteriorate as a geometric function of the time between data generation and record construction.

A data record is essential. Being there is not enough. Many people have been there. The children being studied have been there longer and have had a much richer experience than the researcher, but they have not recorded their experience. Without a robust data record, those hours in the field, however interesting and rewarding, will not have been research, only the stuff of fond memories. Human memory can be wonderful, but it is not a good place to store data for any but the briefest lengths of time.

- Allow 3 hours for record construction for every hour of data generation, more if one is transcribing interviews.
- From the very beginning, allow additional time, at least 1 hour for every 3 hours in the field, for interpretation.
- No one ever allots enough time for interpretation.

A common error is not to earmark enough time in one's research plan for constructing data records and for interpretation (we focus on interpretation in the following chapter). Allot the time. Write it into the plan at the beginning of the research. Write into the plan entire days devoted to the data record. Sit down with a calculator and do the math: If I am planning 30 hours of fieldwork a week, that means I need 90 hours for constructing the data record and another 10 hours for interpretation. That's 130 hours. A week has 168 hours. That leaves 38 hours for sleeping, eating, taking care of my kids, classes, and so on. If I sleep 6 hours a night, that leaves minus 4 hours for everything else. Maybe I need to work on my plan a little more.

Constructing data records in timely fashion is essential when working with children. Interviews with children are typically brief and informal, and easily forgotten. Observations are likely to be interrupted often. A participant observer—for example, a volunteer counselor—must rely heavily on memory and cryptic, hastily scribbled notes. The practice of reconstructing fieldnotes weeks or months later by sitting down with participants and trying to figure out what they were doing or saying as you both try to decipher your notes or understand a muddy recording is a suspect practice at best and abusive of people's time. With children, especially young children, the strategy also is ineffective.

This chapter explores, first, what a data record is; second, how it is constructed; and, third, why a rich data record is important.

The Data Record

Many treatments of research skip over the process of constructing a data record and imply that analysis (we use *interpret* and *analyze* interchangeably), for example, coding, is performed on raw data. This is a serious omission. Notes taken in the field are incomplete, reminders that allow one to write the full narrative description later. Tapes must be transcribed, and artifacts sorted. The data record is constructed from the raw data generated in the field. The data record results from transforming raw data into a form that is organized (that is, easily accessible) and flexible (that is, accessible in many ways).

In the field, the researcher generates data. These data take various forms, the more forms the better. The researcher brings these raw data to a study (assuming one has the luxury of a study) in notebooks and bags and piles them, for the sake of discussion, on a desk. Large piles of raw data can intimidate even the experienced researcher—"What do I do with all of this?" Until the piles are turned into an organized and flexible data record, very little can be done.

At her desk, the researcher constructs a data record and interprets it. It is sometimes claimed that researchers should but "present the data and let them speak for themselves." If it were so easy. We have yet to hear our data speak. Instead, they sit there, inert, and continue to sit there until worked on. The longer they sit untouched, the less they will have to say. The first step is to get them into a form that makes working on them possible. The work done at this point will save anguish and frustration later. The quality of the work done early will affect the quality of work done later.

The distinction, then, between raw data and a data record is crucial. The notes one takes, the drawings one makes, the tapes one records, and so on, in the field are raw data. When the shorthand notations and the cryptic and hurriedly written fieldnotes are expanded into full narrative and entered into a word processing program or a data analysis package, then fieldnotes become part of a data record. When audiotapes are transcribed or when videotapes are logged (described below), they become part of the data record. Building a data record is not peculiar to fieldwork-based research. All raw data need to be worked on before they can be analyzed—questionnaire answers must be taken from the answer sheets and entered into a database, as must test scores or any other recorded descriptions, whether narrative or measurement.

Although interpretation is ongoing, it does not become a primary activity until a data record is constructed. The primary activity in the field is generating data. The reason for stressing the distinction between data generation and interpretation is that it is tempting to move immediately from level one, the immediately visible, to level three, the invisible. If, however, one begins interpreting in the field and records the interpretation rather than the concrete particulars of actions and interactions observed, later, when one discovers that the initial interpretation was deficient, there is nothing in the data record to reinterpret. Another way to look at it is that moving to a generalization without a robust record of concrete particulars is not finding it out, it is making it up.

Constructing a Data Record

- Assume you will remember nothing. Always over-annotate at every stage of the research process.

The first step in data record construction is annotation—making sure that everything is described in enough detail to be immediately recognizable. Annotation requires answering the basic journalist questions—who, what, where, why, when, and how—for every entry in the data record. The tendency is to believe that one will remember why this particular drawing from Melissa was collected or why a particular episode involving Kim and Maurice was recorded. In the field, one gathers many drawings, encounters many Melissas, and witnesses many vivid events. The day just completed, which stands out so clearly in the evening, will soon become one of many days.

Consider the mysterious entries in one's schedule book—phone numbers without names, first names without last names, names without instructions about what one is to do with this person and where. Assume you will remember nothing and tag everything with detailed information. Adding too much detail is possible, but extraneous information can be discarded; missing information often is unretrievable.

A robust data record is multidimensional. As Luria noted, we should "view an event from as many perspectives as possible" (1979, p. 177). Because so much interpretive work is done alone, the temptation is to favor those data generation strategies one finds most comfortable. For example, I am most at ease conducting interviews and must be careful not to construct data records heavily weighted with interview transcripts. Rich data records present many perspectives.

Raw Data

- Always keep raw data. You never know when you will have to go back to them.

Maintaining raw data (of any kind) is essential in case a question comes up later than can be answered only by returning to the original data. With any form of raw data, make a copy and store the copy in a different location from the original; for example, keep one in the office and the other at home. When using a notebook computer, store the raw fieldnotes and create a new computer file before transforming the notes. Always back up on disk, not just on the hard drive. Backing up the hard drive on tape is a good idea.

Why might one want to return to the raw data? Here is an example. A few weeks before Buck's (Daniel's son) third birthday, his 9-year-old sister, Scooter, figured out that he used "got-for" for "forgot," as in "I got-for my book." He had been saying this, we immediately realized, for a long time, but in the past we had been hearing got-for as a curious use of an extra preposition after "got," thus understanding "got-for" as "got," basically ignoring the "for," and completely misunderstanding what he was saying. We thought he was telling us, for example, that he had his book when he was telling us he didn't. We were not sure why he was telling us he had something he did not appear to have, but one comes to expect certain contradictions from toddlers, at least this one, and most likely they come to expect the same from adults. No doubt he was frustrated that we were not sympathetic to his predicament. Now imagine having recorded Buck's conversations and discovering that one had misinterpreted the verb "got-for" for months, and that in one's transcriptions one had ceased hearing, as we did, the "for" and transcribing it as "got." Now imagine that the original tapes had been copied over. Imagine also having begun to draw conclusions about Buck's language use based on the fact that he appeared to be talking about getting things that he had not gotten and now no longer being able to distinguish between his use of "got" and "got-for."

Fieldnotes

The discussion on turning notes taken in the field into fieldnotes that are part of the data record will be brief. The trick to constructing a strong narrative in the data record is to treat notes taken in the field as reminders from which the larger narrative is built. "Transcribing" what is in a notebook from handwritten to word-processed form results in thin description. H. Russell Bernard (1988) refers to what is written in the field as "jottings." He reserves the term *fieldnotes* for what the jottings are expanded into.

The written descriptions, or field jottings, in that pile on the desk are very important, but making them part of the data record requires work. The researcher begins with these jottings and then, with headnotes and the experience of having been there, writes narrative description that goes beyond these initial notes. The goal is what Norm Denzin calls "thick description":

> Thick description . . . does more than record what a person is doing. It goes beyond mere fact and surface appearances. It presents detail, context, emotion, and the webs of social relationships that join persons to one another. Thick description evokes emotionality and self-feelings. It inserts history into experience. It establishes the significance of an experience, or the sequence of events, for the person or persons in question.

In thick description, the voices, feelings, actions, and meanings of interacting individuals are heard. (1989, p. 83)

We recommend formatting fieldnotes with very large margins. The margins provide a place for notes. I prefer single-spacing to keep the volume of paper down. Each page should have a running head that provides annotation—who, where, when. Some data analysis packages number each line, which can be useful. Keeping a running time is useful. Every 5 minutes works well. It also is useful to have a consistent system of conventions. For example, I always use square brackets to separate comments from the description. The example below illustrates the suggested format.

045
101591
After School
1600-1730

the time they are finished.

1635

All the children in the blue group get up and throw their napkins in the trash can. There is a lot of jostling near the trash can. It is the playful jostling of children who enjoy being with each other. The pokes and pushes are all given and taken with smiles. Many of the boys take jump shots and try to bounce their napkins off the wall. TK raises both arms into the air when he makes his shot. DB stops at "leaders' table" to get her clipboard. She pulls her hair into a ponytail and fastens it with a blue and orange "scrunchy" she was wearing on her wrist. She yells at the boys to pick up the napkins that missed the can. JS groans but picks them up and slam dunks them. The kids are going up the stairs laughing and talking. RG stops at the top of the stairs and shouts down, "Come on, DB. You're always so slow." The kids laugh and more shouts of "slow DB" come down the stairs. Someone yells, "DB is a pokey-do!" [I am struck by the casual friendliness of the relationship between the kids and DB, so different from between kids and teachers. I think I notice this more because it occurs in a school building, but what is happening is not "school."]

1640

By the time I get out on the playground the kids are already choosing teams for kickball. I look for a place in the shade. It's very hot. I sit down on the "sitting log" next to DD who can't play because she cut her foot the night before and it is heavily bandaged. I ask her if it's okay if I ask her some questions with my tape recorder going. ES comes over and asks if she can talk too.

Audio and Video Tapes

Transcribing tapes is very time-consuming. It also can be incredibly frustrating as one finds oneself leaning forward in the chair trying to get closer to the words that, despite numerous replays, remain inaudible.

The first thing to decide is the level of accuracy desired. All transcriptions are approximations. No transcription, even assuming wonderful clarity on the tape and no covering noises, is exact. Even if one gets the exact words, missing are the tone, the pace, the emphasis, the nuances, and so on. The nonverbal sounds, the grunts and "uhs" that people make when talking, can only be approximated. The rhythms of speech, the actual time it takes to say something, are missing from most transcriptions. Good transcription requires a set of transcription conventions (see Box 7.1 for an example). A good set of conventions can make the transcriptions richer, but human speech is very complex, and getting it on paper can never be exact, even with adults who know they are being recorded and speak in a way that facilitates recording.

The level of accuracy required will depend on one's purposes. Microanalysis, for example, requires greater accuracy than more conventional forms of analysis. D'Amato (1986), who was very interested in the rhythms of classroom responses, transcribed a classroom episode in real time (see Figure 7.1). Transcribing at this level of accuracy is extremely labor-intensive. Although it does not use real time, Sacks's (1974) transcription of the telling of a joke remains a wonderful example of painstaking transcription that re-creates for the reader an actual exchange between young boys. Although less time-consuming than D'Amato's efforts, Sacks's transcriptions probably are more exacting than one may often need.

Bruce Jackson sees value in transcribing tapes yourself: "I was happy for the labor [of transcribing the tapes] because I learned a great deal listening to those tapes line by line, again and again" (1987, p. 81). Transcribing tapes requires a foot-operated transcription machine that automatically backs the tape up a preset amount each time it is paused and on which the speed can be adjusted. Transcribing from a recorder is not worth the effort.

Even if one prefers and can afford to have tapes transcribed, it is important to regularly transcribe portions to check the accuracy of the person doing the transcription. People who have no trouble transcribing

---

Box 7.1
Transcription Conventions

Transcription format adapted from
Sacks, Schegloff, and Jefferson (1974).

1. Regular uppercase and lowercase type is used to indicate speech.
2. Double parentheses, (( )), are used to provide information about a speaker's tone of voice or about nonverbal speech activity.
3. A double oblique, //, indicates the point at which a speaker is interrupted and stops speaking.
4. Underscoring (or italics) indicates emphasis placed on the underscored (or italicized) word, achieved through pitch changed or increased volume.
5. A colon, :, within a word indicates that the pronunciation of the preceding syllable or syllable part is prolonged (e.g., "n:o" signifies elongated pronunciation of the "no").
6. Letters preceded and followed by a single oblique, /d/, represent phonemes.

Transcription format modified from
Sacks, Schegloff, and Jefferson (1974)

1. Four dashes, ——, indicates that a speaker pauses to rephrase or self-correct.
2. Ellipses, . . . , indicates omitted material.

Additions by author for this study.

1. (?) indicates indecipherable sounds.
2. [description], indicates description of people's action.
3. "child/children" and "girl/boy" indicate the voice cannot be identified.

SOURCE: From Hong (1995).

---

dictation can have their skills tested by tapes of conversation and may have difficulty understanding children's speech, especially if the child speaks a dialect. Some years ago, even though it was one of the few times

In an attempt to preserve the flow of talk in the lesson, the transcript has been organized in terms of "strips" (a use that basically accords with Goffman's (1974) use of the term). A strip is all the talk done in a 5-second period. If all the strips of a transcript were joined end to end, one would have a written version of some of the information contained on a strip of audiotape or videotape. Here is the first strip of the lesson:

:00   :05

                                                          Claradine?
                                                                   Science
Science
    ROOOOO
          I know what that
                                                          Ahhhhhhhhhhhh

Each strip is organized in terms of lines to introduce separation among speakers. The top line is always reserved for the teacher's comments. The second line is reserved for talk done by a child to the teacher; additional lines also may be used for this purpose when more than one child responds. The lines below the second line are otherwise used according to the temporal order of the children's comments. Thus, this first strip begins with a child saying the word, "Science." The child is trying to read the words Ellen has written on the blackboard. Overlapping that child's speech, another child barks, "ROOOOO." Overlapping the bark, a third child says, "I know what that." The teacher then calls on Claradine, whose hand is up, and Claradine responds with her idea about what the teacher has written, saying, "Science." Meanwhile, a fourth child has said, "Ahhhhhhhhhhhh."

SOURCE: From D'Amato (1986, p. 21).

Figure 7.1. Transcription Example

I had funds for transcription, I had to transcribe one tape myself because the midwesterners I had hired could not understand the thick Virginia eastern-shore accent on the tape. On another tape, an interviewee with a more penetrable—by Midwestern ears—Virginia accent referred to a school named Broadus Wood (after a local politician) numerous times. The person doing the transcription heard the phrase as "brought us wood" and managed also to hear the sentences in which the name appeared in a way that the transcription made some sense.

Logging

Generally, one transcribes audiotapes, especially interviews. At times, one may prefer, if one has many tapes and is interested only in certain topics, to "log" the tapes. Logging videotapes is the norm. Unless one views videotapes merely as audiotapes with pictures and is interested in what is being said rather than what is being done, transcribing them is an immense task—how much does one describe?

The first step in making a videotape part of a data record is to make it accessible. Reading a data record of a half-hour episode on a playground generally will take much less than 30 minutes. Viewing a video of a 30-minute recess takes 30 minutes. As one's video collection grows, making it accessible becomes increasingly important.

Logging a tape consists of dividing the tape into short segments using a consistent set of criteria, for example, by activity, by topic, or by actors' entry and exit. Each segment begins with the time recorded on the tape—always use the date and running time option—and has a brief description of what occurs in that segment. Logging audiotapes is more difficult because one does not have the running time referent. Machine counters often are not consistent across machines. It can be useful to log transcriptions themselves by topic or some other important criteria as a precoding step. Doing so can make computer searches more efficient.

Once a tape is logged, then one can access specific segments and within the segment expand the logging process by describing the action in more detail and introducing codes. A shelf of videotapes is inaccessible. A well-constructed log book makes the tapes accessible and turns the raw data of tapes into part of a data record.

Hui-Fen Lin (1993, 1995) experimented with ways to cheaply and easily move visual data from videotapes onto paper. She paused the video image she wished to copy and then traced it on a piece of tracing paper taped to the screen (Figure 7.2). If she wanted to record an episode, she paused the tape every few seconds and traced each image (Figure 7.3). She then took these tracings and scanned them into a computer file. At that point, she was no longer tied to the actual tracing and having to copy it. She also was able to enter verbal information onto the

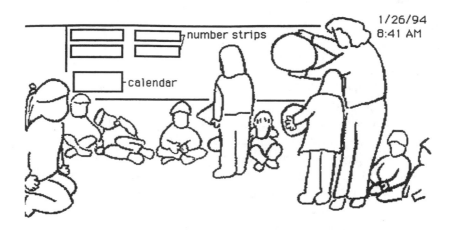

number strips

1/26/94
8:41 AM

calendar

Example 9:   Teacher demonstration—orbiting and rotating
Date: January 26, 1994
Time: Group-time

Mary calls on Elena to stand in the middle of the meeting rug as the
sun and Ivana to stand beside Elena as the earth. Mary herself
plays the moon.

Figure 7.2. Tracing From Video
SOURCE: Lin, 1995, p. 74.

image, for example, dialogue or children's names. This strategy allowed
her to show the reader what was occurring in the classroom she was
studying, but without identifying children or teacher the way a
photographic image would have. Hsueh-Yin Ting (1992) used simple
drawings based on a video to show children's movement and interactions
in the block corner (Figure 7.4).

As always, back up raw data, and that includes tapes. Copying tapes
results in a loss of quality. Work off copies rather than the original. That

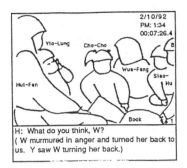

H: What do you think, W?
(W murmured in anger and turned her back to us. Y saw W turning her back.)

(Y turned his back to us,too)
H: (to W) W, after C, it'll be your turn. Turn back. Y is doing what you did.

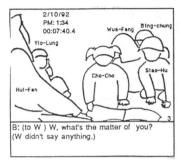

B: (to W) W, what's the matter of you?
(W didn't say anything.)

W: (to Y) Don't you imitate me!
Y: No,...(Y murmured back to W.)
(H helped Y turned back.)

W: Get out of my place!
Y: Get out of my place. (Y's voice was very soft.)

W: (to Y) Don't you imitate me!
(Y looked at W with his mouth pouting .

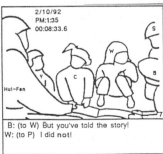

B: (to W) But you've told the story!
W: (to P) I did not!

B: But I am mad at her.
(W lowed her head.)

Figure 7.3. Tracing an Episode
SOURCE: Adapted from Lin (1995, p. 74).

way, if the tape being used is damaged or lost or stolen, the original still is available, and one does not have to make a copy of a copy.

Instruments

We discussed using instruments in Chapter 6. Data generated with and on instruments are raw data. They must be put into record form. If, for example, one does "snapshots" of children by noting on maps of the classroom, as Ting (1992) did, children's location and activity every 5 minutes, one must work on these maps. First, the sheets of paper need to be copied and annotated. Then one needs to find some way of "reducing" the data from many sheets to many fewer sheets. A stack of 300 sheets of paper recording children's movements over a 3-hour session across a week are not accessible. Figure 7.6 in the case study by Hsueh-Yin Ting that follows shows one way Ting turned her raw data on children's movements within a classroom into an accessible data record.

Artifacts

Photographs need to be printed or made into slides; drawings, copied; video recordings, logged. Artifacts themselves must be organized, when possible, into file folders, as well as logged, that is, described in enough detail that one knows what is where. The task is to get the piles into manageable, accessible form. It is unlikely, for example, that everything in the weekly six-page newsletter to parents at the day care center relates to one's research. Highlight those areas that do.

A very useful advance in computer technology is the scanner, mentioned above, which makes it possible to copy written material directly into computer files. Doing so can make the work of analysis much easier. Like everything else, artifacts should be copied. Non-paper objects should be photographed or videoed, and stored.

The Importance of the Data Record

The data record is, to borrow Fred Erickson's phrase, the evidentiary warrant that underlies interpretation. It is not only the record of one's being there, it is what was amassed while there. It is what one works on as one interprets. Research without a rich data record is simply making

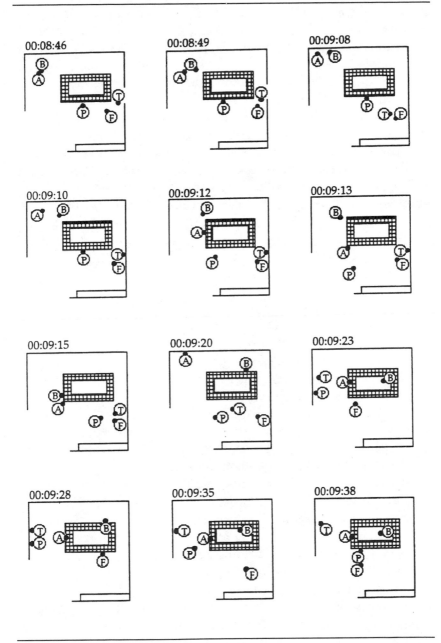

Figure 7.4. Drawings From Video (Dots indicate direction child is facing.)
SOURCE: From Ting (1992, p. 100).

it up. People who make it up generally do so based on observations and experience—"Just the other day I was visiting a summer camp"—but not on a substantial record of observation and experience. Beware of the sage without a robust data record. As the first three rules of real estate sales are "location, location, location," the first three rules of fieldwork are "Record it. Record it. Record it."

We have not up to this point explicitly addressed *validity*, at least not the term. We have preferred to talk about *accuracy* and *precision*. We have two reasons for doing so: first, the baggage that the term *validity* carries in most introductory discussions of research; and second, the limited perspectives on validity in these discussions.

Validity as defined in the dictionary, "well grounded or justifiable," is an important concept. It should be clear that the importance of the data record is that without a robust data record, analysis is not well grounded or justified. A robust data record does not guarantee well-grounded interpretations, but it is the *sine qua non* of good interpretation, necessary but not sufficient. Whether or not the final research report is well grounded or justifiable depends on every aspect of the research process, from planning through writing.

The baggage "validity" carries is measurement baggage. Validity is often used not to refer to the research as a whole but to specific measurements, usually involving instruments, taken in the research. Within the psychometric tradition, validity is used to describe tests, which are often used as instruments in measurement-oriented research. Because of the measurement baggage, some researchers prefer other terms: Geertz (1973), "assertability"; Campbell (1978), "plausibility"; Denzin (1989), "verisimilitude"; Erickson (1989), "trustability."

Introductory research methods textbooks contain long discussions of "threats to validity" (see Krathwohl, 1993, pp. 454-478). The threats discussed—for example, local history, maturation, mortality, and selection—need to be considered in all forms of research, but the textbook discussions invariably locate the threats within measurement, often experimental, research. If, for example, half the kids in the Cub Scout pack being studied quit during the course of fieldwork, then "mortality" must be addressed, but the interpretive researcher will get little help from the standard texts. In fact, how the researcher deals with this challenge will depend very much on the context, where it is conceivable that the mortality is less a threat than an important finding. One can imagine some kids as seeing Cub Scouts as something to do until Little League begins.

Because the issue of expanding perspectives on validity goes well beyond the present discussion of the importance of the data record, we will address it in Chapter 10.

An essential concept in social science research is that one does not analyze social interactions and social processes themselves. One records interactions and processes and then interprets the records. At the same time, the interpretive process begins from the moment one steps into the field, through all the many hours in the field, and through the many more hours working on the data record and writing. Insights can happen at any time. Good insights should not be ignored. Our intention in distinguishing recording from interpreting is to emphasize the importance of the data record.

The purpose of research with children should be to get at and underneath the day-to-day realities of those kids. To return the analogy of three levels borrowed from Maclean, getting to the invisible is done through the data record. One will first see the invisible in one's data record and then in the field.

Conclusion

- Touch the data.

Every data record will be different, as each research project is unique, but a good data record always will be well organized, that is, easily accessible and flexible, accessible in many ways. One way to ensure construction of a viable data record is to handle the raw data as much as possible and in as many different ways as possible. Touch the data. Spread it out, stack it, sort it; spread it out again, restack it, resort it. Use lots of Post-its. Handling the data gets additional data out of memory and into the record. It turns abstract information into concrete data.

Getting Into the Peer Social Worlds of Young Children

Hsueh-Yin Ting

*National Hsin-Chu Teachers College,
Taiwan, Republic of China*

Qualitative research is context-sensitive. The researcher adopts different roles, and uses different strategies and methods, depending on where she is and what she is doing. The wisdom of qualitative research lies in reflexive decision making in context. When one studies children, the age of the children is one of the contextual factors that influence decision making.

In this essay, I talk about some of the decisions I made while studying young children's peer social world. One study was done in a day care classroom and focused on what I called "children on the edge," that is, children on the fringe of the children's social world. The second was done in a multilingual/multicultural preschool classroom and focused on peer grouping.

I will address two issues generally: how I established a researcher role that helped me get into the peer social world, and how I used video to record children's interactions in that world.

The Researcher's Role

Discussions of research often talk about the importance of being unobtrusive, as though we can become like just another piece of furniture in the room. No matter how unobtrusive a researcher tries to be, the nature of the context changes when she enters. Monitoring the effect of one's presence is important because that presence can affect the interpretations of both researcher and participants.

My first challenge was to get close enough to the children's peer world to be able to observe it while affecting it minimally. I wanted to be able to view interactions that occurred while children were not under adult supervision. As an adult, however, my size and my perceived adult competence make me distinctly different from children. As an ethnic Chinese adult whose English is less than colloquial, even though there were Asian and Asian American children in both studies, I also stood out, more in the first study than in the second. More important, as an adult in a context where the other adults were in authority, I was perceived as having authority. My goal was to minimize the children's perception of my authority. Reducing my perceived authority was my "pass" to their social world.

I found that it is possible, using Corsaro's (1985) "reactive strategy," to establish a role in a classroom different from the other adults there. Corsaro noted that adults in authority usually take action first and the children react. I reacted only when the children approached me. My taking a reactive role helped the children distinguish me from other adults in the classroom. The children usually behaved differently in the adults' presence to avoid adult intervention in their activity. I did not intervene in children's activity. I was particularly careful not to intervene in conflicts.

In both studies, I entered the classroom without being formally introduced by the teachers. I sat near a center and observed. When children asked me what I was doing, I told them I was there to watch them playing. I never spoke to the teachers about the children while the children were there. If I needed to talk to teachers, I did it after school. I did not want the children to see me as a spy who would tell the teacher what they were doing. I wanted to be viewed as a loyal friend. By not acting like an adult in the day care and in the classroom, I was able to get into parts of the children's social world that are not easily observed by teachers.

Role defining is a continual and interactive process. During the first few weeks, as I was observing them, the children were also observing me and trying to figure out who I was. Some asked me if I was somebody's mother; others asked me what I was doing there.

(10/03/96: second week of observation)

I am sitting beside a table, writing fieldnotes. A 4-year-old boy comes up to me and asks, "What are you doing?" I reply, "I am writing." "What did you write?" "I wrote down what I see in the classroom." He points to a line on my notes, "Read these lines." I read them, pointing to each word as I do. "It says, 'At 10:30, in the gross motor area, there is no adult there.' " He smiles and asks, "Is that exactly what is written there?" I say, "Yes." He smiles. No more questions. He sits beside me and plays with the small blocks.

Children's Resistance

Normally, participants decide whether or not they want to be part of our studies, but with young children, consent is given by parents

or guardians. Once the parents sign the form, children find themselves being studied whether they want to be or not. That does not
mean that in fact children do not resist. I found that it was at times
difficult to accept that some children rejected me (ironically, when I
was interested in children's rejection of each other).

(09/25/93: first week of observation)

I am observing next to the block center. N comes up to me and punches
me twice in the shoulder. His little fists do not hurt me. Not knowing what
he means by hitting me, I react with a smile, trying to show him my
friendliness. He comes up and punches me again. Instead of stopping
him like a teacher, I decide to react as a peer might. I ask, "Why did
you hit me? I don't like that." He says, "I hate you." I ask, "Why?" He
replies, "I don't know. I just hate you." M (girl) walks by. He hugs her
and says, "I don't hate you (to M), but I hate you (pointing at me)." He
then moves a few steps away and shouts to the whole room, "I hate
that woman over there!" Feeling hurt and embarrassed, I don't know how
to react. I sit there and look at him. He finally leaves when the teacher
calls, "N!"

This happened in my first week of fieldwork during what would
be my first really intensive study. I felt hurt and embarrassed when
N proclaimed his hatred for me in front of the whole class. Later,
the teacher told me that N does not like outsiders to come into
the classroom and responds similarly to most outsiders. I felt a little better. I did have some empathy for N—he did not have the option of refusing to sign a permission form and this might have been
his only opportunity to express his unhappiness about being observed. Still, I had difficulty dealing with my "N problem." For the rest
of the study, I tried to stay away from N when I observed in the
classroom.

Ethical Dilemmas

Deciding not to intervene brings with it an ethical dilemma. I had
to be "loyal" to the children to be accepted into their peer world. I
wanted them to feel safe enough to act the way they would if there
were no adult around. That meant not only that I did not intervene,
but also that I did not talk to the teacher about much of what I saw.
I did not find the role easy. As an educator, I felt continual responsibility to protect and educate children. At times, I had to struggle

with my decision to intervene only if there was clear danger of physical harm.

In my communication with the teachers, I was also "reactive." By being reactive—that is, by talking to teachers about children only when they asked and by being circumspect when I did—I was able to remain "loyal" to the children. I also was able to correct a mistake I made early in my research, that is, unintentionally communicating to teachers that I was seeing things that they were not.

Recording Children's Interactions

Getting physically and socially close to the children was only the first step. Finding ways to record the richness and complexity of their interactions was my second challenge. I found that video and audio taping and a strategy I called "snapshots" were most useful in recording the subtlety of children's verbal and nonverbal interactions.

I found at times that doing research in English rather than my native language made it difficult to pick up all that children were saying to each other. I also found that the nuances of nonverbal communication made it difficult to record interactions in narrative fieldnotes. I felt that if I could draw pictures of what I was observing, my record would be more accurate and closer to the multidimensional aspects of interaction, but drawing well and rapidly is not a skill I possess. I discovered video and audio recording to be most useful. I could listen to children's conversations repeatedly and gain understandings that initially eluded me. Being able to view the interactions repeatedly and at times to review them frame by frame was invaluable for doing microanalysis of children's interactions. Unlike adults, whose language abilities are well developed, children's interactions are marked by nonverbal signs and body language. For example, spatial distance often is an important clue for understanding children's peer relationships. Having a video record also allowed me to ask the children to view their interactions and to comment on them.

Using Video

There is probably no "best" way of using video, but I believe that there are "better" ways. How one uses it depends a lot on the context. I spent a lot of time in both studies experimenting. A good quality camcorder and microphone are prerequisites. When I use video, I always consider three factors: least obtrusiveness, best view and clear sound, and safety (both of the participants and the equipment).

Least Obtrusiveness

A camcorder can influence what one is recording. Using one is much more intrusive than using a pen and a small notebook. It attracts children's attention, and I found that a warm-up period was necessary to satisfy the children's curiosity and let them get used to the machine's presence. When I introduced the camcorder, well after the children had gotten used to me, I let them look through the viewer. Most were satisfied after one look. For those who asked to look repeatedly, I had to explain that the camcorder was not a toy. I found that the degree of obtrusiveness depended on children's previous experiences. In both sites, children were accustomed to being observed and videoed. There was little "performing" for the camcorder. The children seemed to know it was not a toy and that it should not be touched without my permission.

One discovery I made was that a camcorder left running without my attending to it, that is, looking through the viewer, was less obtrusive than when I was there operating it. I often left the camcorder on a tripod recording activity in one area of the classroom.

Best View and Clear Sound

A camcorder has a limited view range. With peripheral vision, the human eye can see 180 degrees or more. The camcorder can see only a piece of that. The restricted locations for placing the camcorder in a classroom limit it even more. I spent much time experimenting with where to place the camcorder.

In the first study, the classroom was large (40 by 28 feet). I decided to video children's interactions in the block center because it was a popular area and because it did not have the number-of-children-allowed-at-one-time restriction that some other areas did. I tried three different spots (on a weekend when the room was empty), eventually settling on a fourth (see Figure 7.5). The first was on top of the piano, the back of which served as one border to the block area. The camcorder was out of the way, but the height made it difficult to adjust, and from there I could not record both activity in the area and children entering and leaving the area.

I then tried putting it on a shelf on one side of the area at eye level with the children. Getting children coming in and out from that angle required my moving the camcorder back and forth, and I couldn't

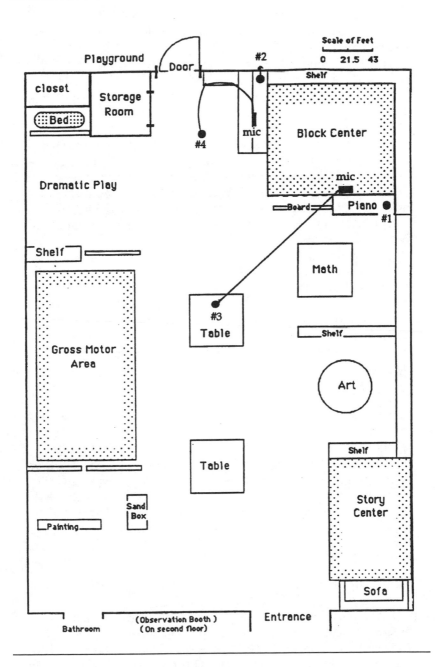

Figure 7.5. Camera Placement
SOURCE: From Ting (1992).

monitor it because the viewfinder was on the left and the only place I could sit was on the right.

I felt it was important to be able to view children entering the area because in earlier observations I had noted that children usually stood near the entrance and watched for a while before entering. This onlooking behavior appeared to be an important part of children's selection of play groups. I tried a third position, on a table outside the area, near the entrance. Because of the distance, I was able to get a wider angle that included the area and the entrance; however, the distance created a problem in recording conversations in the block area. I solved this problem by using an extension cord with my PZM mike. I taped the cord to the floor so the children would not trip on it. I tried using a wireless transmission microphone but was not satisfied with the quality of the sound.

This location gave me a good angle on the block area, but it was very obtrusive. The tripod occupied a table normally used for play dough, and even though the cord was taped to the floor, children were very aware of it and always were careful not to step on it. I finally moved the tripod to an area near the door to the playground, away from children's normal traffic patterns during the free play period (the door was not used during this segment of the day). It was less noticeable there. I could easily adjust the camcorder. In fact, I could easily scan the whole classroom if something interesting oc-curred elsewhere. My point is that a lot of time and experimenting goes into something as seemingly simple as picking a location for the camcorder.

The classroom for my second study was quite small (20 by 31 feet), actually two connected rooms. I stopped using a tripod after the teacher twice tripped over one of the legs even when I set it up in the most out-of-the-way spot I could find. I decided to hold the camcorder, but supporting the machine's weight for 90 minutes each day was difficult, and after a few days my arm was quite sore. Over the course of the study, I found other spots for the camcorder.

Safety

I was most concerned with the children's and teachers' safety, but, of course, I also had to consider the equipment. The equipment, which was of professional quality and quite expensive, was on loan from the university, and I was responsible for it. Even though I would like to have been taking notes on the classroom as a whole while the camcorder was recording one area, I had to keep one eye on the equipment. One day, the teacher told me that while I was not look-ing, a child had moved the microphone, hiding it under the carpet. It was clear she wanted me to watch the equipment more closely. After that, I stayed close to the camcorder and did not try to observe the rest of the room.

Snapshots

I was very interested in how children grouped themselves during the day. One way I did this was to record their positions every few minutes. I tried recording by hand and with a still camera, but neither method worked well. I found using a camcorder to be very effective. From the observation booth, I scanned the room every few minutes, and during the intervals, I zoomed in to focus on target children. From the observation booth, I was unable to record children's con-versations, but I was able to track their movements in detail.

The classroom for the second study had no observation booth. Moving between the two rooms with a camcorder every few minutes to record children's locations was clumsy. I found it more practical to do the recording by hand on small maps of the classroom.

Audiotaping

Although I made heavy use of video, at times a camcorder was simply too obtrusive or impractical. A small, high-quality audio re-corder is much less obtrusive and more flexible. Particularly in the second study, where the small classroom made using video difficult, I always carried an audio recorder. I turned it on whenever I heard an interesting conversation or when I talked to children. I found the recordings helped me recall events that were not recorded com-pletely in my fieldnotes. I also found the audio recorder useful for recording conversation in places where I could not fit. For example, one day some children hid in a "cage" they had made out of blocks. The audio recorder could enter a space that I could not. One caution I offer is to take notes even when one is recording, because without some description of the context, it is very often difficult to tell children's voices apart.

Transforming Video Data

My next challenge was to get the video data on paper. The visual nature of the data presents both challenges and possibilities.

One way to build a data record is through narrative, a commonly used strategy (e.g., Corsaro, 1985). I feel that narrative does not adequately present the important nonverbal parts of children's interactions and sought ways of presenting the data pictorially.

One thing I did was to use series of pictures (see Figure 7.4). Each picture shows the children's position in the block area at a certain time. The small dots show the direction they are facing. From these simple pictures along with some contextual information, the reader can see what I saw, for example, that the two groups in the block area seldom interacted even though they were playing in the same area very close to one another.

These pictures, however, did not allow me to show the reader things like body language, which often was very salient. Recent technology makes it possible to easily turn video images into photos, but using photos of children violates the promise of confidentiality. Even with pseudonyms, the children's faces in the photos are theirs. I used a technique that was later further developed by my colleague, Hui-Fen Lin, tracing a video sequence frame by frame and scanning the images into a computer file (see Figure 7.3). The images protect the children's identity, but they make body language very visible and become a powerful piece of visual evidence. I must admit, however, that I found the process very hard on my already poor eyesight, and I probably will not use it again.

I transformed the snapshot data using non-pictorial figures. Figure 7.6 gives an example. The figure contains three parts. The first part shows all children's locations across the 42-minute period. The second part is an analysis of grouping and shows the same information, but by group rather than children (by this time in the study, groups were identified). The third section adds contextualizing narrative. The uppercase letters identify children. The letters in parentheses (part 3) after the children's initials indicate nationality.

Conclusion

I am very much a beginning researcher with much to learn. I learned to do qualitative research in a second language, even though in my second study, a group of the children in the multilingual, multicultural classroom spoke Mandarin. I am now back home in Taiwan and beginning a career here of studying children who speak my first language.

Date: 3/30/94 (Wednesday)
Time: 9:55 a.m.-10:37 a.m. (42 minutes)
Child #: 14/15
Absent: E

(1) The Children's Locations Through Time

	9:55 a.m.	10:04 a.m.	10:13 a.m.	10:20 a.m.	10:25 a.m.	10:37 a.m.
(Block)	J, P, δ, W, M, R, O	J, P, W, M, R, δ, [O], S, A, B	J, P, W, M, -R-O, [S], A, B, δ	J, P, H, W, M, A, B, δ, -S	J, P, H, W, -M, A, B, S, δ, M	J, P, R, [O], -W, H, Y, D, -S-A-B, -M
(Drama)						
(Art)	A, B, S, ©	-A-B-S				
(Paint)	D, Y, @	D, Y, H	-D-H-Y	D, Y	D, Y, [R]	-Y-D-R, N, δ, S, K, @, -O-K, W, M, δ
(Snack)			D, H, Y	-D-Y-H, R	-R, O, K	
(Math)						
(Carpet)	H, N, K, δ	N, K, -H	N, K, δ, O, R	N, K, O, δ, S	-N-K-O, -S, N	A, B, -N
(Other)						

(2) The Analysis of Grouping

	9:55 a.m.	10:04 a.m.	10:13 a.m.	10:20 a.m.	10:25 a.m.	10:37 a.m.
(Block)	J, P, W, M			H	-M	-W
(Drama)		H			M	-M
(Snack)						M, W
(Paint)	D, Y		(snack)	-D-Y-H, D, Y, H, -S		-D-Y, D, Y, -S
(Art)	A, B, S	(block)			S	
(Block)						
(Art)					-N (snack	
(Carpet)	N, K, δ	-δ	O, δ			

Context

1. (L has gone back to her home country. O is the new student.)
2. The airplane project is going on these days. The block center is set up as an airplane and it is very popular. The teacher allows the children to hang their name tags in the dramatic play center while playing in the block center. In other words, a total of 8 children can play in that airplane. The student teachers sometimes play with the children.
3. The Russian family coordinator is in school today, but it is not clear where she is in my record.

Figure 7.6. Non-Pictorial Figures

@ = Jenny δ = Student teacher © = Family coordinator "[ ]" = Plays alone "_____" = Staying over time
(The adults' locations are shown only when they are obviously interacting with the children.)

(3) Contextualized Analysis

—J (Ch), P (Ch), W (Af), and M (Af) play in the block center (the airplane) for a long time. However, J (Ch) and P (Ch) stay together for most of the time. After M (Af) leaves the block center at 10:25 a.m., W (Af) also leaves later and they both move to each other's snack together.

—L (Pa) has gone back to her home country, so R (Pa) does not stay with any groups for long. She plays in the block center with the other four girls for a short period of time. Later, she is called to water the plants (her job today). After that, she eats snacks and plays in the art center alone. Later, she moves to the block center and plays with J (Ch) and P (Ch) again.

—D (Ch) and Y (Ch) stay together all the time. H (Ch) plays with them from 10:04 a.m. to 10:20 a.m. and then leaves for the block center without hanging his name tag. (R's name tag is still there although she leaves to water the plants.) Later, at 10:37 a.m., D and Y also move to the block center after some children leave and there are spaces for them. After they get in, H moves out of the "airplane" and meets with D and Y outside the airplane. (The girls are playing in the airplane.)

—A (Ru), B (Ru), and S (Ru) approach the block center by acting like dinosaurs. After they hang their name tags and get in, A (Ru) and B (Ru) build another construction beside the "airplane" and play on their own. S (Su) plays alone by himself for most of the time, and he moves in and out of the block center twice.

—N (Vi), K (Pa), and O (Af) (the new child) play in the brown carpet with a student teacher for a period of time. Later, O (Af) and K (Pa) both go to have snacks, while N (Vi) moves to the art center, still with a student teacher. O (Af) plays in the block center before 10:13 a.m. and at the end at 10:37 a.m. She cannot really get in the children's play. Sometimes she just stands beside and frowns at the girls who are involved in the airplane drama and ignore her being there.

SOURCE: Adapted from Ting (1992).

Figure 7.6. Continued

I hope that some of what I learned in my experiences will be helpful to others.

Reference

Corsaro, W. (1985). *Friendship and peer culture in the early years.* Norwood, NJ: Ablex.

8

INTERPRETATION
IN CONTEXT

One of the key points that distinguishes interpretive research from other genres of inquiry is its iterative nature—steps of the process inform one another in ways that are not sequential. Instead, the process is recursive. A diagram might help to highlight the differences between much of the dominant research on children and the interpretive approach. In traditional portrayals of theory-testing research, the process is seen as relatively linear (see Figure 8.1).

Work proceeds through an identifiable sequence in which researchers design the study, choose samples, collect and analyze data, and write up results. In this simple view of research, any deviation from this sequence, particularly within a statistical design, is seen as capitalizing on chance and changing the representativeness of the results. Most quantitative researchers would agree that this conception of the research endeavor is a bit naive, depicting a mythic image of the process. This is the predominant portrait in most introductory research and statistics texts, however, and it shapes perspectives on educational research in ways that contrast sharply with an alternative interpretive view.

AUTHORS' NOTE: Written by Beth.

Design ➤ Sampling ➤ Data Collection ➤ Analysis ➤ Write-up

Figure 8.1. Traditional Views of the Research Process

Interpretive research is designed to maximize the opportunity to change focus, modify questions, find new ways of generating data, identify issues that are unaddressed within current data sources, and shape writing through local ideas. The steps within the process inform one another so that coherence is achieved through convergence of concepts and experience. Rather than proceeding in a straight line, this process seems more appropriately described as a bowl of spaghetti—tangled and holistic (see Figure 8.2).

Although this is often only the ideal, with the pressures of fieldwork squeezing out time to do substantive interpretation and writing, conceptually this notion is very important. The iterative approach works to keep interpretation, and all other aspects of the research process, contextualized. The point is to keep ideas and understandings as close to the field as possible to provide both relevancy and vibrancy that generates interpretation close to the local source.

In this chapter, I will discuss interpretation in context, describing our understanding of this process at the heart of interpretive work. I explore two complementary contexts for interpretation—connecting interpretation to local contexts while embedding understanding within theoretical frameworks. The process of interpretation is illustrated by example—I interpret data related to one child, a kindergartner I call Jared. Excerpts of fieldnotes and interviews are provided to show how Jared can be characterized as nested within multiple contexts that constitute how he is constructed by others. I blend theoretical concepts with information about the local setting to build a case for our interpretation of Jared's kindergarten experience. This example illustrates the situated nature of children's lives—the notion we have made the main theme of this book. We are interpreting Jared in context.

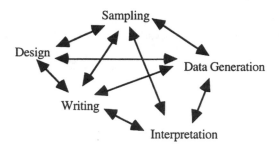

Figure 8.2. Interpretive Research

What Is Interpretation?

> In the social sciences there is only interpretation. Nothing speaks for itself.
> Confronted with a mountain of impressions, documents, and fieldnotes,
> the qualitative researcher faces the difficult and challenging task of making
> sense of what has been learned. I call making sense of what has been learned
> *the art of interpretation.* This may also be described as moving from the
> field to the text to the reader. The practice of this art allows the field-
> worker-as-*bricoleur* (Levi-Strauss, 1966, p. 17) to translate what has been
> learned into a body of textual work that communicates these under-
> standings to the reader. (Denzin, 1994, p. 500)

Interpretation is a complex, recursive, multistep process that is
characterized by theorists and methodologists in very different ways.
Denzin describes it above as the process of moving from field to text to
reader. This characterization positions the researcher within a certain
task (generating data, dealing with the text of data, and constructing a
text, and crafting a narrative for a reader to consume). He also has
described it more procedurally as deconstruction, capture, bracketing,
construction, and contextualization (1989). From this perspective, interpretation is a matter of relationships to data, that is, how the researcher
works to develop multiple standpoints to data generated in fieldwork.
Stake (1995) alludes to categorical aggregation (accumulation of instances of concepts of importance) or direct interpretation. A number of
theorists set their process into trinities: Strauss (1987) describes induc-
tion, deduction, and verification (focusing on the analytical processes);
Huberman & Miles (1994) delineate the process of data analysis as data

reduction, data display, and conclusion drawing/verification (making the task, like Denzin, related stuff you do with data); and Wolcott envisions a trio of description, analysis, and interpretation (which moves from telling about to explaining). Interpretation is in the eye of the beholder, framed by disciplinary traditions and perspectives on what it means to understand "reality." For some, it is a step-by-step process that is highly analytical and prescriptive; for others, it is mystical and full of personal vision and intuition.

Whether you position your description of the process close to the procedural tasks (such as reconfiguring data into displays) or within analytical processes (connecting descriptions to theoretical constructs in textual form), interpretation is complex, confusing, and completely resistant to recipe. It also has elements that are learnable and that can be critiqued methodologically. Our discussion of the process will wobble somewhere in the midst of this science-art dichotomy. Interpretation is both taking apart and putting together, it is analytic and synthetic, it is descriptive and evocative, and it is beauty and beast. It has objective and subjective elements that bounce up against each other in ways that meld the terms. It is, as we have said before, romantic science—poetic but filled with hard work and drudgery, creative and analytic. It is accomplished through plodding persistence. Interpretation is meaning making that is active and embedded throughout the work of interpretive research:

> Interpretation is a productive process that sets forth the multiple meanings of an event, object, experience, or text. Interpretation is transformative. It illuminates, throws light on experience. It brings out, and refines, as when butter is clarified, the meanings that can be sifted from a text, an object, or a slice of experience. So conceived, meaning is not in a text, nor does interpretation precede experience, or its representation. Meaning, interpretation, and representation are deeply intertwined in one another. (Denzin, 1994, p. 504)

From Descriptions to Explanations

Many discussions of interpretation (which probably would be called analysis in most texts) present concepts such as coding, memoing, and themes, with methodological definitions and perhaps short examples of data segments. Although these examples are illustrative, they lack a context within specific research questions and therefore do not highlight the *process* by which a researcher *builds* understandings across varied data sources and experiences. Given our fondness for contextualizing activity, I will take a different tack in our discussion of interpretation. In the remainder of this chapter, I illustrate the process of interpretation by taking you along with me as I analyze data about one child's kindergarten experience. I present data and interpretive work that connects our understanding of Jared in increasingly elaborated ways, moving from everyday observables to rich descriptions to theorized explanations. I focus our interpretations on the ways that the context in which Jared goes to kindergarten provides us with an interpretive map—it helps us see how Jared is constructed by those around him, and it provides clues as to how to find that out.

As I present these data and my interpretation of them, I also will utilize a qualitative data analysis program called HyperResearch to show how computers can support the interpretation process. I want to be clear from the outset that computers and analysis packages are *supporting tools* only and that nothing replaces the mind and experience of a good interpretive researcher. Most computer programs are merely high-tech scissors and folders that allow paperless sorting and organizing. For an excellent review of data analysis programs, see Weitzman and Miles (1995). No computer program will ensure that you have gotten it right or protect you from doing it wrong. Data analysis programs can make analysis more efficient if you know how to take advantage of their organizational capabilities. In many cases, you could do what you need to do within the confines of a good word processor. Programs typically have a nonproductive time connected to learning their quirks and rules. The key is to be patient, read the manual, and have the luck of having someone around you who already has done the dirty work of learning the program.

Notes on Method

Before moving on to the process in a concrete example, it is important to give you some idea of what I mean by several important terms. Although I assume that you have had some experience with field-based research, I'll go over a couple of basic concepts so that we develop a common language. In the next two sections, you will find very brief discussions of coding and memoing, which form some of the key processes I engage in when I interpret data. These include descriptions of how I use the terms and suggested readings that could broaden the view presented here.

Coding

I see *coding* as labeling themes that are represented by chunks of data. From this perspective, codes are merely the signifiers for ideas—analytic categories that a researcher has identified in the data. More important than the code itself is the idea that the researcher is trying to communicate with that code. The very first thing you need to think about when you consider coding is what you hope that code will help you do. Are you trying to communicate your participants' language and ideas, or are you trying to uncover theoretical dimensions played out in participant activity? Being clear that a code is a simple tool to do other things with complex ideas will help you from reifying your codes or forgetting that what you are really trying to understand are the meanings in which those codes are embedded. A code is secondary to its category.

Codes take many forms, depending on when they are generated in a field research project and the researcher's purposes for using them. In its most simple form, a code is a label that says that the researcher thinks that this excerpt of data is an example of this idea. Some things that might be important to look for when coding are *things that recur* in a set of data. *Patterns* also can be fruitful to explore. A pattern is something that recurs in a predictable way. Equally important are breaks in patterns, because they can indicate shifts of one kind or another in the dynamics of a setting. Searching for things that appear to be *salient* also can inform analysis. Salience is interpretive (it is of importance primarily to the researcher), but it should represent something that could be recognized by participants in the field. Salience might come up in recurring events or patterns but also might come out of the blue. Finally, *threads* are interpretive elements that the researcher weaves through events and images in the fieldwork that provide a coherent way of thinking about the topic of interest of the research.

Another distinction could be made between *external* codes, which can be seen as codes that come out of theoretical and conceptual perspectives brought to the project, and *internal* codes, which are issues that come up within your reading of the data. These are not independent entities in most research, but thinking about them as slightly different helps me look at how theory and fieldwork inform each other. There are other ways to think about how to code data, and most researchers develop their own strategies as they become more experienced and as they work within a given project. The key is to find some way to think about coding that is explicable to yourself and to those with whom you might share results.

In terms of the mechanics of coding, they are also without ironclad rules. Reading, rereading, and reading again seem fairly consistent among researchers. I usually suggest that people try to dismiss the urge to begin coding right away, instead giving themselves time to get a sense of the bigger picture. To prompt this opportunity, try reading through a set of notes at least once without writing instruments. Then go in and take marginal notes. This will allow you to take the time to read data and think about it rather than jumping to take it apart. There are many techniques that can be used to segment data, for example, domain analysis à la Spradley and in vivo codes à la Strauss. Each researcher and project pull tools together to answer the question at hand. The more techniques you have available to you, the more likely you will find the one that will be the most useful at that moment.

Codes have a very personal meaning, and in many research projects two researchers will code segments of data differently. The meaning of coding in interpretive research is quite different from in other forms of inquiry. The presumption that a reader can understand the process of analysis from merely perusing the codes used (often presented in an appendix in dissertations and journal articles) reifies coding more than is warranted. Coding is just a piece of the interpretive act and supports the interpretive framework. Codes represent ideas rather than truth. Instead of searching for the perfect code to attach to a segment of data, it might be more fruitful to consider the case that you could make for the code you have chosen.

In addition, you need to think about what using that code will allow you to do. Codes are a means to an end, so they should get you someplace. Coding is a process of data reduction, putting together interpretations so that they are more manageable for both the researcher and then eventually for the reader. For this reason, it is important to code at a level of specificity that will not multiply the amount of information you already have in your fieldnotes. Having 20 different codes to differentiate interactions among children in a first-pass analysis probably will provide you an opportunity to agonize over which code to use rather than a chance to understand how interaction occurs in a setting.

How do you know if the codes you have generated are helpful? There are several questions that you can ask yourself that can provide insight into their utility. First, try putting your codes together and read them like a narrative. What kind of story do they tell? Is it a descriptive story? Then you are just beginning. Are they an analytical story? Then you are farther along. Is the field represented at all in your codes? If not, how can you bring it back in? Another question to ask is, "How do these codes help me understand the world here?" The "how" question is much more important than the authoritative yes or no type of question. Again, what can you know from your codes about your field experience? Finally, coding is a data reduction process. No one can manage the mass of data generated in an interpretive study. But what do these codes leave out? In their simplification of life in context, do they oversimplify and trivialize?

Box 8.1
Suggested Resources on Coding

Emerson, R. M., Fretz, R. I., & Shaw, L. L. (1995). *Writing ethnographic fieldnotes*. Chicago: University of Chicago Press.

Huberman, A. M., & Miles, M. B. (1994). Data management and analysis methods. In N. K. Denzin & Y. Lincoln (Eds.), *Handbook of qualitative research*. Thousand Oaks, CA: Sage Publications.

Miles, M. B., & Huberman, A. M. (1984). *Qualitative data analysis: A sourcebook of new methods*. Beverly Hills, CA: Sage.

Spradley, J. (1979). *The ethnographic interview*. New York: Holt, Rinehart & Winston.

Strauss, A. L. (1987). *Qualitative analysis for social scientists*. Cambridge, UK: Cambridge University Press.

Wolcott, H. F. (1994). *Transforming qualitative data: Description, analysis and interpretation*. Thousand Oaks, CA: Sage.

Memoing

Memos elaborate the researcher's understanding, building from the codes by making connections and positing hunches about what is going on. Put more simply, memos are written notes to yourself about the thoughts you have about the data and your understanding of them. People often miss important chances to memo, overestimating their capacity to remember their own brilliant (and not so brilliant) ideas. For the same reasons that we write down our field observations so that we have concrete records of the experience, the conceptual process of interpreting data needs to be preserved in the form of memos. They are at a higher level than the codes in that they are conceptual and theoretical in nature, exploring the meaning of your observations or interviews. Memos often catalyze a new round of coding as you begin to make connections and distinctions in your understanding. They can be seen as the paper trail of your interpretive work, representing the false starts and dead ends as well as the ideas that prove to be building blocks of your analysis. I've never heard anyone complain that they've spent too much time memoing. A crude analogy might be that memoing is like flossing your teeth—it's something that is not too exciting, but if you are persistent, you probably won't regret it.

Box 8.2
Suggested Sources on Memoing

Corbin, J., & Strauss, A. (1996). Analytic ordering for theoretical purposes. *Qualitative Inquiry, 2*(2), 139-150.
Emerson, R. M., Fretz, R. I., & Shaw, L. L. (1995). *Writing ethnographic fieldnotes*. Chicago: University of Chicago Press.
Strauss, A. L. (1987). *Qualitative analysis for social scientists*. Cambridge, UK: Cambridge University Press.

With that brief description of the ideas we use for methodological tools, I move now to an illustration of interpretation. It is thick with data excerpts to provide you with at least part of the experience of swimming in the data to come to interpretive ideas.

Jared Through Observation

The data come from a year-long interpretive study of standards for readiness in kindergarten and first grade. From past research (Graue, 1993), I knew that children were constructed as students in particular ways within a local definition of readiness. I was interested in learning how ideas about readiness were constructed and communicated within a local school community and across grade levels. What student characteristics and activities were salient in the local framework for readiness? What roles were constructed for teachers and parents for the education of kindergartners and first graders? How were expectations shaped by local cultural values and enacted in decisions relating to young children? These questions framed my study and the data generated. They provided a foundation for the categories used to understand the data and propelled me to follow certain types of ideas. They provide the core for the analysis I present in this chapter.

In the course of this study, weekly visits were made to a kindergarten and first grade at Solomon Elementary, a K-5 school serving a middle-class and primarily White community. Parents were interviewed at the beginning of the school year and again at the end; teachers were interviewed in August, December, and May; children were interviewed in May; and materials were collected throughout the school year. For the purposes of this illustration, I pulled all references to Jared in fieldnotes and interview texts and include representative excerpts. In addition, I utilize data illustrating local expectations for kindergarten and first grade.

I begin our exploration into Jared's kindergarten life by culling excerpts from observations made in his classroom over the course of the school year. I read fieldnotes for the entire kindergarten year, then identified sections in which Jared was a part. These sections were coded using HyperResearch by highlighting the section of text and attaching a code name to it. These segments were then sorted and printed out so they could be examined separately. For the purposes of this chapter, I have chosen a representative group of coded fieldnotes that provide a glimpse across the course of the year as well as across classroom situations. In the next section, codes represent descriptors of Jared within the context of an observation—things he was doing or things commented on by his teacher. They include little reflection and are close to what we call everyday observables. It is important to remember that the observations were framed within MY interests in readiness—I focused on particular incidents, interactions, and language markers with ideas about readiness in my mind. The headers are from HyperResearch and provide the following information: the code, the location, and the date of the fieldnotes. As you read these notes, try to picture Jared and how he made his way through his kindergarten year.

CRYING, char 307 to 1449 of page 1 of Sept. 3

First day of school A little before the bell rings, Mrs. Warren heads out to the playground to meet her class—"I'll bet I have some nervous kids & parents." She meets them outside the kindergarten door and they file into the classroom as she asks them one at a time "Do you have anything in your backpack for me?" The children are to check in their backpacks, take out anything that needs to go to Mrs. Warren, and hang the backpacks up in the coatroom. Notes go in Mrs. Warren's mailbox above the cubbies. Some children come into the classroom with their backpacks and wander; others leave them in the coatroom. Mrs. Warren reminds them to put them in the coatroom. They head for the rug area for the most part, with many standing and talking among themselves, fiddling with toys or charts around the edge of the area. Jared has a sad look on his face and he is clinging close to Mrs. Warren.

Mrs. Warren: Jared, you can sit right next to me . . . OK? Let's all have a seat. [The group is seated around the rug—were they in a circle or in a general group?] Are we all ready? [Mrs. Warren surveys the group and checks that they are all comfortable.]

IMMATURITY, char 5442 to 8703 of page 1 of Sept. 24

Mrs. W: This morning we are going to work on the shapes you drew last week—they are shapes of you! Do you remember when I drew around you and it kind of tickled, didn't it? Christopher, sit up, please. You need to fill in the shape of your body. In the shape of your face what do you need to see?

Class: Eyes!

Mrs. W: And what shape do you need to smell?

Class: A nose.

Mrs. W: And what do you need here? [Mrs. Warren smiles and points to her mouth]

Class: A smile!

Mrs. W: And what do you need so your head doesn't get cold?

Class: Hair!

Mrs. W: When you do your fingers, what do you notice? [She holds her hand up and points to the ends of her fingers]

Class: Fingernails.

Cara: Fingernails and fingernail polish—like me!

Mrs. W: Some of you do have fingernail polish on, don't you? When you do your clothes, you can do what you are wearing or you can draw what you WISH you were wearing—your favorite clothes if you want. If your favorite shorts are red, you can color red shorts. Or draw what you have on today. If you are wearing a belt—draw in a belt!

Obs: The children are looking at one another pointing to various items of clothing as Mrs. Warren describes them.

Mrs. W: Your shapes have shoes—right? Now your crayons are good for drawing in the face and for zippers and things like that. I have some other crayons that would be good for coloring BIG spaces that you can borrow. I'll bring them out when you get started. Carlie's mom is here to help us weigh and measure. She will take you down by the office a few at a time to do that. Marta, Cara, and Carlie, will you please go with Mrs. Ansell? You should go find the shape with your name on it.

Obs: The children scatter around the room, looking for their shapes. I help children who cannot find theirs—notably Allison and Lester. Most of them find their shapes first, then go to get their crayons. As the children start to work, Mrs. Warren puts on a Hap Palmer record and a song that is about me (I can't remember the name). I move about the room watching children work. Mrs. Warren remarks about Allison, who is busy working on the head of her shape. She has drawn hair and eyes with eyeballs. Mrs. Warren says that that is pretty impressive. Next she comments on Jason, who is working on a very intricate pattern on a shirt. He says that he is doing an army shirt and is working on blending two colors. As she walks past David, she sees that he is laboring over very large shoes with a small crayon.

Mrs. W: David, will you color that other shoe the same color, then switch to a fat color for the pants?

Obs: Mrs. Warren comments about Jared's picture when he is out of the room getting weighed and measured. She says that he is very immature but that his picture has every body part that you would expect. In contrast, David is really pained to get this job done—it's really hard for him.

FOLLOWING INSTRUCTIONS,
char 48 to 3947 of page 1 of Feb. 13

The children are on the carpet with Mrs. Warren, who is writing on the board and talking to the group. Karen and two moms are working around the room putting materials out on tables. There are pink, red, and white pieces of paper, doilies, and heart-shaped pieces of paper.

On the chalkboard is

> Roses are red
> Sugar is sweet
> _____
>
> Roses are red
> Violets are blue

She is talking to the group and they are spelling out messages to put on Valentine's cards. I am not taking notes but they spell "I love you" and "Happy Valentine's Day." She sits down on her chair and the children turn to face her.

Mrs. W:　And you will get a piece of paper to make your card. Remember we talked last week about the long way and the short way of folding a paper? Well, you are going to do a long-way fold—you're going to make a card like from a store. And after you fold it, it will open up. At the table you will find some fancy lace [she picks up a doily that is in a circle about 3 inches in diameter and shows it to the group]. It can make a fancy background for things you might put on your card. [She picks up a heart that has a picture of something—I don't remember] I found this kind of heart at the school store. It's not so fancy, but it would look really nice. There are some Valentine's pictures on the table under the Orange star. [She bends over and speaks directly at Trevor, who is sitting in front of her] Trevor—you should stay looking at me. [to group] You will need glue for the Valentine's pictures. Some of them used to have their own glue but it dried up. Remember—Mrs. Warren would like you to use tiny dots of glue. Not a puddle because that will ooze all over the place. There are lots of things that you could put on your card—a garden of flowers—anything that you would like. Did Miss Gordon show you how to make hearts in art class?

Class:　We had a sub.

Mrs. W:　Oh, OK. Well, here. You fold your paper and you draw a candy cane shape on it—that seems a little silly to do a candy cane to make a heart but that's the way it works. The candy cane is drawn on the folded side.

Obs:　She holds up a piece of paper that she has folded in half and then draws the following:

Obs: She then cuts the heart out and shows it to the group.

Mrs. W: You might want to practice on a couple. It looks a little like an ice cream cone.

Max: Or a raindrop.

Mrs. W: Or a raindrop—yeah. [she opens up the piece of paper] You need to begin thinking about a message. [Cory is talking out loud] Cory, who is talking now?

Cory: You.

Mrs. W: Then listen please. You can use one of the messages that we thought up this morning—or you can make up one of your own. You will need to decide who your Valentine is for—for your mom or your dad or both. That's for you to decide. Now I am going to send you off to your tables. Please listen for your name. [as Mrs. Warren calls children, they get up and sit down at a table]

Mrs. W: If you do not like your color of paper, what should you do?

Class: Raise your hand.

Mrs. W: Just let us know and we'll get you another.

Obs: I am standing at a table with a group of children. They immediately begin to write. They are asking for the spelling of various words and getting help from other children and me. No one begins by cutting out shapes or by pasting things on their paper. This is what Jared does on the inside of his card:

> I LOVE Y
> I LOVE YOU
> DAD

CRYING, char 9428 to 12978 of page 1 of May 14

Mrs. W: Choice time is no longer choice time if you haven't gotten your work done. I will come around and tell you where you need to go get to work. Marta, will you get scissors and cut this please. Trevor, will you get up and go walk around the room 3 times and then come sit down here to work on this paper? [she then says the same to Jared and Kelsey and asks me to work with them.]

The paper has the following addition problems.

6 +7	8 +7	3 +5	9 +10
8 +7	14 +7	6 +8	11 +8
13 +7	1 +0	9 +9	16 +3
3 +2	0 +1	7 +11	11 +9

At the bottom of the page was a key that had the numbers 1 through 26 matched with letters of the alphabet. The children were to solve the problems, then use the letters as a key to find the words.

Jared, Trevor, and Kelsey are sitting at the table with me working on the worksheet. Jared uses the counters for 8 + 7 but uses his fingers for 10 + 5. He alternates between various strategies to solve the problems. Kelsey tells me that 14 + 7 is 23. I ask her if she is sure and whether she would like to use the counters. She tells me that she is not allowed to use the counters. Her dad tells her to concentrate. She turns around in her chair and puts her head down for about 1.5 minutes. She then turns back and writes 21 on her sheet and smiles.

9:12

Jared: [working on 7 + 7] I have to use the counters.

Kelsey: I have to go to the bathroom.

Jared: [counts the bears and beams] 14.

At this point, Jared and Trevor begin to have a dispute. They whisper, and Jared begins to shake his head and turn red.

Jared: He says I don't know anything! Yesterday he said I didn't know anything about GI Joe and I do!

Me: Well, I think that you seem to know quite a bit about lots of things—look at how well you're working on that paper.

Jared: But he says I don't know anything!

Me: Is he right?

Jared: No.

Me: So have you got anything to worry about?

Jared: No.

Jared is counting out blue bears to solve a problem. With a basket of bears of all colors in front of him, Trevor takes a couple of Jared's bears from the group he has been counting. Jared jumps up and runs around the table to me, doing something that seems like crying. Trevor drops a large number of bears into the pile that Jared was counting and Jared spins around saying—"Now I don't know how many there are!"

Me: Well, let's count them again—we'll do it together.

I ask Trevor to work from the bears in the basket and he hisses that he wants blue bears. I point out that there are still blue bears in the basket—at the bottom—and he glares at me. I ask him to try not to be so crabby and he spits, "Don't you ever call me crabby." I tell him that I will never use that word with him if he is not acting that way and we shake on it—that seems to satisfy him and he seems happier. He begins to twirl his pencil around saying that it's not sharp enough. I tell him that I'll sharpen his pencil if he would count out the next problem. [he has only done one problem so far] While I'm gone, Jared tells Trevor the answer. They are grinning when I come back. Trevor writes the answer and then asks, "Jared, will you help me again?" Kelsey has answered 13 + 7 as 02. I ask her what the answer is and she says "Twenty." I tell her that it looks like 2 to me—we get the number chart and I ask her to find 20 on the chart. Jared pipes up that it is right under the 10. She goes back to the table and erases 02 and makes it 20.

The observations shared above are good examples of how we need to think beyond description to the notion of inscription (Geertz, 1973). I created my own version of Jared's life, situated within my own experience. The data are presented in fieldnote form yet are already theorized. They represent a research focus and experience base that bear the marks of my previous work as a kindergarten teacher and someone who had done fieldwork in similar settings.

These observations were made with particular intent—I was interested in finding out how K and Grade 1 teachers thought about and communicated issues of readiness to various audiences. I observed in these classrooms with the voices of the teachers, parents, and children ringing in my ears. I focused on specific things given my past work related to readiness. Jared came in and out of focus because his mother had voiced concern about his age when he started kindergarten. Also, I sensed that the teachers at Solomon valued certain skills and dispositions in their students. The segments of data are not just snapshots of Jared's kindergarten experience; they are labeled with interpretations about how Jared fits into a framework for the idealized kindergarten child at Solomon Elementary. The codes represent ideas about those skills and dispositions—a concern about emotional maturity is shown through the segments on crying, and about the ability to stay on task and do an activity through the segments on following directions and immaturity. I was able to identify the codes through my past experience as a kindergarten teacher, as someone who has listened to many, many discussions about readiness, and as a participant in the educational life at Solomon. As they stand, they are like pieces to a puzzle—descriptions that are fragmented images of a child in context. How to piece the puzzle together?

One way is to look beyond the surface for patterns. That is the purpose of the following memo, written to unpack both the observations and the reasons I looked at things the way I did.

Memo 1: Observations of Jared

Jared was a child with all the classic markers that would tag him as a readiness risk. He was young relative to the entrance cutoff, he was a boy, and he was on the smallish side. Was Jared unready? What kinds of things come up in the observations? Did he cry frequently? Jared could be described as a sensitive child who over the course of the year finds ways to work within the demands of the kindergarten classroom. In these observations here, his crying was a salient characteristic. He cried the first day, but so do many children. He cried in an interaction with Trevor in May but I often felt like I was going to cry when I talked with Trevor, he was a master of manipulation. Those are the only times that I remember seeing Jared cry but I was in the classroom about 20% of the time over the year. He DID participate in all the activities that his peers were involved in and he was pretty successful. His literacy and numeracy skills were right on track. He found ways to negotiate his way through many challenging situations. What does it mean if other people think Jared cries all the time? It might be fruitful to try to understand how others around him saw Jared. What are the standards for being a successful kindergarten student?

This memo reflects on Jared as an individual—I compare him to traditional characteristics that foretell readiness problems, I scan the corpus of fieldnotes to look for patterns in crying (see, counting is useful in a variety of settings), and I identify other sources of information that might help me understand Jared in new ways.

To get to know him better, and to understand how I developed a more contextualized understanding of his experience, I explore the ideas of those around him. I will try to get a sense of what it means to be a kindergarten student in this classroom at this time. In the next section,

---

Box 8.3
Note on Methods

As we work with data, we use various strategies to help us manage the process. One strategy Beth uses is to go through the data in a number of ways to provide more than one perspective on her developing understanding. Particularly with interview transcripts, she first chunks the data analytically by the concerns that structured the questions. This is, at least in part, to remind her that interview texts are responses to particular questions, motivated by a specific research agenda. After coding and sorting according to those categories, she goes back again and codes according to issues that come up within the text. These categories might be theoretically oriented but are more locally informed than the broad interview categories.

I illustrate this process. I will piece together the views of two people who were very important in Jared's educational experience—his mother and his teacher. You will find excerpts of interviews as well as analytic memos that I wrote during my work that track my developing understanding of Jared's context.

In the appendix, you will find an interview transcript that has been coded with analytic categories that motivated the interview questions. These are ideas that I used to elicit certain kinds of cultural knowledge from my conversation with Mrs. Millard (Jared's mother). Any response she gives needs to be thought of as coming out of an intersection of my interests and her concerns. The entire transcript is provided to show how Mrs. Millard interpreted and responded to the questions. My understanding of that interview, which includes both my intentions in asking questions and the interpretations I made from the responses, are developed in Memo 2. Finally, I share coded excerpts of interviews with Jared's mother and his teacher related to Jared's kindergarten experience.

During interpretation, work iterates between coding and memoing. Here is an example of a memo that gives a quick reading of the general issues that came up in Mrs. Millard's interview (shown in the appendix). It was written for the purposes of this discussion, to provide the reader with an overview of the questions that frame a context to the responses given. In particular, it focuses attention on the conceptual issues that shaped the questions and gives an eye to more in-depth analysis later. Read the coded sections that are presented later with this memo in mind.

Memo 2: August 4, 1995

This interview was conducted at the end of Jared's kindergarten year. It was designed to get a sense of the issues of importance for parents as they approach another transition point in their child's school life. In the case of Mrs. Millard, the major issue is concern about Jared's immaturity and how that will affect his work in first grade.

Overview: This question is posed to explore the kinds of things that are important to parents of kindergarten children at the end of the school year. Mrs. Millard is concerned about whether Jared is emotionally ready for first grade given Mrs. Warren's reports that he cries easily. She thinks that time will help him get over this. She is pleased with his learning this year as well as how Jared has made friends. She's also worried about the length of the school day next year.

Describe K: This question focuses on the issues that shape how parents think about the kindergarten experience. She thinks that kindergarten was fun for Jared and that he has become "more worldly" (something that is not necessarily positive to his mom).

Communication: Framed to get a sense of the kinds of feedback parents have gotten from the school about their children, Mrs. Millard focuses primarily on discussion of Jared's immaturity. She talks about his relative age in the group and strategies used by Mrs. Warren to help Jared over his crying in class.

Expect 1: The end of the year is a transition point and we were interested in finding out how parental expectations about first grade were connected to their recollections of the kindergarten year. Mrs. Millard hopes that Jared will be reading by the end of first grade and thinks that kindergarten helped by giving him experience in a school environment. She doesn't think that first grade will be as much fun as kindergarten and just hopes that he learns what he needs to learn for that grade.

Miscellaneous: This question is a catch-all, to provide parents a chance to voice (or revoice) things that are important to them or that they think will be important for me to know. Mrs. Millard is pleased with Jared's kindergarten experience but would suggest that more effort be put into helping children get important information back and forth between home and school.

Summary: Issues of age and maturity are pervasive in this interview. Mrs. Millard has seen growth this year but is concerned about whether he has matured enough to meet the challenges of a more rigorous program in the next year. She sees Jared this way because of feedback she has gotten from Mrs. Warren over the course of the school year.

Through my discussion with Mrs. Millard, we began to see Jared as a child who was interpreted through concerns about maturity and with an eye to preparing for the next life (his growth in kindergarten is measured by his ability to meet the demands of next year's program). At this important time at the end of his kindergarten year, Mrs. Millard looks at Jared through two lenses—through the kindergarten stories told by Mrs. Warren and through the future prism of expectations about first grade. How did these concerns come about, and how did his mother build the image of her son that she has in May? One way to explore this issue is to listen carefully to both Jared's mother and his teacher as they spoke over the course of the school year. The next section does just that, exploring discussions about Jared that occurred with Mrs. Warren and Mrs. Millard in interviews.

All the interviews with Jared's mother and his teacher were read and re-read, then segments were identified that dealt directly with Jared and his kindergarten experience. For the purposes of the analysis here, I looked for examples that specifically dealt with concern about Jared's age, whether to enter him in kindergarten, and maturity. As I identified these themes, I also began to think about how the expectations of kindergarten or first grade might set the stage for perception of Jared as a child who was immature. How did expectations set people up to make certain decisions about Jared? This question flagged the social nature of the characterization process, nesting descriptions of Jared in a particular context of ideas. With this in mind, I also noted issues of expectations in the transcripts. In the next section, I've pulled coded excerpts that build on the notions developed thus far—concern about age and immaturity. They are presented in chronological order in terms of when they were generated over the course of the academic year.

AGE, HOLDOUT, IMMATURITY char 1646 to 4110 of page 1 of Jared mom pre int (August)

P: His age. . . . He just turned 5 on July 31 and a lot of people, you know you get so many different ideas, but some say, "You know he really is too young." "He's the first child." "He's a boy." And that played a lot on my mind about whether or not to send him to kindergarten.

Int: How did you decide?

P: I talked to my pediatrician and I talked to the school here. And they both said that there was absolutely no reason to hold him back. But I was starting to doubt myself. All these people would say these kinds of things. You know he's a good size for his age . . . he's outgoing . . . he's not shy . . . he's smart. . . . I just felt that there was no reason not to send him. But so many other parents were going "Oh, no, you really should not send him." So I started to doubt myself. So I felt a lot better when I talked to the pediatrician and then I called the school and then I talked to Mrs. Warren when I came to the screening and she too felt that there was no reason that he should wait.

Int: How did you find out about . . .

P: I guess it started with my next-door neighbor. She has a daughter who has a birthday at the same time of year, July. She's 7 now but when she was 5 her parents didn't send her to school. She started when she was 6. Why I thought she knew more about than I did, I don't know. . . . She said don't send them when they are so young. Da-da-da-da-da-da . . . Then I asked friends that I worked with who had kids in school and they were about 1/2 and 1/2. Half were saying "For crying out loud, send him" and half were saying, "No, I'd never send a child that young." So I was all concerned. So then I talked to the pediatrician. He said that a lot of parents hold their kids out because of sports. He said a lot of parents would hold them so that kids would do better in sports when they get further on in school . . . in high school. You know they'll say, "He's small for his age and this will help later." They want them bigger for sports. I think that's terrible. And I called the school—I talked to somebody in the office. They had recently had a meeting and they were really encouraging parents to send kids when they were 5 because they thought that kindergarten really was the first step in socializing kids to school. Especially if you have some kids who went to preschool and some that didn't. You really need to try to get them all at the same point for first grade. So I thought that was good.

EXPECT K, char 247 to 1604 of page 1 of Jared mom pre int (August)

P: Well, just that this is really the big start of what I hope is a good long education. To make him like school . . . I want to go to school . . . So that he'll continue on and really want to learn. I guess I look at it as the foundation for whether school is going to go well in the future or not. And I think it is a good chance for him to learn the basics: to know how to socialize, he doesn't know how to share well, he doesn't know how to wait. He's terrible about waiting his turn. That kind of thing. The everyday kinds of skills to deal with people, that he needs . . . that's what I'm expecting.

Int: What are the positive things you're thinking about? What are you hoping for him?

P: I hope he'll come out knowing how to write the alphabet. And he already can count pretty well—I'm not worried about that. Like I said, learning how to wait his turn and learning how to not interrupt people when they're talking. Education wise, I really don't know what to expect from kindergarten. You know, when I was in kindergarten. When I was in kindergarten, you took a nap and you played and I think now it's more education now. They're actually learning how to start to read or maybe basic numbers or arithmetic, I don't know how far they go but . . . I do sense and I don't know if I'm correct that they do more now than they did when I was a kid.

IMMATURITY, char 2273 to 5577 of page 4 of Warren 2 (January)

T: Occasionally I will come across a child that I would really rather see in a preschool program but the parents never do that.

Int: What kind of kid do you think that is typically good for?

T: It is mostly emotional immaturity. I am real worried about Jared. I am looking ahead to first grade and academically he may be ready but emotionally he is just barely keeping it together here. I need to talk to his parents about it. Typically kids that I would like to see wait a year are relatively bright and they are going to catch on as soon as they are ready for the rigor of the program, but they maybe need another year in preschool where they are interacting with 4-year-olds because they are really on an emotional 4-year-old level. If they come to me I may suggest keeping them another year so they can mature a little. If they are slow academically, occasionally you find that they are slow and immature and then they end up in programs like the 5-year-old option. But what you will generally find out if they are behind academically because of the immaturity they will catch up. But if they are overall slow you don't really want to keep them back because they can't get good service and they can't prove the lag if they have been retained so it is better to push them ahead and allow them to fail so someone will say, yes this kid needs help.

Int: For Jared . . .

T: It is the immaturity and the emotional instability right now. He is a bright kid, very capable of learning but the emotions will get in the way of that learning if he is intimidated by the expectations of first grade.

Int: What kinds of things are you seeing in the classroom?

T: Tears every day. If he is chosen to be the flag holder, if I won't hold his hand going down the hall, if somebody looks at him cross-eyed, if he bumps himself. It has been building up so I need to call home and find out if there are any tensions going on at home as well. And then I will kind of watch him through the spring and I will alert the parents early on that I am a little concerned about the emotional stability and what things are going to be like in first grade so we don't hit them all of a sudden with, "let's hold him back." Maybe he will develop during the spring too and won't need to be held back. Usually a child that I am worried about it shows up this early in the year. Every once in a while you get somebody right the last month of school, and all of a sudden everyone is going full tail to head and all of a sudden this child is kind of being left behind socially and emotionally and then you worry about first grade and it is too late really to pull back and say, "Lets wait a year" and then you kind of worry about whether you made the right choice, but somebody who is emotionally immature, these kids are moving ahead now and he is emotionally not. He is spending all his time in the block corner, he doesn't come to do the work at the tables. Even the kids who like blocks, they'll either self choose or else just one word from me is enough to get them over here. But he spends 95% of his time playing with the animals and the blocks if I don't redirect him. It is not even going over to the dramatic play or trying the art or anything else, it is that spot. And that is a secure spot where he can play.

IMMATURITY, char 208 to 1641 of page 1 of Jared mom 2 (May)

Int: What kind of things have you been thinking about as Jared approaches finishing kindergarten?

P: Oh, is he ready for first grade, mostly emotionally, I guess his biggest problem at school has been crying at times and that kind of thing. Academically, apparently he is doing just fine.

Int: Can you tell me a little bit more about the social part?

P: Just from what I hear from Mrs. Warren, he just cries easily like if he thinks his turn got missed, he will cry easily or if somebody teases him he will cry, that kind of thing.

Int: Do you see that kind of thing at home?

P: Yeah, sometimes, mostly when he is overtired.

Int: How do you think that might impact how he does in first grade?

P: Oh, I am just afraid that he will get teased more about it if he does cry and that would make him cry more and it would be kind of a vicious circle.

Int: Sure, sure. So what do you think needs to happen, what will get him to the point where he is socially more ready?

P: I think just maybe time and maturity. I'm not sure, I mean we can work on it at home but I think it is more a matter of aging and . . .

DESCRIPTION OF K, char 1456 to 2199 of page 1 of Jared mom 2 (May)

P: Oh, how much he really has learned! I mean as far as a little bit of reading and writing and a little arithmetic, actually I was surprised how much they did learn for kindergarten.

Int: How did what they learned connect or not connect with what you expected? Was it different than you thought it would be?

P: It was more than I thought it would be.

Int: So going in, what kind of things did you expect?

P: I expected them to learn their alphabet and everything and counting and that kind of thing but I really didn't think they would get into words as much as they did and I didn't think they would get into like adding and subtracting like they seemed to.

Int: And how do you feel things went?

P: I think very well.

EXPECT 1, char 8462 to 10068 of page 1 of Jared mom 2

Int: What do you think his first-grade year is going to be like?

P: That is hard, I don't know. I am not really sure. I expect as far as learning things, I expect him by the end of the year to be reading fairly well, but other than that I don't know how much they get into math or any of the other subjects.

Int: How do you think kindergarten prepared Jared for first grade?

P: Well, I hope it prepared him well in that he did have to learn to sit and be quiet and follow directions and you know . . . just the school environment, it is different than being able to play and run around all the time. Like I say I am just concerned that it is all day long, in comparison, kindergarten was so short.

Int: Yeah, the morning just flies. Do you have a sense of how it might be different?

P: I think he will find that it . . . I hate to say it, but not as much fun . . . that it is more geared for learning things than just getting in the school environment for the first time.

Int: What kind of things are you hoping that he is going to learn?

P: I guess just learning what he is supposed to be learning at that age, you know as far as subjects goes and then growing out of this crying easily and you know, maybe learning how to solve problems more effectively.

IMMATURITY, SCHOOL COMMUNICATION,
char 4832 to 7301 of page 1 of Jared mom 2

Int: What were the conferences like?

P: Well, the first one was mainly how he is doing, what he is learning, what he needs to work on, you know, what letters he knows . . . pretty much academic type of things and some on the socialization part. The second focused more on his immaturity and easy crying and that kind of thing because she said he was doing very well otherwise but that was really what she wanted to talk about.

Int: Did you request the conference?

P: I requested it but Mrs. Warren said that she had debated because she thought it was important but she said it had been getting better but she was just going to let it go a little bit to see and if it hadn't gotten any worse she was going to let it go but if it had gotten any worse she was going to call me. She said she had seen an improvement from the beginning of the year with that toward the end of the year. She did see an improvement so that's why she was feeling more comfortable with it, it was improving as the year went on.

Int: That idea of immaturity is really interesting to me, was that something that you think he came in with?

P: Oh, yes and again I think he is THE youngest one in the class, he won't be 6 until July 31 and I don't know if I just had it set in my head that he had a late birthday so he was immature or if actually he is a little less mature than some of the older kids, I don't know. But I had it set in my mind that he would probably be a little less mature than most of them.

Int: You think time is the thing that is going to help him out with this?

P: Yeah, I do.

Int: How did Mrs. Warren talk about how that immaturity affected how he did in class?

P: Well, I think she had to do some kind of behavior type modification, maybe you would call it, apparently, like for example, if he wanted to hold her hand at recess or something and he came crying to her, then she wouldn't do it but if he came and asked nicely, "Mrs. Warren, I would like to hold your hand now." Then she would let him to try to show him that if you ask appropriately or do things appropriately that is better than crying and getting out of control about it. Another example was, I guess it was the flagholder person, everyday that she made a list because he felt one time his turn was missed and he was very upset so to visualize it she made up the list so every day he could see the name ahead of him being crossed off so he would know his turn didn't get missed.

Looking at these segments along with the previous data, some themes begin to emerge. What follows are some memos that you can use to track how I came to think about how Jared was being constructed by his mom and teacher in the context of the kindergarten program.

Memo 3: Summary of Issues in Coded Segments

Age/holdout/immaturity: Jared just 5 at entrance to K. Mother talked with pediatrician, the school and neighbors about whether to enter him in school. His doctor and the school said put him in; others brought up his age and hoping he would do better in sports later if he were older. Parents in this community consult others about their child's kindergarten entry rather than assuming that the child will go when s/he is age eligible (NOTE: confirmed through interviews with other parents).

Expect 1: is worried about the length of day; thinks that grade 1 will be less fun and that he will learn to read.

Expect K: (pre) K is foundation of schooling, will learn the basics (mostly social stuff), not sure about education types of objectives; (post) learned much more than expected, particularly in terms of 3 R's.

Immaturity (parent view): questions whether Jared is ready emotionally, lots of crying; worried he would be teased in Grade 1. Needs time and maturity; in conferences was told about progress socially and academically—second conference focused on immaturity although teacher saw improvement; Jared is the youngest in his class; teacher used behavior modification to help him find alternatives to crying in school.

Immaturity (teacher view): certain children would benefit from delaying kindergarten entry—Jared is a good example; he's academically ready but emotionally immature—bright but his emotions get in the way. Spends all his time in the block corner.

Summary: Immaturity is a strong theme in these discussions as well, beginning with checking the expectations of others before Jared began kindergarten and continuing with concern about his ability to meet the expectations of his teachers. A classic discussion of maturity and readiness is provided here, with concern about Jared's gender, age, and profile as a bright immature. Both his mother and teacher are worried about how Jared will adapt to the rigors of first grade, which is characterized by a change in activity and expectations. How have these ideas been developed within the Solomon Elementary community? Are there long held meanings about children that can be seen in policies and practices in the school? Broadening the analysis to explore demographic characteristics, teacher beliefs, and other issues should help us understand more about how Jared is placed in a specific social and historical spot which allows people to only see certain things about him and his growth.

Jared's Community Context

Jared is living his first elementary school experience in a particular community, at a particular time. Who he is is shaped by those around him, their material circumstances, and their expectations for success. For this reason, it is important to examine more general characteristics of the school community. Solomon Elementary is a school of high-achieving middle-class families that have advantages in almost every aspect of their lives. Glancing through the information in Figure 8.3 gives a sense of its high standards and affluence in a primarily middle-class school district.

These numbers portray a certain kind of school—relatively affluent and high achieving. How do these numbers play out in the lived schooling experience at Solomon? One way to cross check would be to ask Mrs. Warren, who had a double-edged perspective—she is both a kindergarten teacher and a Solomon parent. This is how she described the Solomon community:

> The community here is primarily, I would say, socially economically upper middle class, upper class, a lot of doctors, lawyers, professors. We have a few pockets of lower income people, but they don't tend to stand out a lot. . . . Our parent population is a very involved population. They do a lot of volunteer work, they are very active determining or influencing policies that go on at this school. They care extremely a lot about their kids' education and we have had parents even try to transfer in because the reputation at this school has been gaining. . . . It is wonderful. I am spoiled and I have to say that. Mainly because the kids come in so ready, because the parents are so supportive we have very little by way of personal home life to fight against. . . . My classroom tends to operate on what I perceive as an early first-grade level, for the most part. If not in the beginning of the year they move into it very quickly by January. So my expectations are very high . . .

The high hopes and standards that come with these conditions are represented in many ways in the Solomon culture—through teacher and parent expectations and intense parental involvement in all aspects of school life. Parents and teachers want the best for children and work to find ways to provide it.

Among the ideas that are intertwined with high expectations are strongly held notions of what it means to be ready for kindergarten or first grade. Ready students are mature enough to meet the demands of a rigorous education program—they are able to fit into a system that requires focus and a level of sophistication. These considerations of child readiness came out of concerns about whether students could measure up to the standards of next year's teacher and how they fared in comparisons to their classmates. In the next section, I include excerpts from Mrs. Warren's interviews that provide even more context about how Jared is portrayed. This portrayal comes out of a set of ideas about how children grow and develop and what roles teachers and parents should

27th in child poverty	27th in single parent households	3rd in composite percentile of CAT grades 3 & 5	Median family income: $50,000	% of boys held out of K 90-91: 17%

Figure 8.3. Characteristics of Solomon Elementary and Rankings Among 28 District Elementary Schools

take to facilitate that process. Although Jared is not the topic of conversation, Mrs. Warren's view of him is situated in the broader images of teaching and learning portrayed here.

MATURITY char 7221 to 9766 of page 2 of Warren 1

T: Academic abilities don't jibe with maturity necessarily. You can have a kid reading on a second-grade level and not be terribly mature. That when you get at cross purposes with parents because they come in thinking, well, their kid is already reading at a second-grade level, you've got to push them up a couple levels and they don't realize what the child needs in a kindergarten setting is to learn how to socialize with other kids. To learn to be independent, to learn to have patience and take turns. I find kids can have different agendas. The class the year before that, Lenore and I both thought were very strong . . . they were immature in some ways but very strong academically. We started getting some complaints from some teachers and I think what happened was new kids that pulled it down for the rest of them and it made it sound like the whole group was not ready. I don't think that was the case, I think a few kids can give the group an immature . . . and it depends if those kids are clustered in one teacher's class and that teacher does most of the complaining.

EXPECTATIONS IN K, char 3968 to 6085 of page 3 of Warren 1

Mrs. W: The kids, early on will be free play, but eventually I start building jobs into there and they become responsible for doing as many as three or four jobs throughout the week and then they have to learn how to balance their work and play time. That also tells me a lot because eventually you will get kids who would rather work than play and those that would rather play than work. Then you are kind of pushing them that sit and do worksheets all day into the block corner or the housekeeping. You try to push the kids that would rather be in the block corner over to the work tables, but it tells a lot about their learning styles and giving them a sense of responsibility, feeling of choice. I like the feeling of choice a lot. But the whole day can't be that way. It is divided between this is the time when Mrs. Warren will tell you what to do and this is the time where you can choose what to do.

EXPECTATIONS IN GR. 1, char 21 to 1414 of page 4 of Warren 2

Int: Have you gotten any other feedback from the first-grade teachers concerning kids you have sent on?

T: Not this year, we get very minimal feedback. We may get it from a teacher maybe . . . these kids are coming in so low, what is happening down there? Maybe she just happened to get a group of kids that were low, the mix or whatever and then it looks like the whole kindergarten isn't doing its job. We seldom get praise, we seldom get teachers telling us that these kids are really flying. I think because they come in at a certain level and a status quo is formed and if they don't come in higher, the status quo is never enough. If we sent them all in reading, well, they're not reading high enough. We seldom get praise for where they're coming in. I always feel like these kids are really great when they leave me.

EXPECTATIONS IN GR. 1, char 2367 to 3688 of page 3 of Warren 3

Int: How do you think the ideas of readiness are different between kindergarten and first grade?

T: I sort of get mixed messages because if I ask what they want and I have in the past, I always get, "Well, I would like them to know their numbers to 10, we would like them to know their ABC's, and we would like them to be able to sit and listen." But the complaints I get are that they don't have perfect handwriting, you know they don't have in-depth phonics knowledge or whatever. ,

Int: So the first set seems more general.

T: Well, I feel like if I ask what they want I get real minimal expectations, but when they get the group and look at the group, it is like their expectations are either based on their image of the prior year and it took me a long time to get used to the fact that every year when I get my new group and they can't line up and they can't sit still, it is like getting hit with a brick wall because you are looking at the spring's expectations. I do worry if these kids can sit and listen, you know we purposefully stretch our listening time, direction-following time and those kind of things. So that even though all they want is for them to sit and listen I feel like you know, if they aren't just great little direction-followers then it kind of comes back at me like if I didn't do my job.

Memo 4: Mrs. Warren's Ideas About Teaching Kindergarten

Mrs. Warren talks here about how she makes decisions about children over the course of the kindergarten year. Two major themes can be seen: how Mrs. Warren uses the notion of maturity to interpret children and how Mrs. Warren's job as a kindergarten teacher is framed, at least in part, by her colleagues. Mrs. Warren pays close attention to children's maturity—a mature child is one who will be a success in kindergarten and first grade. She distinguishes between academic and maturational strengths, with being socially and emotionally ready being one of the main goals of her kindergarten program. One of the barometers of maturity is a child's ability to choose appropriate tasks in kindergarten. Appropriateness is defined in part by whether it is a task chosen by the teacher. One of the reasons Mrs. Warren is so attuned to her students' maturity is that she hears about it from her first-grade colleagues. Her effectiveness as a kindergarten teacher is judged by whether students come to first grade able to be engaged by the curriculum. The standards are set by previous groups of students so children not meeting those criteria are seen as deficient. Curriculum and evaluation therefore are set by expectation, and thresholds are set up for children at each grade level by the grade above rather than being generated by the needs of children. From this perspective, Jared must be able to meet the standards of highly able and privileged students.

Some Words From Jared

There has been lots of discussion of Jared and his program, but we have heard from Jared only in the context of observations and through other people's eyes. In this section, we will look at some of Jared's ideas about going to kindergarten through an interview I did with Jared and two classmates, Trevor and Bill. These interviews were conducted at the end of the school year and focused on student's ideas about kindergarten. Although this was a group interview, I include only those sections that include Jared's responses (to keep this chapter from ballooning to 2,000 pages). Shifts to other speakers are shown with ellipses (. . .).

> *Int:* I want you to imagine that there is a brand new child in your class—this child doesn't know anything about kindergarten and doesn't know what it is like. I would like you to tell this new child what you do in school.
>
> *Jared:* Well, the good thing is there's a lot of work to be done but there's not much play time. Mostly I like the play time better but not the jobs. You have to work.
>
> *Int:* Can you explain the difference between play and the jobs?

Jared: That means working and playing means playing with your toys.

Int: Who makes up the work thing?

Jared: The teachers make up the work and the kids make up the play.

Int: And you like to do the play things better than the work?

Jared: Yep. . . .

Int: I want you to think about what you would tell this student about what you shouldn't do in kindergarten. What things would get you into trouble?

Jared: If you wouldn't do some things that the teachers tell you.

Int: Like what?

Jared: Like if one of the teachers says to go pick up that stuff and you don't do it and she says it again and then you don't do it and then if she says it again and you don't do it. And then she says, "You're on time out!" . . .

Int: Jared, can you think of things that you like and don't like?

Jared: Well, the bad news is that I don't like people when they hurt my feelings or do something bad to me. But the good news is I like playing with each other all the time. I can play with friends a lot—that is Trevor and Bill and Daniel.

Int: Can you think of something that is really easy?

Jared: The easy work is that when you do something easy, a job then, you get it done so fast and then if it takes you so slow then you won't have time to play then you have to set it down in a box and then we have to finish it tomorrow. . . .

Int: Can you tell me something that is hard for you to do?

Jared: What's hard is all the work in school that I can hardly believe it. I wish that nobody came to school, nobody, except me. Because I hated school. I started here and then we had to do some jobs. I like it at home . . .

Int: Are there any things that you have to learn before you leave kindergarten?

Jared: You have to learn to walk in the hall and be quiet and don't say any jokes.

Memo 5: Jared and Kindergarten

Jared's discussion of kindergarten circulates around issues of who controls child activity. One of his main concerns is the difference between play and work—defined by who chooses the activity. Again and again Jared brings up the fact that jobs get in the way of his doing what he wants, which is play. The criterion that Mrs. Warren uses to judge whether a child is ready—his willingness to engage in tasks that he doesn't define—is just the criterion used by Jared to describe his kindergarten experience. Because he resists that standard, he is caught in a bind—both in classroom interaction and in his definition of being a kindergarten student. What is interesting is how he has picked up on that issue as something that is salient in kindergarten experience in much the same way that Mrs. Warren has framed it.

Readings of Jared's Experience

In the previous pages, I presented excerpts of data about Jared's experience in Mrs. Warren's kindergarten. These excerpts were framed by my interest in issues of readiness and were interpreted with those interests in mind. Along the way, I presented snippets of interpretation—narrations of our emerging understandings of how Jared was constructed by school people and his family. Next, I present a couple of alternative readings of these data, informed by divergent theoretical positions and resulting in different portrayals of how Jared made his way through kindergarten.

Reading One: An everyday observable reading of Jared's experience would look at the interpretations of important participants at Solomon Elementary. It would involve careful listening to Jared's mother and his teacher and would probably also listen to him. It might construct a picture of him as a child who was classically at risk for readiness problems and who in fact had them over the course of the kindergarten year. If approached from a maturationist perspective, Jared would be read as an unready child—his birth date, sex, and social-emotional maturity provided barriers to his success in kindergarten early on. His mother voiced those concerns on kindergarten entry but chose to enter him in kindergarten anyway. Those markers proved true for most of the year but faded at the end of the school year. If Jared's experience was approached from a more interpretivist perspective—that of rich descriptions, Jared would seen as *constructed* as an unready child—that the ideas of the teacher and community framed him in a particular way. All of Jared's activity over the course of the kindergarten year would be perceived within this interpretive framework, one that served as lenses that only allowed him to be seen as unready.

Reading Two: Utilizing an activity theory reading of Jared's experience, we can ground the interpretivist reading in a way that helps us see the *process* of meaning construction. It situates meaning within an institutional context characterized by particular resources and opportunities. Utilizing the interpretation of activity theory developed by Eisenhart and Graue (1990), we explore the following aspects of meaning making: actors, interpretations, task structure, and motives.

Actors-*who is involved in interpreting Jared?*
What roles are they given and what roles do individuals take on?

The field is crowded with people whose voices can be heard as they interpret Jared's experience. Both his mother and his teacher have been highly involved in his experience over the course of the semester. The role of parent is defined in this context as someone who gathers information to optimize her child's schooling. The role of teacher is defined as someone who helps children access excellence. Children are defined in terms of their social-emotional readiness to undertake the challenging kindergarten curriculum.

Interpretations-*the meanings held*
of institutions, actions, people.

Kindergarten wasn't necessarily a place for children to get ready for school—there was a presumption that children would come in with enough readiness to be able to benefit from extremely high standards. If children were bright, with some social-emotional immaturity problems, then they were seen as needing more time to develop. This interpretation fit Jared to a tee for most of the kindergarten year. He was seen as immature and lacking the emotional tools to meet the challenges of the Solomon kindergarten.

Tasks-*resources available to actors and*
structures for interpersonal relations.

Academic task structure: characterized by Mrs. Warren as junior first grade, by Mrs. Millard as more academic than when she was in kindergarten and by Jared as too much work and not enough play. To teach responsibility, Mrs. Warren increased the amount of teacher-directed activity in the classroom, requiring students to choose work activities over their own play. One way that she assessed maturity was to see who chose work on their own and who had to be guided toward it. Because Jared needed help selecting jobs, Mrs. Warren thought he was not as ready as he should be. And Jared thought that school wasn't as much fun as he thought it could be.

Participation structures are rules people use to interact with one another. Teachers and parents had a collaborative relationship at Solomon, with parents taking the lead on finding out what they needed to do to ensure their child's success within a highly competitive environment. Within an active social network, parents talked to each other about the curriculum and their child's experience within it. Jared's mother was not at the center of this network and in some ways she did not experience the pressures to conform in the way that other parents did.

Motives-*goals and objectives assigned*
by members of a community.

The motive for all actions at Solomon was to ensure that children could excel in the school setting. Being average was not necessarily enough—it was very important for students to rise to the top of the class. For this reason, parents and teachers searched for strategies to help individuals improve their chances of advancing to the top of the group. This included watching children to make sure they fit into the curriculum designed to maximize the potential of a very able group. Mrs. Millard chose to enter Jared into kindergarten because she had been told by her pediatrician and schoolpeople that there was no reason not to (although she had alternative advice presented by others as well).

An activity theory reading of Jared's experience provides multiple perspectives on community, institution, and kindergarten curriculum. It situates judgments about children in the multiple fields of influence that shape home school interaction, and it forces us to pay attention to the varied voices that narrate those influences. Jared is constructed in particular ways, in this particular kindergarten, in this local community, at this time and place. Expectations for adult activity and child ability are threaded through with consciousness of power relations, resource allocation, and near and distant goals. This theoretical reading allows us to look beyond the surface of simple descriptions, connecting actions to ideas and activities to philosophy.

Conclusion

In this chapter, we explored what to many researchers is the most mysterious aspect of interpretive research—the process of interpretation. Through my struggles with a very small set of data, I illustrated how I try to connect description to interpretation through understanding of context by slowly widening our focus to include as many relevant aspects of experience as possible. Among these aspects is the contribution of theory, which grounds our interpretations by providing ways of looking that go beyond the data. In the next section, we look at a specific example of how theory has been used to read a field experience and the data it generated. Anne Haas Dyson provides a Bakhtinian narration of the intersections of social world and literary practice to illustrate theory in practice in qualitative research.

Making Sense in Children's Worlds: The Meaning of Tina and the Weeping Superheroes

Anne Haas Dyson
University of California, Berkeley

Tina, 7 years old and a second grader, is sitting next to her good friend Holly. She is not talking (unusual for her) but is quickly and for the most part, steadily, writing a story for the classroom Author's Theater (when the children choose classmates to act out their written stories). When the composing period is over, her notebook contains the following newly completed text:

ods tare wry 4 x-man	Once there were 4 X-men.
in the x-man fote othr	And the X-men fought others.
own x-man died	One X-men died.
and the rast uavy they wrey	And the rest of them were
sad they criyd	sad. They cried.
Storm flow away	Storm flew away.
rogue stry to criy	Rogue started to cry.
Jeen Gray cam	Jean Gray came.
Black Momy cam to	Black Mommy came too.
They all fote	They all fought.
and the x-man won	And the X-men won.
rogue found storm	Rogue found Storm.
She was making weather	She was making weather.
and they all lived	And they all lived
happy eave after the end.	happy ever after the end.

Tina's story, I imagine, is not particularly impressive or even meaningful to readers (especially those who know nothing about the *X-men* [Lee, 1963] team of superheroes). For me as researcher, however, this text mediated a key incident in the history of Tina's social imagination and literacy use: It suggested a moment of "ideological becoming" (Bakhtin, 1981, p. 341).

This interpretation—this way of articulating the social meaning of Tina's textual actions—results, at least in part, from the interplay of analytic attention to the details of Tina's classroom life, on one hand, and, on the other, reflection on, and appropriation of, theoretical constructs about the nature of language use itself. As anthropologist Clifford Geertz explains,

> It is with the kind of material produced by . . . almost obsessively fine-comb field study . . . that the mega-concepts with which contemporary social science is afflicted—legitimacy, modernization, integration, conflict . . . meaning—can be given the sort of sensible actuality that makes it possible to think not only realistically and concretely *about* them, but, what is more important, creatively and imaginatively *with* them. (1973, p. 23)

Thus, a researcher begins with some basic theoretical constructs—some definitions of what one is studying. Such definitions help one draw boundaries around the phenomenon being studied; they guide methodological decisions about what is relevant and what is not in a study of, for example, writing development. At the same time, however, the details themselves (children's actions and reactions) enrich, extend, or challenge those very constructs.

In the following pages, I aim to illustrate this interaction between theoretical constructs and local materiality. To do so, I draw on a recent study in Tina's urban primary school, a school that served children from strikingly different sociocultural backgrounds. (For descriptions of study methodology, including site, see Dyson, 1995, 1997.) I first define the theoretical construct about literacy that guided the study. I then describe how this construct influenced methodological decisions about how to pay attention to children and their writing and, also, how it guided efforts to find a language of analysis. That language—that vocabulary for telling the story of what happened in this class—is critical to interpretation, for it is the language that mediates the theoretical constructs and the everyday.

To go some way toward achieving these grand ambitions in a few pages, I will use a common strategy of the interpretive researcher. After providing the basic definitional and descriptive information, I will tell a short story—more accurately, I will provide an analytic summary of a long story. In Erickson's words,

> I think what qualitative research does best and most essentially is to describe key incidents in functionally relevant descriptive terms and place them in some relations to the wider social context, using the key incident as a concrete instance of the workings of abstract principles of social organization. (1981, p. 22)

The key incidents herein include those linked together by Tina's X-men story. Through constructing these incidents (i.e., through deciding what to highlight and what to gloss), I constructed as well an interpretation that sought to explain at one and the same time the local and theoretical significance of those weeping super-heroes.

Basic Definitions and Methodological Decisions

In any study of literacy development, a basic definitional question is, What is "it" that develops? Where does one look for "it"? To make sense of Tina's "writing," for example, should I attend primarily to the text on the page, to her topic, story structure, and spelling? Or perhaps what matters most is the behavioral evidence of individual mind at work, her engagement in the processes of planning, monitoring, and revising (Graves, 1983). Yet again, perhaps writing is a kind of social and cultural happening—an "event" (Heath, 1983; Hymes, 1986); in that case, the focus should be on the "components" of the event, including the relationships between participants (including Tina, her peers, and her teacher), their norms of interacting, available symbolic tools, and communicated messages.

In making sense of Tina's writing, I attended to all these matters—and more. I adopted a "dialogic" definition of literacy (Bakhtin, 1981, 1986; Volosinov, 1973). In this definition, the text—its content, structure, and style—*does* matter. Moreover, the struggles of a writer like Tina to get words organized on paper matters too, as does the organized social event in which the writer participates. In completing her X-men story, Tina engaged in a classroom composing event as she made choices of text topic, theme, and structure. In this way, she had her say, so to speak, about the nature of superheroes. In fact, from a dialogic point of view, the text is literally just that—a say, an "utterance" addressed to others (Bakhtin, 1986, p. 60).

From a dialogic perspective, however, there was more than just a social event going on through Tina's writing; there was also an ideological one. Tina used written signs to bring order to her written thoughts and simultaneously to reach out to others. But those signs were themselves symbols of societal order—they were public signs, drenched in community experience, not just her own experience. In learning to write, children, like Tina, are learning the signs or words available in certain situations to a boy or girl, to a person of a particular age, ethnicity, race, class, religion, and on and on. They are also potentially becoming ideologically aware, as they adopt or resist the expected words.

In the words of Bakhtin's colleague, Volosinov,

> A verbal performance inevitably takes its point of departure from some particular state of affairs. . . . Thus the printed verbal performance engages, as it were, in ideological colloquy of large scale: it responds to something, objects to something, affirms something, anticipates possible responses and objections, seeks support, and so on.
>
> *Any utterance . . . is only a moment in the continuous process of verbal communication.* But that continuous verbal communication is, in turn, itself only a moment in the continuous, all-inclusive, generative process of a given social collective. (italics in the original; 1973, p. 95)

Child writers, like adult ones, are active contributors to a local "state of affairs"—an ongoing social dialogue—that both draws on and influences larger cultural ones. Their authorial choices are influenced by social identification and social struggle. Thus, to make sense of Tina's text as a particular "moment in . . . a given social collective," it is important to know the meaning of superhero stories in the classroom collective as a whole, as well as the particular meaning of Tina's story in her own evolution as a writer and as a participant in that collective.

Among the relevant questions are, for example, who usually appropriated the cultural materials (i.e., the signs) of superhero stories in this classroom? For what evident social purposes? In what ways was Tina's X-men product representative of the superhero stories produced in the community? In what ways was it representative of Tina's own usual story lines? What social interactions (or conflicts) were evident during its composing and eventual presentation on the classroom stage?

In my study of Tina and her peers, I was concerned with just such questions. I aimed to illuminate the social and ideological dynamics undergirding writing development and, more particularly, the links between learning to write and learning to negotiate one's place in a complex community of differences. Thus, I gathered data (fieldnotes, audiotaped records, and written products) on the class as a whole, paying special attention to the Author's Theater events, *and* I also gathered similar sorts of data on the composing events of selected child participants, like Tina. In collecting that later data, I followed the social history of particular child products, like Tina's X-men story, by observing their talk and behavior on consecutive "free" writing days. Of course, I had to watch all the videos, cartoons, and television shows the children referenced to figure out how the children appropriated and transformed the available characters and actions.

To construct interpretations of the data sets, like the series of events connected with those weeping superheroes, I needed to develop coding categories—specialized vocabulary for telling analytic stories about what happened in this class. It is this vocabulary that mediates between the theoretical notion of dialogism and the children's recorded behaviors.

I developed one set of coding categories for describing the social processes evident in children's interactions (e.g., affiliating with others, resisting others, distancing oneself from them, or, more equitably, negotiating with them) and another for the ways in which written texts figured into those processes (e.g., as props [often with minimal writing] for Author's Theater productions, as representations of valued characters and actions, as reinforcers of textual authority, their right to say how the world is). Finally, I appropriated Volosinov's (1973) terms "reflection" and "refraction" to describe the ideological processes through which texts reflected and distorted the children's professed values, interests, and beliefs about human relations. (Coding categories, with behavioral indices and data examples, are available in Dyson, 1995.)

Especially in the public forum of Author's Theater, social processes like affiliating with selected others intersected with the ideological processes reverberating in the classroom community as a whole, and thus emerged authorial processes: conscious decision making about the portrayal of human relations and human experience, that is, about composing stories.

To illustrate this dialogic way of paying attention to and interpreting child writing, I offer below a brief interpretation of Tina's superhero story. The interpretation is in narrative form, a form that allows me to capture the interplay between Tina and the classroom community as a whole.

The Case of the
Weeping Superheroes

The Author's Theater was an extremely popular activity in Kristin's room. For many children, the theater promised the opportunity of public play with one's actual or desired friends; a "finished" text was the desired ticket to this public play. The children's "finished" texts were generally very brief—and sometimes literally invisible; a good oral storyteller could compensate for a nonexistent text, as long as the paper was held very close to the chest.

For weeks, the boys had been dominating Author's Theater with their stories of ninjas, ninja turtles, and X-men—and, for weeks, Tina had been begging for a part to play, with limited luck. The only boy who regularly included girls in superhero dramas was Sammy, and he, like other boys, picked only Melissa or Sarah, two slender, middle-class, and outgoing white girls—just as were the ninja's "foxy babes" in the popular media stories. They never chose girls of color, like Tina and her friend Holly. Tina had had it. Usually, when she wrote in her journal (titled *The Peace Book*), she wrote brief texts expressing her love of family and friends. On this day, Tina enticed her friend Holly to write an X-men story with her. (X-men stories were particularly appealing, because the X-men superhero team includes "strong" and "tough" girls, including girls of color.) "And no boys," she said firmly to her friend, "'cause the boys doesn't let us play."

Sitting side by side, Tina and Holly began playfully to plan their story. Their story, composed by authors situated in the social world very differently from the usual superhero authors, revealed a complex, contradiction-ridden response to the emerging class dialogue about gender and power. When the children began, Tina planned to be the X-men character Rogue, but she quickly became "the toughest guy in the world. . . . We're all Blobs!" (Blobs are huge, fleshy mutant humans, virtually indestructible and very bad guys.) "'Cause if somebody threw a metal ball at me, the energy go right through me and I would never know. And we're sisters robbing the world. . . . And we'll never get sick. And we'll never die."

The sisters evolved, Tina becoming Uncle Blob, Holly niece Blob. As the girls became more and more animated, they moved to the classroom rug, deep in play. In the drama, Uncle Blob Tina captured the female X-men character Rogue, cutting off her long hair. Uncle Blob drank that hair, absorbing its fiery power, giving just a small bit to his begging niece Holly Blob. "The only thing you can do," he tells the girl, "is just shoot out fire at them [the X-men] and then just call me." (There are shades here of the ninja stories and of the girls who call them for help.)

Class composing time ended before the children had put pencil to paper. The next day Tina was absent, so each girl eventually authored her own X-men story. Given the intensity of peer pressure, each girl found it impossible to write the planned drama. For example, on the day Tina attempted to write her X-men story, both girls and boys begged for powerful good-guy roles—and expressed great unhappiness with the unapologetic bad guys Tina had in mind, as is illustrated below. Tina is sitting during composing time with Holly, Liliana, Sarah, and James. She is preparing to make a list of her actors.

Holly: Can I be Rogue?
Tina: You're all bad guys. I got all the part of you all.
Holly: We're not bad guys.
Tina: But so! You can't beat me! Hey-hey-hey-hey! You can try to beat me all you want.
Liliana: Are you Jean Gray [another X-men character]?
Tina: No I'm Blo::b. You can't kill me::::.
Liliana: A BOY::.
Tina: So! I wanta be a boy.

Still, the pressure continued. Holly wanted to be Rogue, and Monique wanted Storm. Sarah said she would be any good-guy girl, and then James asked to be Wolverine. So Tina relented, with evident exasperation, "You don't want to be a bad guy? OK. *Fine.* You're not a bad guy."

In the midst of these classroom negotiations, Blob was abandoned and the X-men resurfaced. Tina spent the entire composing period negotiating who was going to be whom in her story. She did not, however, actually write a text. Tina tried to present an Author's Theater anyway, one dominated by female characters. But she seemed overcome with shyness and, moreover, her actors found her story too "confusing." She decided she needed more than a mere ticket. She needed to actually "finish," as she told her teacher. That is, she needed some written representational material to cue her oral storytelling, and she also needed, it seemed, the authority that having something written could provide.

The next day, Tina did indeed "finish" her text and, also, her Bakhtinian utterance—her response to the class. She did it carrying a text and, buttressed by that text, speaking loudly and clearly. During composing time, Tina sat next to Holly (who was writing, once again, about friendships). Tina wrote the story with which this chapter section began. That story was not only unusual for Tina (given her typical texts about loving people and things); it also was an unusual superhero story in her class: There was a predominance of women, enacted primarily by girls of color; there also was a death among the good guys; and, most strikingly, a good cry by the superheroes.

During the peer enactment of her story, Tina reinforced the disruption of the usual gendered order:

Tina: (reading) "One of the X-men *died* . . . And the rest were very sad. They cried." Everybody [all of the child actors] cry now, even the *boys.*

Tina had not been able to enact a Blob story; however, she did not go quietly into the realm of the more conventional superhero story. Although she was held back by the social milieu and its dominant "routes and directions" (Volosinov, 1973, p. 91), she was not silenced by others' resistance. She negotiated, given her own affiliations, and, when temporarily overwhelmed, she raised both pencil and voice and tried again. Her struggle seemed to be a decisive experience in her own "ideological becoming" as an author (Bakhtin, 1981, p. 341), that is, in her deliberate and selective appropriation of others' words.

As an activist girl—and an experienced writer of relationships—Tina was helping to change the possibilities for superhero stories in the local culture of the classroom. Although conventional male-exclusive superhero stories continued, they were "dialogized," to use Bakhtin's word (1981, p. 426); that is, they were rendered a possibility among other possibilities. These new possibilities—and the ideological refractions that accompanied their social evolution—elicited a composing time response from Sammy . . . but that, as they say, is another story (see Dyson, 1995, 1997).

Coda

The first time I read Bakhtin's final essay in *The Dialogic Imagination* (1981), I appropriated appealing phrases, writing them out the slow way—longhand, in a curvy cursive—in my reading journal. I especially liked his notions about "the ideological becoming of a human being," which is evidenced in "the process of selectively assimilating the words of others" (p. 341). But I had only a vague, shadowy notion of what exactly that meant.

In a similar way, when I first began observing Tina, I had only a vague, shadowy notion of what exactly her writing "meant." I selected key incidents, filled with social struggle, writing them out the slow way—longhand, in a curvy cursive—in my project log book. The Bakhtinian concept of "ideological becoming" and Tina's everyday actions and reactions illuminated each other, as I appropriated both his words and hers in my own story. Bakhtin, after all, wrote nothing in particular about children's writing development; Tina most certainly never quoted Bakhtin; and, to my knowledge, developmentalists rarely have been interested in dialogic, rather than linear or interactive, changes in child writing. In linking Bakhtin and Tina, I hope I have constructed a reasonable narrative, one that seems carefully grounded in details, and, most important, one that others might appropriate to make sense of the children in their own lives.

References

Bakhtin, M. (1981). Discourse in the novel. In C. Emerson & M. Holquist (Eds.), *The dialogic imagination: Four essays by M. Bakhtin* (pp. 259-422). Austin: University of Texas Press.

Bakhtin, M. (1986). *Speech genres and other late essays.* Austin: University of Texas Press.

Dyson, A. H. (1995). Writing children: Reinventing the development of childhood literacy. *Written Communication, 12,* 3-46.

Dyson, A. H. (1997). *Writing superheroes: Contemporary childhood, popular culture, and classroom literacy.* New York: Teachers College Press.

Erickson, F. (1981). Some approaches to inquiry in school-community. In H. Trueba, G. Guthrie, & K. Au (Eds.), *Culture and the bilingual classroom: Studies in classroom ethnography* (pp. 17-35). Rowley, MA: Newbury House.

Geertz, C. (1973). *The interpretation of cultures.* New York: Basic Books.

Graves, D. H. (1983). *Writing: Teachers and children at work.* Portsmouth, NH: Heinemann Educational Books.

Heath, S. B. (1983). *Ways with words: Language, life and work in communities and classrooms.* Cambridge, UK: Cambridge University Press.

Hymes, D. (1986). Models of the interaction of language and social life. In J. Gumperz & D. Hymes (Eds.), *Directions in sociolinguistics: The ethnography of communication* (pp. 35-71). New York: Basil Blackwell.

Lee, S. (Author and Illustrator). (1963). *The X-men.* New York: Marvel Entertainment Group.

Volosinov, V. N. (1973). *Marxism and the philosophy of language* (L. Matejka & I. R. Titunik, Trans.). New York: Seminar Press.

APPENDIX

The full interview text came from a conversation with Jared's mother at the end of the kindergarten year. We had talked at the beginning of the year, and many of the questions were quite similar.

Overview

Int: This is kind of an overview, what I am doing now is an interview kind of parallel to the one that we did in the fall mainly just to review how the year has gone and things like that. *What kind of things have you been thinking about as Jared approaches finishing kindergarten?*

Mom: Oh, is he ready for first grade, mostly emotionally, I guess his biggest problem at school has been crying at times and that kind of thing. Academically, apparently he is doing just fine.

Int: Can you tell me a little bit more about the social part?

Mom: Just from what I hear from Mrs. Warren, he just cries easily like if he thinks his turn got missed, he will cry easily or if somebody teases him he will cry, that kind of thing.

Int: Do you see that kind of thing at home?

Mom: Yeah, sometimes, mostly when he is overtired.

Int: How do you think that might impact how he does in first grade?

Mom: Oh, I am just afraid that he will get teased more about if he does cry and that would make him cry more and it would be kind of a vicious circle.

Int: Sure, sure. So what do you think needs to happen, what will get him to the point where he is socially more ready?

Mom: I think just maybe time and maturity. I'm not sure, I mean we can work on it at home but I think it is more a matter of aging and . . .

Int: So the summer could be a pretty important time for him. What kind of positive things have you been thinking about?

Mom: Oh, how much he really has learned! I mean as far as a little bit of reading and writing and a little arithmetic, actually I was surprised how much they did learn for kindergarten.

Int: How did what they learned connect or not connect with what you expected? Was it different than you thought it would be?

Mom: It was more than I thought it would be.

Int: So going in, what kind of things did you expect?

Mom: I expected them to learn their alphabet and everything and counting and that kind of thing but I really didn't think they would get into words as much as they did and I didn't think they would get into like adding and subtracting like they seemed to.

Int: And how do you feel things went?

Mom: I think very well.

Int: Any other positive things?

Mom: Let's see . . . just the aspect of making a lot of new friends, we do have some of his friends over to play once in a while so it is nice to have a new group of friends rather than just neighbor kids.

Int: You mentioned a concern about his social readiness, is there anything else?

Mom: Maybe just the length of the day, I think that will be a challenge for him.

Int: And how do you think he is going to handle that?

Mom: I am not sure, you know 3 days a week he is at day care, opposite the kindergarten so you know he is kind of used to being in that setting all day but not quite as structured as what school will be, then a couple days that he is home during the week are totally free time, so I am just a little worried that his attention span will be long enough to really concentrate and do what he is supposed to all day long.

Describe K

Int: How would you describe Jared's kindergarten experience?

Mom: For him I think it was fun, he seems to enjoy it. He likes going to school. He didn't like doing the homework that she sent home, he complained about having to do that at home but basically he liked school and I don't know if he liked it so much because it was just going and being with the other kids or because of the actual things that they were doing. For me, it was also very positive but I don't know they aren't your little 4-year-olds anymore, you know they kind of get a sassy mouth and they come home with all these words that they never used to know and that kind of thing, so in that way it was kind of . . . oh I wouldn't say negative but it was a little harder on me.

Int: And he is your first child, isn't he?

Mom: Right.

Int: So this is all new for you.

Mom: Right.

Int: How is he different now than he was in September?

Mom: He is just more worldly, I think. Although, a lot of the things he says I am sure he really doesn't understand, but he sounds tougher and more sarcastic.

Int: Any other differences?

Mom: No, not really I don't think.

Communication

Int: *What kind of information have you gotten from Mrs. Warren to help you understand how Jared is doing?*

Mom: Well, do you mean like has it been written?

Int: Any sources that you had, so if you could tell me about all the different ways you found out about what was going on in school?

Mom: Okay, you know the things I found out about what the whole group was doing was through notes and that kind of thing. Specifically to Jared it was usually, the conferences, I had two conferences with her and then one time I just stopped in to pick him up after school and I had a chance to talk to her.

Int: What were the conferences like?

Mom: Well, the first one was mainly how he is doing, what he is learning, what he needs to work on, you know, what letters he knows . . . pretty much academic type of things and some on the socialization part. The second focused more on his immaturity and easy crying and that kind of thing because she said he was doing very well otherwise but that was really what she wanted to talk about.

Int: Did you request the conference?

Mom: I requested it but Mrs. Warren said that she had debated because she thought it was important but she said it had been getting better but she was just going to let it go a little bit to see and if it hadn't gotten any worse she was going to let it go but if it had gotten any worse she was going to call me. She said she had seen an improvement from the beginning of the year with that toward the end of the year. She did see an improvement so that's why she was feeling more comfortable with it, it was improving as the year went on.

Int: That idea of immaturity is really interesting to me, was that something that you think he came in with?

Mom: Oh, yes and again I think he is THE youngest one in the class, he won't be 6 until July 31 and I don't know if I just had it set in my head that he had a late birthday so he was immature or if actually he is a little less mature than some of the older kids, I don't know. But I had it set in my mind that he would probably be a little less mature than most of them.

Int: You think time is the thing that is going to help him out with this?

Mom: Yeah, I do.

Int: How did Mrs. Warren talk about how that immaturity affected how he did in class?

Mom: Well, I think she had to do some kind of behavior type modification, maybe you would call it, apparently, like for example, if he wanted to hold her hand at recess or something and he came crying to her, then she wouldn't do it but if he came and asked nicely, "Mrs. Warren, I would like to hold your hand now," then she would let him to try to show him that if you ask appropriately or do things appropriately that is better than crying and getting out of control about it. Another example was, I guess it was the flagholder person, every day that she made a list because he felt one time his turn was missed and he was very upset so to visualize it she made up the list so every day he could see the name ahead of him being crossed off so he would know his turn didn't get missed.

Int: What would you like to know more about?

Mom: I really would have loved to have been a mouse in the corner and really just seen what he did every day, how he acted with teachers, how he acted with the other children and I know teachers really can't give you that sense. They can tell you he is doing fine or he listens well or he doesn't listen well, whatever the case may be but I think kids are so different when they are not at home and they are not with mom or dad, yet you never see that because if you are there then they are like they usually are, do you know what I mean? I guess I really would . . . I mean I say academically I know he does the work well and I know he is smart enough to do it and everything I would really have liked to have been the mouse in the corner, just watching him, just to see how he interacts with everybody.

Int: How did the report card help you, did it help you out? Did it give you much feedback?

Mom: Yeah, actually I was surprised how complete and what it all hit on. And it did show me that she did obviously think he was doing very well and that we really didn't have any big areas to worry about.

Expect Grade 1

Int: *What do you think his first-grade year is going to be like?*

Mom: That is hard, I don't know. I am not really sure. I expect as far as learning things, I expect him by the end of the year to be reading fairly well, but other than that I don't know how much they get into math or any of the other subjects.

Int: How do you think kindergarten prepared Jared for first grade?

Mom: Well, I hope it prepared him well in that he did have to learn to sit and be quiet and follow directions and you know . . . just the school environment, it is different than being able to play and run around all the time. Like I say I am just concerned that it is all day long, in comparison, kindergarten was so short.

Int: Yeah, the morning just flies. Do you have a sense of how it might be different?

Mom: I think he will find that it . . . I hate to say it, but not as much fun . . . that it is more geared for learning things than just getting in the school environment for the first time.

Int: What kind of things are you hoping that he is going to learn?

Mom: I guess just learning what he is supposed to be learning at that age, you know as far as subjects goes and then growing out of this crying easily and you know, maybe learning how to solve problems more effectively.

Int: How do you think you are going to find out what they do in first grade?

Mom: I suppose just through the conferences and everything. I would like to say I would be able to volunteer more and do more at school but I am not sure that is realistic to hope.

Int: Sounds like you have a pretty full plate right now.

Mom: Yeah, we do.

Miscellaneous

Int: *Are there any things that I didn't ask you that would be important for me to know?*

Mom: I guess, I mean I have been very, very pleased with Solomon and Mrs. Warren and the whole situation but the one thing that has concerned me and other parents that I have talked to in other schools in that I think they depend on the kindergartners to tell you a little too much, I know they try to send notes home a lot but if Jared didn't bring them home you know then I didn't know about them. And I know one field trip in particular I didn't get the permission slip back because I knew nothing about it in time. I don't know if there is a way at the end of the hour they could say, "Now everybody get your papers, you have to take them home." I know they are trying to teach them responsibility but at the same time if the parents aren't getting the papers and notes and things then it is not working.

Int: So if you could imagine the very best system for getting information between home and school, what would that look like?

Mom: Oh, boy . . . I don't know. I know you can't mail everything and they can't call with everything, I guess you really do have to rely on the kids, but it just should be a little more formal. Like Jared would just come home with all these papers just rumpled up in his backpack rather than in, like maybe if they each had a nice envelope that went back and forth with correspondence between the parents and the teacher, I don't mean like for his school papers and stuff . . .

Int: But for important information.

Mom: Yeah, any correspondence that the teacher might want to send me, you know.

Int: What is important for you to let the school know so they can do the best job for Jared?

Mom: I guess, his personality, you know, what he is like, you know, if he does have a short attention span I think it is helpful to know that ahead of time, although then you might kind of do a self-prophesying type thing, the teacher might think he's got one just because I said it and she may not find it is a problem but think it is because I said so but at the same time I guess they should know how I feel about his behavior.

Int: Anything else?

Mom: No, I guess not, I guess they will probably see pretty much of this age that the kids are pretty much equal in academic standing. I don't know how they group them as far as learning to read and that kind of thing but I mean they can tell that probably very easily from the first week of school.

Int: Do you have any questions for me?

Mom: I don't think so.

9

WRITING AS CONTEXT

Writing should be the easy part. You already have danced the fieldwork dance, balancing your desires for generating information against the needs of your participants to live their lives. You've asked important questions, listened carefully, gathered useful and useless information, and smiled as you realize you've put the microphone plug in the earphone jack when you are almost finished with an interview. You sorted through the mounds of information, trying to find patterns and knit together a picture of something, then another thing, and then something completely different. Now you just have to write it up. That's it, right?

If only it were that easy. More and more, qualitative researchers are understanding that rather than being an afterthought or merely a mode of communication, writing is part and parcel of the interpretive act. Qualitative researchers write all the way along, inscribing their understandings in fieldnotes, interview questions, analytical memos, and finally in a text the tells the world about some aspect of the process. Instead of being neutrally located outside the researcher's persona, free of the push and pull of personality and politics, writing is rhetorical, situated, and mysteriously as analytical as "analysis." We often do not know what we know until we write, forced into the situation of saying something about

---

AUTHORS' NOTE: Written by Beth.

what was nothing before. Through our writing, we create a reflection of our knowing—or at least a reflection of the part we are willing to share in public places.

Curiously, texts on qualitative methodology focus little on writing.[1] In this book, we will work against that standard and look closely at both the discourse on and the act of writing. We will explore the context in which qualitative researchers are now thinking about writing as well as walk through what we see as some of the important issues in the process of writing. We will focus on how narrative forms shape what is known by both writer and reader and examine the use of a particular genre, the vignette, as a way to sharpen analysis and to crystallize issues deemed important by the researcher for the reader. We begin by situating writing as a research-long process.

- Writing is part of a chain of textualizations that begins with framing the problems and runs through fieldnotes, transcriptions, and books written from a study.

"Writing up" is a curious misnomer when applied to interpretive research. The practice of writing is undertaken at every step of the research process—the researcher is authoring both her own experience and her understanding of others as she generates data, formulates interpretations, and develops a case for others to read. Atkinson (1992) describes the process of textualization in this way:

> Before we come to "write up" the ethnographic report, we have already "written up" our observations and reflections concerning "the field." Indeed, "the field" that is reported on the basis of fieldwork is not a pre-given natural entity. It is something we construct, both through the practical transactions and activities of data collection, and through the literary activities of writing fieldnotes, analytic memoranda, and the like. Writing up, then, is not the mechanical collation and reportage of raw data. It is part of a complex layering of textual production. The ethnography is a version of social reality that is inseparably a matter of textual representations. (p. 5)

What does this mean? First and foremost, it means that research is interpretation all the way down (Geertz, 1973). Transforming observations into text frames the author role very early in the process and makes each subsequent textualization reliant on those earlier links in the chain.

Using Atkinson's ideas, interpretive work is very much like a collage—a multilayered, multiphasic representation of both knowing and known.

- Writing is an interpretive activity that shapes how we know as readers as well as how we know as researchers.

Just as the role we enact as researchers provides us with very situated perspectives on the topic of interest, the role we take as writers allows only certain things to be explored, by us or our readers. The boundaries of writing have broadened considerably in recent years, making choice of writing style a methodological, theoretical, and even political decision. How we choose to write allows us to tell only certain things and allows our readers to experience a particular set of understandings.

John Van Maanen (1988) provided one accounting of the written forms typical in ethnography, exploring how the author is positioned and culture is presented. *Realist tales* are the most common, in which third-party descriptions of lived experience hide the author by separating methodology from cultural account, relying on experiential authority and interpretive omnipotence to portray what appears to be an unmediated perspective on the native's point of view. This displacement of the researcher from the story appears to heighten the objectivity of description by distancing the knower from the known. In contrast, the author is front and center in a *confessional tale*, which aims to show how the process of fieldwork produced certain kinds of understandings. My discussion of failing Matthew, presented in Chapter 5, is an example of a confessional tale, with its focus on how my misguided attempt to broaden his teacher's view on him backfired and got him into trouble. Confessional tales make the author part of the interpretive process by linking role with understanding in explicit ways. Narration still occurs, but the narrator becomes part of the play, standing on stage with the other actors. Both reading and writing confessional tales is different from the realist genre, creating new spaces for understanding and positionings for all involved. Finally, an artistic form of writing, which Van Maanen calls *impressionistic tales*, presents both a cultural scene and the writer's knowing in a startling dramatic format. They are highly personalized and often seem more like a novel than interpretive research. The stylized form challenges both writer and reader to remember the fact that any story can be told in many ways and that any analysis is ongoing and partial. Other authors have pointed to other forms of writing (see, e.g., Richardson, 1994). The point to take away from these categorizations is that narrative forms bring certain things to light and hide others.

The choice of textual genre is shaped by our ideas about what it means to know and how that is related to methods of representation, to conceptions of author positioning, and to the politics of narration jointly held by author and publishing venue. Certain genres are not welcomed by some groups of readers and adherence to particular "standards" of writing (such as strict interpretations of the APA manual) is used to police the boundaries of acceptable textual formats. The genre therefore shapes what can be known by individuals and groups who share notions of a field. Laurel Richardson is right when she reminds us that "How we are expected to write affects what we can write about" (1994, p. 520).

- Writing represents the author as much as it represents the field.

There is something very self-disclosive about writing. No matter what the presence of the author in the text, it tells us something. The writer's identity is reflected in both how he or she comes to know the subject of interest and the way that subject is portrayed in writing. According to Norman Denzin:

> Representation, of course, is always self-presentation. That is, the Other's presence is directly connected to the writers' self-presence in the text. The Other who is presented in the text is always a version of the researcher's self. Krieger (1991) argues: "When we discuss others, we are always talking about ourselves. "Our images of "them" are images of "us." (Denzin, 1994, p. 503)

A good example of this could be the differences between my portrayals of Jared and Trevor in Chapter 8. I was drawn to Jared because he fit the prototypical readiness problem described by scores of early childhood teachers. He was relatively young compared to his classmates, he had been in a baby-sitting setting rather than preschool in the time before he started kindergarten, and his teacher felt that he was emotionally immature. I found him to be engaging, creative, and responsive to his classroom environment—in a word, I liked him. I could have had a similar connection to Trevor—his teacher was very concerned about his readiness for first grade—but he and I did not hit it off at all. I saw him manipulating Jared in ways that seemed to cause myriad problems—they often seemed to be the context for Jared's frustrations. Trevor also managed to irritate me, or should I say, I found myself irritated by Trevor. His sarcasm and nasty humor did not bring out the best in me.

Who is framing whom in this situation? My portrayal is not very flattering. Its perspective tells as much about me as it does about Trevor. I depict him relationally—in the context of my coming to know Jared. Because of my interpretation of his relationship with Jared, I write about him as a villain. With that script comes certain assumptions about interactions and ways of framing his relations with others. It portrays my failure to connect with Trevor and my irritation about what he does to Jared. Even when I am not written into the story, I am there. The picture is much more crowded, recalling the motif of the collage mentioned earlier.

- Writing is not a neutral activity, reporting the facts. It is strategically undertaken to tell a particular story to a particular audience.

As a writer, you have choices. You choose the particular question framing, you negotiate fieldwork positions, you marshal evidence in particular ways. The choices you make shape what you can do at a later point, and they reflect an agenda you hold for your work. Whether you choose a researcher-absent position that focuses on your rendering of participants' experiences, whether you insert yourself visibly into an account that presents a dialogic framing of coming to know, or whether you create a fiction to teach the reader about the field, these choices frame reality for both reader and writer. They produce a way of knowing that helps us see the world. These are powerful choices that include and exclude certain topics, people, and theoretical terrain.

The texts we create construct a sense of what is, beginning with the language we use and extending to the genres that carry our ideas. The productive process of writing is charged in ways that are muted when we do not think of the implications of our choices.

Language does not "reflect" social reality, but produces meaning, creates social reality. Different languages and different discourses within a given language divide up the world and give it meaning in ways that are not reducible to one another. Language is how social organization and power are defined and contested and the place where our sense of selves, our *subjectivity*, is constructed. (Richardson, 1994, p. 518)

Taking these implications into consideration changes the way we work as readers and writers. As readers, it forces us to consider how our knowing is shaped by the narrative forms deployed by an author. We must look not only at the theory, method, and interpretations but also at their staging in text. As writers, we need to interrogate how we put together our arguments, stories, and discussions, exploring how the choices we make compel us to see things in particular ways. These choices can be exciting, liberating, infuriating, and deliberate, but instead they often are taken for granted and mechanical. We must focus more carefully on how we frame our work, taking responsibility for the blind spots it engenders and the illumination it allows. Writing is not just telling what is—it is shaping and contouring perspectives in ways that have implications for all involved.

In the rest of this chapter, I describe a couple of ways that you can help readers see things—ways that set up conversations in particular ways. I begin by talking about a tried and true way of showing: data displays.

Data Displays

You know how they say, "A picture is worth a thousand words." Sometimes *they* are right. Sometimes writers need to find alternatives to straight text to help a reader see relations and themes that arise in interpretive analysis. There are a number of alternatives to the fieldnote excerpt in narration style that characterizes most interpretive research.

> *Data display*, defined as an organized, compressed assembly of information that permits conclusion drawing and/or action taking, is a second, inevitable part of analysis. The researcher typically needs to see a reduced set of data as a basis for thinking about its meanings. More focused displays may include structured summaries, synopses (Fischer & Wertz, 1975), vignettes (Erickson, 1986), networklike or other diagrams (Carney, 1990; Gladwin, 1989; Strauss, 1987; Werner & Schoepfle, 1987a, 1987b), and matrices with text rather than numbers in cells (Eisenhardt, 1989a, 1989b; Miles & Huberman, 1984, 1994). (Huberman & Miles, 1994, p. 429)

Huberman and Miles detail a variety of ways that data can be displayed to highlight salient themes in analysis. In this chapter, I will focus on two distinct versions of displays: matrices and vignettes. In some ways, these two forms seem very different. Matrices, which some people see as translations of traditional data tables in quantitative work, compartmentalize data presentation so that readers can see categories arrayed against each other. It is in the juxtaposition of categories or ideas that meanings are illustrated for the reader, often pointing to underlying mechanisms that drive social relations. In contrast, vignettes are narrative snippets that crystallize illustrative issues in the field. They are stories framed by the writer to make an interpretive point. In matrices, it is the fracturing of data and their relations to the lived experience of participants that helps us see things in new ways. With vignettes, it is the synthesis or integration of common elements that provides insight. I will begin with matrices.

All of us become known for certain things—infamous and famous. One of the main things I became known for when I was doing my dissertation was my passion for constructing tables of various sorts. What began as a strategy for helping me see new things in my data became a very useful writing strategy to share those understandings with my readers. It even earned me the illustrious title of "Table Queen" bestowed by fellow grad students who watched in bemused puzzlement as I spent hours arraying and rearraying my data trying to make sense of what seemed like indiscernible patterns. I have no idea why I started doing it—I had a copy of Miles and Huberman (1984) on my shelf, but I never read it very carefully. Constructing tables became a way of helping me make meaning when none was immediately apparent.

The example I will share comes from interviews of parents of children about to enter kindergarten. In this study, I was working to understand how various participants thought about readiness for kindergarten. I had asked the parents what kinds of things were coming to mind as their child approached school. The topic of readiness came up again and again, without my prompting. When I went through and coded sections of text related to readiness, there were differences in the ways parents talked about it, ways that at first did not make sense. Some parents were more confident than others about their child's readiness. Two characteristics have been linked in the literature with ideas about readiness—child sex and age. In this group of parents, the sex of the child did not seem to matter, but when I arrayed the discussions about readiness by child age, from youngest to oldest, a strong pattern was evident—the older the child, the less concerned his or her parent was about readiness.

I could easily have stated that in a couple of sentences in the case; that would have been an efficient way to communicate to the reader. Efficiency, however, is not always as persuasive as descriptive contrast. Including the material in Table 9.1 provided a rich data source for the reader to follow along with my analysis path and spoke much more forcefully than a simple summary ever could.

This is how this table was narrated in accompanying text:

> Looking at the ways that parents talked about readiness, some interesting patterns can be discerned. The parents most sure about their child's readiness had children who were in the oldest part of the kindergarten age range if overage children were not considered. Those in the middle were confident at the time of our conversations, but were worried enough last year that they held their children out. Greg would have been 5 1/2 if he had entered kindergarten by age eligibility only, Alice would have been 4. Of the two parents who had some current readiness concerns, their views were quite different. Rick had been held out the year before and he still didn't seem interested in school. Alyson, on the other hand, seemed ready to her mother and to her pre-school teacher but her mother was worried that her birthdate, which put her in kindergarten at not quite five, would work against her. The age pattern was relatively consistent for these parents: older children were usually seen as more ready. (Graue, 1993, p. 126)

The combination of excerpts of parental discussions on readiness paired with the influence of child age on parent perspective allows us to see the variance in parental ideas as more than difference in opinion. Instead, it allows us to see how ideas are set within a complex web of meanings, in which conceptions of readiness are situated within particular life experience given meaning through personal interpretations of child characteristics. In this group of parents, the calendar helped determine who was ready for kindergarten.

The next example includes children's perspectives in addition to those of adults. In the process of trying to understand how middle school students and their parents were experiencing a reformed mathematics program Mathematics in Context (MiC), particularly as it related to assessment, I interviewed both groups. In trying to interpret the interview data, I was confused about what responses meant. There were subtle differences among parents and among students, but the differences were not obvious. When parent and student excerpts were paired, patterns began to be discernible. Table 9.2 contains quotations from student-

TABLE 9.1. Pre-Kindergarten Parental Talk About Readiness

Child Name	Birth Date	Talk About Readiness
Sam	10/4/83	They [his preschool teachers] say he's more than ready for kindergarten; that he can do just anything that was ever asked of him. That he has a very good vocabulary and that he understands bigger words, he also is fairly enthused about what he's doing so he's able to follow through on that so they've never really had any problem with him.
Tammy	10/18/83	She's ready and I'm ready . . . I guess probably her maturity. I don't want to call it maturity, but I guess that's what it is. She's grasping so many things and concepts. She seems to have an excellent capacity to remember. . . . Also ready in that she seems to be real inquisitive about things.
Alice	9/22/83	I think that she is mature enough now. Last year she could have went to school—she'll be 6 in September. We waited the extra year, because we felt that she really wasn't ready . . . I think I just watched her, how she interacted with other children when we'd go to the park. She seemed like she wasn't catching on to just coloring or scissor cutting. Most of it I think was just interaction with other children that she'd meet on a day-to-day basis.
Greg	2/17/83	Last year he would have been starting out with cold feet, which emotionally, maybe he just wasn't quite ready. Whereas now, I think that he is real ready.
Rick	5/27/83	I'm a little apprehensive. I'm not sure that he is socially ready; he's just not interested in school.
Alyson	9/5/84	Mostly if she's ready. She'll be 5 on September 4th and I've talked to the teacher and she seemed to think that Alyson was plenty ready 'cause she can say her alphabet or most of it and count and her name and stuff. She seems to be doing a lot better—she's been in preschool for 2 years. It's something that kind of goes through my mind. I'm kind of scared—this is my first time.

SOURCE: From Graue (1993).

parent pairs that illustrate how dyads of parents and students shared ideas and language related to the mathematics program. They are presented in an extended excerpt (Graue & Smith, 1996), including some of the accompanying narrative interpretation to show how data displays and text can work together.

Among the students marked as average and high ability, at least two distinct voices could be heard. One group provided the support noted earlier while

TABLE 9.2. Student-Parent Views on Reformed Mathematics Program

Student	Parent
Elizabeth: You learn *more like the basic idea of stuff* and get to do more with it—not just problems, a lot of the same kind of problems on a worksheet . . . *The math we did last year we just learned one basic thing and we did a lot of those kinds of problems over and over again.* And this year you get to do it a couple of times and then you use it in the next kind of problem.	**Elizabeth's mother:** *Not to expect to see the number of problems over and over again to be practicing. But it seemed like there's a lot more of an understanding of what she was doing.* . . . This year, I think she felt it was sometimes a little too easy, but most of the time I think she felt it was challenging enough. She never really got stuck on any kind of problem where she really didn't understand it. But it wasn't that it was always super easy but a lot of it she would get done in class. . . . Elizabeth is a really good student and so for her it's like, well she thinks she's supposed to catch onto something right away. But then she feels, well, that's just because it's easy and if it's hard, then she kind of blames herself. It's like "I'm just stupid. I can't get it."
Chester: *It's a little bit more challenging. Last year I was in a good math group— a better math group and a lot of times I wasn't challenged. But now I'm challenged and I actually like to do the stuff because it's fun and so I enjoy doing the math problems.*	**Chester's mother:** *He really enjoyed it.* . . . *I think it challenged him. He has been challenged in math, so that was good.* . . . *I think there were parts that demanded some thinking from him.* I think he's pretty sharp at picking things up rather quickly. It wasn't the kind of thing that he could just whip off real quickly. He needed to think, which I thought was good.
Jorge: It's hard and easy. You had to explain it—sometimes that's hard. You've got to tell what you did and stuff. *The easy is like adding—you could add, multiply—that's easy.*	**Jorge's father:** *As far as Jorge has gone, it seemed to be fairly smooth sailing for him. No major obstacles that he had.* He normally does fairly well in math and now this new program that he was in, I don't think it would be a problem for anyone as far as changing to a new system.
Erica: Well, it's fun, *it's different.* We have a lot of different things that we didn't do in elementary school. Like in elementary school, we would just do one thing like division and work on it for 4 weeks and then go on to a different thing. Here we do lots of different things.	**Erica's mother:** The arrow math, it seems to me it was easier for her to understand longer problems—problems that built as she went along. . . . She's a very good math student and really does a lot on her own. So I didn't get involved with that too much. . . . Math seems to come easier to her this year than other years. And I think a lot of it had to do with Mr. Varso and maybe the introduction of the geometry and algebra—new concepts. *She likes to try new things and the way that it was taught.*

SOURCE: Graue and Smith (1996).

the other group voiced concern about how the curriculum supported their child's needs. In trying to understand how these ideas were constructed, we noted that the most striking similarity was the degree of consonance between parent and child, even in the words used to describe their experiences in the reformed mathematics program. Listen to those who supported the program; they also echoed the excitement of the new approach heard earlier.

These parents and students saw the potential of a new vision of mathematics represented by the MiC program. They appreciated the range of problems encountered and the way students were challenged to facilitate growth. In particular, both Elizabeth and Erica and their mothers enjoyed a move away from monotonous drill and practice—they were doing a variety of things and felt that it enhanced their learning. Finding the activities easy was seen as a plus because it meant that they were working at a level appropriate for their ability. This new mathematics program was good because, as Jorge said, "It's hard and easy." They were challenged but not bored. Their words seemed to be a chorus in the reform song, remaking the meaning of mathematics through their new classroom activities. They did not find the change in activities to be a threat; in fact, they found the new forms refreshing in many ways.

The third group seems on the surface to be much the same as those just described—they had life long experiences of success in mathematics in school and were considered average or high ability. They told a different story, however. This group did not take in the rhetoric of the mathematics reform. Instead, they used what might be seen as the more traditional criteria of ability in mathematics and progress through the curriculum to judge the efficacy of instruction. They worried about not reaching their potential, about being slowed down by others who were less able.

These students occupied positions of privilege because they were perceived to be more accomplished in traditional mathematics settings. They had always been in the elite group, doing different kinds of mathematics at a brisker pace than their classmates. Two complementary conceptions of the mathematics program were woven through their comments—conceptions that told of what they valued as they learned mathematics. They portrayed these ideas through language that had been used by their peers, but in very different ways. (Graue & Smith, 1996, pp. 313-317)

The subsequent section of the article provides further interpretation of the meanings of the shared and unshared conceptions of mathematics held by these parent-student dyads. The power of these matrices comes from their ability to show how language can be used in similar ways but with different meanings by groups of participants. Patterns in word use and parallel constructions of the meaning of mathematics are highlighted through the presentation in columns and italicization of like ideas. The shared nature of meaning and language is a good example of a theoreti-

TABLE 9.3. Perspectives of Traditionally High-Achieving Students and Parents

Student	Parent
Karen: *We're all in different levels. I mean, one thing I thought might be better is if they had maybe two or three different groups, even if we all covered the same stuff—we were all doing it at different times. I mean all at different rates.* So people who don't get it could get extra help. There are some who aren't willing to be helped. . . . Maybe part of the problem is accepting that they're not the smartest person in the whole class. . . . I think it's probably different from anything I've ever done in math and I like it, but sometimes *it can be kind of boring. Because if you know something already and she has to keep explaining it to some other kids.* That's why I suggested splitting the class into three different groups. But the only thing about that was you wouldn't want some people to feel bad. . . . I like being ahead so I can explain things to other people that don't understand it. The only thing about that is sometimes you get real frustrated with people because you can't explain it.	Karen's mother: *Last year she was able to move through the material at her own pace—not necessarily being at the same pace as the entire class. There were several groups in her class that way.* I didn't perceive that being the case this year. Both of my children *are easy learners who get frustrated working in a group where there are kids that take longer to grasp the idea being presented* and sometimes they feel used because the other kids perceive that they know the answer and then won't try themselves. . . . I talked with Karen and she said that she had approached Mrs. Patterson about having some additional things or more challenging things. Or she would make a comment about, *"This is boring. I already know how to do all of this."* And she couldn't understand why she needed to do it again. . . . They're very happy to keep everybody in the same groove.

cal concept put forward by Bakhtin called *ventriloquation*—that concept was woven into the discussion to theorize in ways that anchors the interpretations presented.

Matrices can provide illuminative ways to show relations found within interpretations of data. Through their structure, they promote certain readings and can anchor narrative interpretations in ways that strengthen a case. They can be particularly powerful when paired within another form of data display, vignettes, which are discussed in the next section.

Vignettes

Intact fieldnotes are not effective narrative forms. They are written to prompt memory and understanding on the part of the researcher, not to

TABLE 9.3. Continued

Student	Parent
Eli: *If one person doesn't understand then everyone else has to sit through the explanation again. So I actually prefer it when I'm sort of on my own* and if I really don't get something then I can ask the teacher and they can usually explain it to me in about 2 minutes. . . . The extra credit and stuff is good, but on the other hand, I do the extra credit but *I can't do that while I'm still stuck being bored with the other stuff. . . . It would be nice if there were some areas that could be more challenging because I'm sort of getting bored.*	**Eli's father:** *Mr. Varso did seem to have some sense of times that Eli was tuning out or a little bored with the standard exercise* and I know on a number of those occasions he tried to identify those times and *develop exercises that Eli could work on either alone or with several other classmates in parallel situations. . . .* I'm not positive that the right way to think about this is just moving kids through the standard curriculum. . . . Eli is quite a gifted math student. In fact, he was just one of the people honored at the Northwest Talent Search. We had contemplated putting him into algebra in sixth grade. . . . *My overall impression is that the curriculum was not as challenging or satisfying as what he was ready to take on. . . .* So that anything that can be done in developing materials that really will identify kids who have native ability and love for math and could really soar— number theory, number games, mental math, I'd just love to see some available to kids who would want to take advantage of it and to parents who could stimulate the kids with that.
Rick: *Well, we could try doing a little harder things. Because I thought what we were doing in the unit was kind of easy. . . .* We'd be on that stuff like a whole week and for a lot of the people, especially at my table, we knew it the first day. We pretty much understood it the first day. So she's got to try and vary it up.	**Rick's mother:** Rick's on the real bright side. *He has been real bored, quite frankly. He doesn't feel he is getting challenged. He says that a lot of the stuff he is doing he has seen since he was in elementary school. . . .* I would like there to be more difficult math in there. He has been messing around with algebra so I guess I would like to start him on that. Take them as far as they can go. It seems like the group, there are kids who can do the math and are real able to do the math. There are kids who are just trying to stay with the program and keep up. And then there are kids who are really struggling. He seems to be in that top bracket. And I think he just needs more.

(continued)

TABLE 9.3. Continued

Student	Parent
Nora: *I'm good at division, multiplication, addition, and subtraction, but in the new kind of formulas where you have to do problem solving and stuff, I'm not that good. [In fifth grade] we had a math meet where you do mental math and stuff and our school won and I was in the top eight or something and I won the math meet in my class.* So they'd say I'm pretty good at math because that's my best subject.	Nora's mother: I'm not real sure that this math challenged her as far as compared to what she had in fifth grade. Because I thought she wasn't doing as much. And of the things I saw, *I thought these are a lot of the things she already knew from fifth grade. So it was like review, which is good . . . but she needs things that would have challenged her more. . . . Just harder stuff I guess. . . . Some students do better at some things than others, but if you're doing that level, I would like to have seen that maybe she got some more ahead.*

SOURCE: Graue and Smith (1996).

communicate to those outside the research context. That is the reason we cannot plunk our notes down on the table and expect journals to publish them. Frankly, nobody wants to read them!

What we must do instead is to translate our fieldnotes and headnotes into forms that are persuasive, accessible, and finely crafted. We must choose the story we wish to tell; frame it rhetorically, analytically, and narratively so that it is of interest to some imagined readers; and develop arguments/images that facilitate that telling. These are all matters of authorial choice that represent how we think about the world and our responsibility as writers. Nothing is obvious. In this section, I will explore my favorite form of telling in interpretive research—what Erickson calls vignettes.

Vignettes are snapshots or mini-movies of a setting, a person, or an event. They tell a story that illustrates an interpretive theme within a research paper. Vignettes sketch images that through their detail illuminate ideas that seem inherently related to "being there." According to Erickson,

> The meaning of everyday life is contained in its particulars and to convey this to a reader the narrator must ground the more abstract analytic concepts of the study in concrete particulars—specific actions taken by specific people together. A richly descriptive narrative vignette, properly constructed, does this. (1986, p. 150)

Although vignettes focus on the substance of daily experience, they are not real life. Threaded through this recounted version is an interpretive perspective, one that positions the researcher analytically. According to Erickson, the vignette's validity is dependent on a complex interaction of descriptive richness and analytic interpretation: "Within the details of the story, selected carefully, is contained a statement of a theory of organization and meaning of the events described" (p. 150). So a good description is not enough—the description must take the reader to a new place, providing connections to theoretical ideas and interpretive insights.

Vignettes are crystallizations that are developed for telling—they are communication tools that help leverage understanding for both the reader and the writer. For the reader, they do what stories have always done for teaching—vignettes put ideas in a concrete context, allowing us to see how abstract notions play out in lived experience. Erickson elaborates this point when he says:

> Thus the vignette does not represent the original event itself, for this is impossible. The vignette is an abstraction; an analytic caricature (of a friendly sort) in which some details are sketched in and others are left out; some features are sharpened and heightened in their portrayal (as in cartoonists' emphasis on Richard Nixon's nose and 5 o'clock shadow) and other features are softened, or left to merge with the background. (1986, p. 150)

The vignette is illuminative for the writer as well. Writing vignettes help prompt certain kinds of understanding—as you try to frame a story and figure out critical issues, vignettes can help show you where you are analytically. My rule of thumb is that if you can't write a vignette, there is something you do not understand. Forcing myself to consider writing a vignette makes me look at both the phenomenon of interest and the nature of my analytical understanding of it. Erickson also suggests that writing a vignette from a variety of perspectives provides another dimension to that conceptualization. Examining something from more than one vantage point illuminates details that are available situationally and highlights how perspective frames knowing.

The degree to which a vignette is directly represented by field documents varies immensely. For some researchers, vignettes are polished versions of their fieldnotes—spiffed-up retellings of something that was observed by the fieldworker in a certain place at a particular time. An example of vignette writing with a realist twist can be seen in a modification of fieldnotes you read earlier in the interpretation chapter. In this vignette, I wanted to show a prominent theme in discussions about Jared—his emotional immaturity. I chose a brief segment of fieldnotes from the first day of school that shows Jared's fearful transition into the classroom and Mrs. Warren's accommodation to it. For the realist vignette, the process involved choosing a salient theme to illustrate, finding a segment of data (fieldnotes, interview transcript), and fine tuning it so that it communicates what you want it to communicate.

A key issue to consider in thinking about vignettes is that they never stand alone: Vignettes are tools for understanding that are complementary to other forms of analytical display. The vignette references other evidence, and you can understand what it means only in relation to the total discussion. As you read the fieldnote version and the vignette presentation in Table 9.4, realize that you are reading them within the context of your understanding developed through a more thorough analysis of the themes in Jared's case. This vignette has connections to broader issues, and it is these connections that help you see the importance of the vignette in the case.

This vignette was chosen to reflect the ongoing concern about Jared's immaturity—something that was a theme in fieldnotes and both teacher and parent discussion. In concert with other data, it could show how Jared stands out from his classmates in his reticence in this new setting as well as Mrs. Warren's attention to those needs on the first day of school. The shift from fieldnote to vignette filled in descriptive gaps to make it more storylike. It moved from speaking to me as a researcher as a kind of memory enhancer to speaking to you as a reader to frame the story. It could be paired with data that illustrate other instances or discussions of perceived immaturity, highlighting the multiple interpretations grown-ups in the setting had of Jared's actions. What the realist vignette cannot do is to tell beyond surface events—it cannot look inside someone's mind to tell us what he or she is thinking, for example. It is anchored in the seeable and misses much of the rich terrain that comes from inference, connecting motive to activity.

These close-to-the-field vignettes are related to another sort of story—fictionalized tales that illustrate, in the same way, important issues. Although their foundation is knowing generated from fieldwork, their representation is less a matter of real time than of impressions of plausible events or interactions. Fictionalized vignettes allow the writer

TABLE 9.4. Fieldnotes and Vignette Versions of an Event

Fieldnote Version	*Vignette*
First Day of School	*First Day Jitters*
A little before the bell rings, Mrs. Warren heads out to the playground to meet her class—"I'll bet I have some nervous kids & parents." She meets them outside the kindergarten door and they file into the classroom as she asks them one at a time "Do you have anything in your backpack for me ___?" The children are to check in their backpack, take out anything that needs to go to Mrs. Warren, and hang the backpack up in the coatroom. Notes go in Mrs. Warren's mailbox above the cubbies.	It is a picture perfect Wisconsin late summer morning—the sun is streaming through the windows of Mrs. Warren's first day of school kindergarten classroom. Mrs. Warren pages through the pile of papers on her already cluttered desk, shakes her head, looks up at the clock, then out the window. The sounds of children playing on the playground fill the room and she strides toward the outside door to meet her class. "I'll bet I have some nervous kids and parents," she says as she heads out the door.
Some children come into the classroom with their backpacks and wander; others leave them in the coatroom. Mrs. Warren reminds them to put them in the coatroom. They head for the rug area for the most part, with many standing and talking among themselves, fiddling with toys or charts around the edge of the area. Jared has a sad look on his face and he is clinging close to Mrs. Warren. Mrs. Warren: Jared, you can sit right next to me . . . OK? Let's all have a seat. [The group is seated around the rug—were they in a circle or in a general group?] Are we all ready? [Mrs. Warren surveys the group and checks that they are all comfortable.]	The bell rings and children sort themselves out into the ordered groups of their classrooms. The kindergartners, looking very small, leave their parents slowly, some with big smiles and others with concerned glances.
	"Good morning children!" Mrs. Warren says with a warm smile. "I'm so glad you've come to kindergarten today! Could you please line up in front of me and listen for directions as we come in. If you have something in your backpack, please let me know. There are places to hang your bag in the classroom—we call them cubbies. As you go in the room please look for your name and leave your things there. Are you ready?" As each child comes in the door, Mrs. Warren leans toward them and asks if s/he has anything in a backpack for her. A stream of brightly colored new shoes, backpacks, and faces flows through the door.

(continued)

to weave together issues into composite tales that illustrate themes that might not have been observed directly. They could have been recounted by participants or they could be created by the writer as a tool for helping the reader see particular concepts. In these fictionalized accounts, the rhetorical aspect of doing a vignette is highlighted: They are framed in terms of arguing certain ideas. The fact that scenes might be fashioned

TABLE 9.4. Continued

Fieldnote Version	*Vignette*
	Mrs. Warren maneuvers the group into the room, reminding those who are wandering about with backpacks that they should go into the coatroom to leave them there. As she shepherds them toward the rug area, the children mill around, some talking to one another, others touching every object in their path. Jared stands out among the group, lagging behind and acting like Mrs. Warren's shadow. With his head down, Jared does not interact with the other children, a panicked look plastered across his face. He looks as if he could burst into tears at any moment. As she surveys the group, Mrs. Warren takes Jared's hand and whispers, "You can sit right next to me—OK?" To the rest of the group, she suggests "Let's all have a seat." As the group settles, she smiles and says, "Are we all ready?" Faces rise up to meet her and the first day of kindergarten begins.

from bits and pieces of field experience rather than intact chunks is premised on the power of story to leverage understanding rather than the necessity for fidelity to certain kinds of knowing (direct observation, for example). They rely on a different kind of authority than realist vignettes. Realist vignettes are framed out of a possessive individualist's view of what is true—personal experience and direct observation perceptions of "what is supposed to occur 'inside' isolated individuals studied 'externally,' from the point of view of third-person observers, socially uninvolved with them" (Shotter, 1989, p. 143). In contrast, fictionalized vignettes gain their warrant from their ability to *tell* something to someone. The meaning created by the vignette is jointly constructed by the author who is speaking to a reader for a purpose.

I always have loved this vignette variation. I find them to be a creative way to bring the reader to the field with me. They make more seamless the interpretations presented in the case by allowing me to contextualize interactions by pulling from data sources that are disparate in terms of time and space but that represent cultural understandings in a holistic manner. They seem particularly effective at allowing characters to speak unspoken words—to frame action in terms of interpretations by actors.

I constructed a fictional vignette to illustrate a number of complex ideas around Jared's perceived immaturity because that was such a strong theme in discussions of school readiness at Solomon Elementary. I wanted, however, to make the issue more complicated than just showing an example of Jared bursting into tears in his kindergarten classroom. I wanted to show how Jared's emotional displays could make much sense in certain situations, when the tears were seen in context. I had come to see Jared's tears in response to frustrations in the classroom, particularly out of the complex relationship he had with Trevor. Trevor knew how to push Jared's buttons and used their relationship as a site to exercise power over someone.

In addition, I wanted to show multiple perspectives on activity in Mrs. Warren's room. In the case of this vignette, I set up a situation that shows the tension between Jared's and Mrs. Warren's conceptions of classroom activity. These themes were generated out of observations and interviews with Jared, Mrs. Warren, and Jared's mother and were transformed into an account of a single fictional event. The following vignette illustrates these points through a story of Jared in the block corner.

Building Images of Kindergartners

Jared stands in the corner of the block area, admiring his tall, tall building. It has three towers, two bridges, and a place for animals—the best he has ever built. Until now he hadn't noticed anything else in the room. When Mrs. Warren told them that it was time for centers, he bounded off to the block corner, ready to begin building this thing he had been planning since he got up this morning. How tall could he make it? How many blocks would the other kids let him have? He smiles, realizing that he is the only one there; everyone else is working on jobs or doing something else. He knew he could do it—his mom called him something, something that he was going to be when he grew up. An archi . . . hmmm . . . what was it. . . .

Out of the corner of his eye he sees a flash of brown. Trevor flies through the air and hits the building right in the middle, knocking over the first, which hits the second, and then the third tower. The animals lie under a mountain of wood and the bridges are flattened. Glancing back only briefly, Trevor walks off to the computer area. "TREVOR," Jared wails. "He knocked over my beautiful building!" Tears immediately roll down his round red cheeks and he is immobilized. "Mrs. Warren. . . ."

Just seconds before the crash, Mrs. Warren looks up from the group she is working with on the other side of the room. Every day this week, she thinks, Jared has played in the block area. Every day this week, he has passed up a chance to do his jobs. He'll spend recess today and all play time tomorrow finishing things that most children had done days ago. How will he make it in first grade? All he wants to do is play! She looks back to her group, then hears Jared's wailing. Oh, boy. And this crying—that's not going to play very well with any of the first-grade teachers either. Slowly she gets up, trying to think of how to smooth this over without playing into his continual need for individual attention. How do you get kids to deal with frustration? And how do you do it with children as immature as Jared? "Mrs. Warren," Jared cries, "Mrs. Warren, he knocked down my city! He broke the buildings!" He is gasping for air and gesturing wildly. The pile of blocks shows no resemblance to the wonderful thing he had done. "I'm a good builder—that's what big kids do!" Jared thinks to himself. "He's crying like a 4-year-old," Mrs. Warren thinks as she shakes her head. Trevor watches all of this from the corner with a slight smile.

This vignette provides opportunities for the reader and the writer to think about Jared in context. It illustrates how meanings for activity are socially constructed and multiple: Jared had planned and carried out a complex block building activity that illustrated motivation, focus, and attention to detail. Building was his work, something he was proud of and that his mother reinforced at home. He saw it as an indicator of his growth that he could make something so elegant. In contrast, Mrs. Warren interpreted his choice of time in the block corner as showing his immaturity. Instead of focus, she saw perseverance of an unhealthy type. She was frustrated by his choice of "play" over "work," and her frustration was complicated by Jared's tears over tumbling towers—what she saw as the equivalent of crying over spilt milk. A mature child would have chalked it up to experience and rebuilt the structure or, better yet, would have gone to another area to work. As a writer, I could pull ideas from a variety of data sources and weave together a story that was never observed in this particular scripted fashion, but was certainly plausible given other experiences with these actors. Along with an analytical narrative, this vignette can show how Mrs. Warren's interpretation of Jared is made with certain goals in mind (developing work habits and maturity for first grade). For the reader, the vignette serves as an integrative source of information, building on the power of story to make the interpretive activity of the researcher more concrete.

What is it about vignettes that makes them so powerful? Why are they compelling to both readers and writers of interpretive research? I have begun to think that vignettes work because of their narrative powers.

They embody many of the critical structural and rhetorical attributes that makes narrative a powerful method. Laurel Richardson (1994) argues that

> narrative displays the goals and intentions of human actors; it makes individuals, cultures, societies, and historical epochs comprehensible as wholes, it humanizes time, and it allows us to contemplate the effects of our actions and to alter the direction of our lives. (p. 200)

Vignettes synthesize ideas in a storied format that tells something important. They represent lived experience in a way that is accessible, concrete, and alive with meaning. They challenge our notions of what it means to know and what is allowed in telling by framing interpretation in literary as well as "scientific" terms. I keep pushing myself to distinguish between vignettes and other forms of stories, told for other purposes. Who creates stories, tales, and vignettes is one issue. The reader and writer must come to terms with whose voice they will allow into the conversation and whether having an author create a voice for someone is palatable. Two polar views of authorship and authority would argue against fictionalized vignettes. On one hand, those who work from a realist perspective would distrust the leap from direct observation to the creation of an event or interaction. The enactment of a fictional interpretation would move the work from research to mere writing. On the other hand, some proponents of narrative might see it as the ultimate usurpation of voice—the researcher absenting the participant to such a degree as to avoid needing observed interaction as a basis for interpretation. From this perspective, vignettes break any chance for more collaboration between participants and writers.

As I try to find a place in relation to these critiques, I keep reading and re-reading Laurel Richardson's answer to the question "How should we write?":

> If we wish to understand the deepest and most universal of human experiences, if we wish our work to be faithful to the lived experiences of people, if we wish for a union between poetics and science, or if we wish to use our privileges and skills to empower the people we study, then we *should* value the narrative. (1994, pp. 218-219)

Richardson's ideas go to the heart of the use of vignettes. Are fictional vignettes "faithful to the lived experience of people"? Not necessarily.

They could be distortions of experience to sell an interpretation; they could be brainstorms of an author with little connection to anyone's lived reality. Equally important, they *can* be, if they represent understandings that come out of sustained inquiry that is well grounded in someone's life. How do we determine which is which? It is a job for the reader to locate the vignette within the rest of the interpretive case. The meanings that come out of the spaces created by the vignette and other sources of evidence provide a source of understanding as well as evidence of its utility. It is the dialogic relation between vignettes and other ways of knowing that is critical to their use.

SUMMARY

Writing is a complex activity that makes or breaks interpretive work. Elegant designs and intricate analyses go nowhere if the case is not presented in an engaging, persuasive, and dynamic manner. Curiously, the facade of formulaic production of the interpretive case has hidden the many choices inherent in writing and often has made for mindless and boring texts. Rethinking our stance on writing makes us much more responsible to both those we portray and those who read our work. Finding our place within the many authorial positions helps us find our voice so that we can help others see our take on lived experience. Deborah Ceglowski illustrates the multilayered nature of this process in the next section, in her discussion of writing short stories.

Writing Short Stories

Deborah Ceglowski
University of Minnesota

Mark, a red-haired, three-year-old, has a runny nose. "Go and get a Kleenex and blow your nose" I tell him. He gets off the bench and goes to the end, rubbing a Kleenex under his nose. The food is laid out in bowls and on plates, ready for the children to pass it down family style.
    Mark looks at me. "I am not going to eat it."
    "Come on, Mark, give it a try," I say.
    "No, I'm not going to try it," he tells me.

So begins "Air Ferns," a short story I wrote to describe how Head Start staff and children interacted with Mark, a finicky eater. I wrote this short story and others like it as part of my 2-year study of how Head Start staff interpret and implement official policies to create a set of localized policies, which I call policies from practice.

In this section, I explain how short stories communicate a holistic and naturalistic understanding of a research project and how short stories, coupled with other types of writing, can expand our understanding of educational issues. I then present a short story and two other texts to demonstrate how different types of text illuminate different aspects of my research study.

"Story" is a word frequently used by educational researchers and has a variety of meanings. Storied narrative (Clandinin & Connelly, 1994) describes the everyday and universal conversation that people share to understand events (Bruner, 1990). Researchers have shown that teachers explain their understanding of curriculum and school policy by telling stories of their personal and professional experiences (Carter, 1993; Clandinin & Connelly, 1996).

One of the reasons that I began writing short stories is that the Head Start staff, like the teachers in Clandinin and Connelly's (1996) study, framed their talk about policy by telling stories about the everyday and special events at the program. In daily conversations with the staff, during breakfast and lunch, before and after school, on the bus, and on the playground, I learned how the staff interpreted and developed policies. When the Head Start staff talked about policy, they framed this talk into a larger story narrative: They talked about how policy "fit" into a particular story. For example, when I first began volunteering, I was uncertain what to wear to work. During the second week of the program, Judy, the teacher, and Susan, the assistant teacher, "explained" the dress code to me:

That day after lunch we headed to the apple orchard to tour the warehouse. Judy turned to me. "I forgot to tell you, you could wear jeans today. Always OK to wear black or white jeans but blue jeans only on the field trip days."

"Why's that?" I asked.

Susan said, "It's the dress code here, no blue jeans for anyone, not even the bus driver or aide. You can't wear those pants for running either, anything with elastic around the ankle.

I looked down at white pants with the elastic around the ankles.

Judy added, "But nice suits, those nylon ones are OK, like the ones Ruth wears. And none of those spandex pants, those really tight ones."

"But stirrups?" I asked.

Judy responded, "Those are OK, I wear them all the time. The other thing is you can't wear those booze or ciggie tee shirts. Yeah, none of those booze or ciggie tee shirts, or sweatshirts, you can't wear 'em here."

Policy analysis situated in interpretive stories, like the dress code story, acknowledges that staff's knowledge about their everyday lives may expand the current understanding of how Head Start policy is interpreted and implemented. My aim in writing stories is to highlight the situational and local nature of this interpretive process by describing how the staff implement policies in response to the ordinary and extraordinary events at the Head Start program.

I describe my writing as short stories because I have borrowed "fiction-writing techniques to tell the story" (Van Maanen, 1988, p. 132). These techniques include dialogue, story line, and representations of the characters' emotions and points of view (Van Maanen, 1988). My short stories are not fictional in the sense that are make-pretend (Bruner, 1993). My fieldnotes include records of all the events and conversations depicted in the short stories; however, the events and dialogues described in fieldnotes are reinscribed in a story to place the reader alongside Mark and the Head Start staff at the lunch table. Van Maanen (1988) calls short stories literary tales because they combine a researcher's sense of what is important at a site with a fictional writer's sense of narration.

I began writing short stories in the first month of my study (Ceglowski, in press) because of two factors: my dissatisfaction with my fieldnotes and my growing understanding that when staff talked about policy, as exemplified in the dress code described previously, they framed their talk in a story. I found that my fieldnotes lacked a sense of the rhythm of the daily schedule, the urgency of the everyday problems at the program, and the tones of the interchanges between the children and staff. Although my fieldnotes indicated what was served at lunch each day, they did not capture how it felt to sit next to Mark, the finicky eater, day after day. What I was learning and experiencing cognitively, emotively, and physically (Bochner & Ellis, 1996) at the program was not evident in the field records. My field records described my understanding of the events at the program, but they did not communicate how I came to this understanding (Bochner & Ellis, 1996).

In my study of Head Start policy, I use short stories to give the reader a lived understanding of the mundane and extraordinary events at the program and situate my understanding of Head Start policy within an interactive context. Norman Denzin (personal communication, June 9, 1994) suggested that the short stories provided a window to understanding how Head Start policy is enacted in the daily events at the program. Short stories connect the mundane and extraordinary events, like eating lunch with Mark, to the larger world of Head Start policy.

Short stories add a different dimension to Head Start policy analysis, which has relied almost entirely on top-down, large-scale studies that tell us little about the daily operations of a program. By examining how staff interpret and implement policies from a different angle (short stories), I present a different frame on understanding policy. Just as a crystal reflects different colors and patterns depending on the viewer's vantage point, different textual representations focus attention on different facets of the topic (Richardson, 1994). How a researcher writes frames what both the researcher and the reading audience will understand about the research topic. My aim is not to replace current research with short stories but to expand the acceptable writing genres so as to expand our frames of understanding (Eisner, 1993).

In the following pages I first present the short story "Air Ferns," then write about the short story in two different ways: (a) a chronicle account that describes events prior to and following the short story and (b) a policy analysis text describing how staff interpret official policies and create local policies. The chronicle and policy analysis texts are akin to different voices describing eating at Head Start. The story version provides an entrée for the reader to enter the lived experience at Head Start, and the chronicle and policy texts analyze how the story developed and how the Head Start staff made sense of this story in relationship to eating policies. The three texts are "nested" together, each providing a different window on understanding Head Start policy.

Air Ferns: The Short Story

I think about the air ferns as I sit across the lunch table from Mark. Mark, a red-haired, three-year-old, has a runny nose. "Go and get a Kleenex and blow your nose," I tell him. He gets off the bench and goes to the end, rubbing a Kleenex under his nose. The food is laid out in bowls and on plates, ready for the children to pass it down family style.

Mark looks at me. "I am not going to eat it."

"Come on, Mark, give it a try," I say.

"No, I'm not going to try it," he tells me.

"OK, but put a bit on your plate, and pass it on; you have to have some on your plate," I tell him.

He dishes himself out three peas and hands the dish on. Then comes the buttered bread; he plops a slice on his plate, beside the three peas. As the food is passed, he adds a meat patty, green jello, and a pickle slice. He sits and looks at the food on his plate, picks up his milk glass and drinks it down. A white mustache outlines his mouth.

"I'm done," he tells me. "I want to clear off my plate."

"You'll have to wait a few minutes until some of the other children are done. How about trying the jello?" I ask.

"I'm not eating it; my mother is making me food at home," he tells me.

"What is she making you?" I ask.

"French fries and fish sticks; she is making me French fries and fish sticks," he says.

Judy looks down at Mark's plate. "Mark, I want you to try that patty; take a bite of it." Judy leans over and cuts a thin slice for him.

Mark looks at the slice and moves it around with his fork. As the children start to finish eating, he picks up his plate and scrapes the meat patty, three peas, buttered bread, green jello, and pickle into the trash. He puts his silverware and cup in a plastic dish pan. He starts to run around the gym, and other kids join in the chase.

"Come back here," yells Judy, "I didn't tell you that you could run around. Now you just sit down here and wait." The kids grow restless waiting for the adults to finish.

"OK," says Judy, "you can run and chase." As the kids start to run, Judy, Susan, and I sit at the table, finishing up our plates.

"You know," I tell them, "Mark reminds me of these ferns my sister told me about, air ferns. The funny thing is that I never saw Paula water these things, they seemed to live on air. One day I asked her, 'How do you keep those things alive?' She laughed, "You just let them go until they really are dry, then add some water."

The next day at lunch Mark sits next to Susan. Mark passes the roast pork on, without taking any.

"Hey," says Philip, "You have to take some, put some of that on your plate."

Mark takes the bowl back and picks out a small piece of pork.

Susan points to the roast pork, buttered bread, mixed vegetables, and pear slice on Mark's plate. "Mark, I want you to take a bite of these things."

Mark eats his pear slice and asks for more.

Susan replies, "First eat some of your other food, then you can have some more."

The children from the special education program are in the gym, doing exercises at the far end. They are lying on mats, lifting their legs up and down to the teacher's count, "One and up and two and up and three and up." Mark looks underneath the table and kicks his leg.

Susan tells him, "If you want some more pear, you have to eat some other food."

Mark replies, "My mother is cooking for me at home."

Susan says, "You've got to sit up and stop kicking or you'll have to go and sit against the wall."

Judy adds, "If you don't eat, you can't have an ice cream bar."

"I don't like those anyway," Mark tells her. Mark continues to kick, peeking under the table.

Susan responds, "Clean off your plate and go sit against the wall."

Mark scrapes his plate and sits against the wall. He watches the special education children run up and down the floor, from one end of the gym near him to the other. He butt slides nearer the piano so that he has a full view of the running path.

At our table, Judy is looking through the roast pork dish, picking out the pieces without fat to put on her plate. I pass the bread by, too much butter to my liking, but load up on the roast pork, fat and all. Judy picks out a few carrots to put on her plate, passing up the peas. The children finish scraping their plates. Judy gets the ice cream bars and starts to pass them out.

"Can't have one today," she tells Mark, who is sitting next to the wall.

"I don't like them anyway," he responds, kicking his feet on the floor.

On the third day Mark is back at the table near Judy and me.

Judy says, "Today, Mark, if you don't eat, you can't have a cookie."

We start to pass the food down the table: hot dogs, rolls, beans, sauerkraut. I look at the hot dogs; bright red and rubbery. Perhaps I can skip those, I think to myself. I take a roll and pass them on to Mark; he takes one and puts in on his plate. Next comes the sauerkraut. I take a large portion and scoop a few pale strands onto Mark's plate. I see the hot dogs next. Four-year-old Ben has the tongs and puts one in his roll. I fluff up my roll, hoping that nobody will see it is empty. I hand the dogs on to Mark.

Ben says, "He doesn't have one."

I look at Ben, and look around the room, knowing that he is talking about me. "He doesn't have one," he repeats, pointing to my plate. Ben tells me, "You have to have one, even if you don't eat it."

Judy smiles at me. She got away with just a roll on her plate, and I got caught in the act. I take a hot dog and put it in my bun. Yuck, I say to myself, and go to the kitchen to get some mustard to put on it. Mark takes a hot dog and passes on the bowl. He eats his hot dog, leaving little on his plate aside from the few pale strands of sauerkraut. He goes to scrape his plate, rubbing the rubber spatula against the sauerkraut, pushing it into the trash.

I wait for the children to finish, place my napkin over the hot dog, and push it into the trash.

Judy goes for the cookies and hands them out. "Here you go, Mark, want one, Deb?"

> I take the chocolate chip cookie and sit to eat it.
> "These are good," says Mark, crunching on his cookie. "Just like the ones that my mother makes."

If you were a finicky eater, you may disagree with the staff who told Mark he had to try new foods and withheld dessert. Or you may ask, "Why is eating such a big deal?" This striking, familiar short story is reminiscent of both childhood and teacher-child interactions. The aim of this story is to place the reader (Van Maanen, 1988) at the lunch table with the Head Start children and staff.

Does this simple short story explain anything about Head Start policy? Certainly there are glimpses of how policy is operating in the short story, but the framework is incomplete. What happened before and after this short story took place? The chronicle provides information about what happened before and after the short story. This information enables the reader to situate the short story within the ongoing events at the program. In the following section, I present a brief excerpt of a chronicle text.

Air Ferns: The Chronicle

> Mark usually ate all his food at breakfast. At lunch, he ate the foods he liked and told the staff he was done. Staff sometimes ignored Mark and other times encouraged him to try a new food. When Mark requested seconds on a favorite food like oranges, Judy, the teacher, Susan, the assistant teacher, Ruth, the site aide, or I would often tell him to taste another food on his plate first. Several times Judy told Mark he could not have an ice cream unless he tried one of the foods on his plate. Mark responded by saying that he did not like ice cream.
>
> In December, Jasmine sat near Mark. Mark served himself a large portion of canned peaches, some meatballs, buttered bread, corn, noodles, and lettuce. After eating the peaches and corn, he stopped eating.
>
> Jasmine asked him, "Do you want Santa to come? You have to eat that food on your plate all gone. He is watching and he won't bring you presents if you don't eat."
>
> Mark responded, "He is going to bring me presents."
>
> Jasmine said, "Not if you don't eat, he won't."
>
> Mark retorted, "Yes, he will."
>
> The following day, Mark served himself fish sticks, mashed potatoes, green beans, buttered bread, and milk. After Mark ate his fish sticks, Judy told him, "You need to eat something besides those fish sticks."
>
> Mark started to cry. Judy asked him, "What is wrong?"
>
> Mark told her, "I feel sick."

Judy said, "You can get up and scrape your plate off now. If you need to get sick go to the trash bin and get sick there. Luci used to make me clean that up and once I did clean it up and then I got sick too." After Mark scraped his plate, Judy and I sat at the table and talked about our children's eating habits. Both of us described our sons as fussy eaters. . . .

On January 5 Judy told Mark that he had to stay at the table until he tried his potatoes. Judy described the meal. "Yesterday Mark ate a bit of potatoes and meat. I told him if he didn't eat, he couldn't go outside. He put the potatoes in his mouth and looked like he was going to gag. I told him, 'If you gag and throw up, you can't go outside either.' He chewed it and then I gave him a piece of meat. Later when he came back to the room, he told Susan that I had given him some more meat and that he drank his milk too."

The chronicle explains how the staff and children dealt with Mark over an extended period, highlighting these events and conversations to the exclusion of other ongoing events. It emphasizes how both the children and staff define Mark as a finicky eater and how Judy implemented an eating policy for Mark. The following policy analysis text stresses how the Head Start staff translate official policies into practice and how, based on this translation, they create local policies.

Air Ferns: Official Policies and Policies From Practice

Meal pattern requirements and guidelines are found in the agency Head Start policies and procedures manual.

During my first lunch at Head Start I learned about the policy requiring staff and children to serve themselves a portion of all foods. This local practice stems from the agency Meal Evaluation form, dated July, 1991, which states that all children are to be "given all the required food components." The Meal Evaluation form, completed by administrative staff during on-site visits, asks:

Are efforts made to encourage consumption
of the minimum portion requirements?

The Head Start staff instruct children to serve themselves a portion of each food. When children complain that they did not like a food, a staff member or child reminds, "You don't have to eat it, you just have to put it on your plate." The children grow accustomed to serving themselves portions of every food and then throwing away those foods they do not like.

In August, 1993, the agency Head Start policy council adopted a new meal pattern requirement policy: "The minimum amount of food will be made available and offered to each child." Changes in the United States Department of Agriculture [USDA] food policies prompted this change in policy. In August, 1993, administrators distributed updated Head Start Policies and Procedures manuals to all programs which contained a copy of this new meal pattern policy. However, the administrators did not point out or discuss this change in policy with the staff.

When Andrea Holland, the agency dietitian, visited, Judy prefaced her descriptions of Mark's eating pattern and the "bite of protein" policy with, "I know I shouldn't be doing this." Judy knew that it was against agency policy to "force" children to eat, but she also knew at first hand that "Mark ate hardly anything."

Andrea asked what Mark ate, how old he was, and whether Judy planned cooking activities to "get Mark interested in trying different foods." Andrea's food activity question referred to an agency policy requiring teachers to plan two monthly cooking activities. Andrea concluded that Mark "must be getting enough foods to make it on."

Policies From Practice

Staff embody varied perspectives when talking about Mark. For instance, Judy and I, positioned as parents of older children, described our own children in their preschool years as finicky eaters. Staff's responses to Mark at lunch time reflected different views on eating, daily circumstances, and moods. At times we ignored his behavior, other times we withheld food or limited favorite foods, and at still other times we told him that he had to eat. These varied responses reflect our different views on young children's eating patterns and how to handle finicky eaters.

As staff continued to discuss Mark and his eating behavior, they formulated a consensus about his eating pattern. This consensus developed during September and October. Regardless of our individual beliefs about how to handle children's eating patterns, we agreed that he was a finicky eater. In October, I nicknamed him "air fern" and the staff, especially Ruth, the site aide, would refer to Mark as "air fern." Children too, aware of our views of Mark's eating, responded by telling Mark to put food on his plate and eat. This is depicted in Jasmine's warning that if Mark did not eat Santa would not bring him any presents. Jasmine echoed the staff's frequent comments telling Mark to eat his food.

Staff formulated policies from practice based on their ongoing interactions with Mark. For example, when Judy told Mark he could not have an ice cream if he did not try some of the food on his plate, he responded by telling Judy he did not like ice cream. In this instance, we learned that withholding ice cream would not encourage Mark to eat. Staff determined that they would have to try other approaches with Mark. Through this trial-and-error process, staff learned what did not work with Mark and Mark learned strategies to avoid tasting new foods.

When Mark cried and said that he would get sick, Judy told him to scrape his plate. Mark continued to use this tactic until January, when Judy announced that he was going to eat his food. She explained that if he got sick, he could not go outside to play. Judy's change in strategy resulted in changes in Mark's eating behavior.

Changes in Mark's eating pattern affected the "bite of protein policy." At the start, staff monitored Mark's eating closely and told him he had to taste a new food. Once Mark grew accustomed to the new policy, he would try foods on his own and sometimes ask for seconds. At the February staff meeting, Susan noted that Mark was trying foods on his own. At this point, staff seldom monitored Mark's eating though they continued to positively talk about the variety of foods he was now trying.

Summary

This policy analysis text illustrates how staff translate official policies into daily events at the program, yet the eating policies themselves are not clear-cut: Children are to serve themselves all foods, staff are to encourage children to eat, but staff cannot force children to eat. In translating these policies into practice, staff assess the situation at hand and through group discussions and trial and error figure out how to handle Mark. This text, like the short story and chronicle, is formulated in an interactional context: staff talking with each other, trying out solutions, and coming to consensus on how to handle a finicky eater.

In writing about Head Start in these three ways, I present three different windows (Richardson, 1994) on policy. In the short story, it is Ben telling Deb she has to have a hot dog even if she doesn't eat it; in the chronicle, Judy the teacher telling Mark halfway through the year that he has to try a "bite of protein"; and in the policy text the multiple contradictory policies that staff translated into daily practice. Each window provides a different viewpoint and together, like a crystal, illuminate different angles, colors, and dimensions of our understanding of policy.

Short stories, through their descriptions and narrative structure, invite readers into the worlds described, to live "their way into the experience" (Denzin, 1994, p. 511). Readers construct various interpretations of the text reflective of their personal values, experiences, and knowledge. Short stories open the door of possibility to understand the relationship between Head Start policies and the daily events, routines, and activities at a Head Start center in different ways.

References

Bochner, A., & Ellis, C. (1996). Taking ethnography into the twenty-first century. *Journal of Contemporary Ethnography, 25*(1), 3-5.

Bruner, E. (1993). Introduction: The ethnographic self and the personal self. In P. Benson (Ed.), *Anthropology and literature*. Chicago: University of Illinois Press.

Bruner, J. (1990). *Acts of meaning*. Cambridge, MA: Harvard University Press.

Carter, K. (1993). The place of story in the study of teaching and teacher education. *Educational Researcher, 22*(1), 5-12.

Ceglowski, D. (in press). *Policies from practice: The stories of the Wood River Head Start Program*. New York: Teachers College Press.

Clandinin, D., & Connelly, M. (1994). Personal experience methods. In N. K. Denzin & Y. S. Lincoln (Eds.), *Handbook of qualitative research* (pp. 413-427). Thousand Oaks, CA: Sage.

Clandinin, D., & Connelly, M. (1996). Teachers' professional knowledge landscapes: Teacher stories-stories of teachers-school stories-stories of schools. *Educational Researcher, 253*, 24-30.

Denzin, N. (1994). The art and politics of interpretation. In N. K. Denzin & Y. S. Lincoln (Eds.), *Handbook of qualitative research* (pp. 500-515). Thousand Oaks, CA: Sage.

Eisner, E. (1993). Forms of understanding and the future of educational research. *Educational Researcher, 22*(7), 5-11.

Richardson, L. (1994). Writing: A method of inquiry. In N. K. Denzin & Y. S. Lincoln (Eds.), *Handbook of qualitative research* (pp. 516-529). Thousand Oaks, CA: Sage.

Van Maanen, J. (1988). *Tales of the field*. Chicago: University of Chicago Press.

Note

1. Notable exceptions are Emerson, Fretz, and Shaw (1995), Richardson (1990, 1994), and Wolcott (1990).

10

CONCLUSION

All research is first undertaken and later communicated within particular social, historical, political, and institutional contexts. These contexts influence topics and subjects of inquiry, the shape reports of research take, the reception the reports receive within the scholarly community, and the actions that result. Research is knowledge production. It is vital to consider the specific contexts within which knowledge production occurs and the markets for which that knowledge is produced.

We first consider institutions and markets. We conclude this chapter and this book with a discussion on expanding existing notions of validity.

Institutional Constraints

Research is conducted within an institutional context. This section focuses on the academic institution, which is the one we are familiar with. We apologize to the non-university-based researcher for lack of attention to your sphere.

Consider dissertation research. The dissertation writer produces knowledge not for the field but, at least immediately, for a dissertation committee. Dissertation research also has its own peculiar constraints. Traditions for the length and structure of dissertations exist within disciplines. These traditions change, in some places more slowly than others, but they exist, and they must be considered. Committees make demands to which a dissertation writer must attend. She does not have an option analogous to finding a different publisher or submitting to a different journal. Finally, dissertations must be completed before one can move on to other things, sometimes by a certain date to qualify for a certain job. They cannot be put into a file cabinet to be completed at a later date while one embarks on other research projects.

Assistant professors working toward tenure face another set of constraints. They write for a field, but they also write for a series of committees at their university. They often feel compelled to conduct certain kinds of research to produce both the number and kind of publications necessary for promotion. They may decide to defer other types of inquiry until after tenure has been granted, work that has a long time line to publication, a category that includes much good interpretive research.

For both the graduate student and the assistant professor, research is instrumental; that is, it provides a way to get somewhere—out of graduate school or into tenure. Assuming tenure survives, with it the struggle for survival becomes less immediate. Constraints still exist, for example, merit-review committees that dole out raises based on numbers of publications in the previous year. Certain types of research on certain topics are more likely to get funded than others.

The audience one writes for always will be ambiguous. In real life, the production of knowledge does not exist independently from the struggle to survive. Research may be about finding it out, but it is about finding it out within existing institutional contexts.

Market Constraints

Whatever the ambiguities, survival and "thrival" require publication. The knowledge produced must be made public. The routes to publication vary. One may begin by presenting a paper at a conference, by responding to an invitation to write a chapter, or by writing with a particular journal in mind. The decisions made at the beginning of the process will have a serious impact on the publication success. Presenting a paper as the first step to getting published is wise. Writing the paper for a conference with a particular publication outlet in mind is even wiser. Presenting a paper at a conference to get the department to pay for the airplane ticket to Chicago may or may not be. My (Daniel's) experience is that I have presented far too many papers that then were filed away never to be worked on again as I worked on yet another paper.

Many factors influence whether a report gets published—the quality of the work, the fit between the venue chosen and the style used, the trends and values that dominate a discipline at a particular moment, and one's particular network of support. Getting published can have as much to do with one's decision-making skills as one's research skills. Decision-making skills include, among others, deciding what kind of research to do, how to present it, and where to send it. Publication also is a matter of who you know. Within the "objective" process of peer review are threaded selected opportunities for writers connected with a guest editor or even a sitting editor who knows exactly who to choose to give a good paper reasonable reviewers. These openings in the system of publication require knowledge and familiarity with the field, the strategies of getting work in print, and acquaintance with those who can provide a spot.

We offer personal examples of our own market struggles. We have both been skilled enough to get out of graduate school and to gain tenure, but we have not had a comfortable relationship with the Early Childhood/Child Development SIG (Special Interest Group) of the AERA (American Educational Research Association). Given that we are both early childhood professors and active researchers, one would expect it to be our academic home.

Beth: I have never had a paper accepted by the SIG. Ever hopeful, I try again and again. Always I slink away licking my wounds from yet another set of scathing reviews. My reactions have shifted from worry that my work was worthless to outrage that my "colleagues" could not understand and appreciate my efforts. I now live somewhere in the middle, content with my scholarship but worried that I have not made it accessible to those who view the world differently from me. I have been able to find groups in AERA who CAN read what I do and help me grow intellectually. I have focused my attention on getting my work published in early childhood journals and have been successful. I have never learned the genre of the EC/CD SIG, but I hope that my work is still valuable, and I have found others who appreciate it.

Daniel: I think I have had papers accepted. I do know that I have never enjoyed the process. The nastiest reviews, bar none, I have ever received were from the SIG. It's curious that a field that views itself as caring engenders the hostility encountered in reviews, but it's an issue of who values what. I operate, like Beth, on the margins of acceptability in the SIG. I have come to encourage graduate students who work with me to submit their papers to other SIGs or divisions in AERA, mainly to protect them from having to deal with this hostility early in their careers. It is not helpful to be told, as one student was, that the title of her paper was "dopey."

Our point is that getting on a conference program or getting published can be likened to a game, or better, many games. Different groups have different criteria for what gets accepted and what gets rejected, who is included and who is excluded. Knowing the rules of the games and finding the right people to play the games with are essential.

The discussion thus far has been a self-centered one—how research affects us academic researchers. Research has the potential to influence others' lives and experiences. Our work has ripples that go beyond our little section of the pond.

Participants

With rare exceptions, the audience researchers write for does not include the people whom they have studied. We have no answer to this problem, but we do believe that interpretive work has an accessibility that allows it to be disseminated beyond the narrow academic market.

Good interpretive work is built on the relationships forged with those with whom one works. Interpretive researchers become part of the experience of others, and those others become part of our experience. The collaborative aspect of this relationship can provide rich insight into the meanings of lived experience less available to more distanced forms of inquiry. It can provide participants with ways of thinking about their lives not normally available. The relationship has implications for participants and their lives that need to be taken seriously. We discussed above what academics get out of their research. What do participants get out of it? We should be about more than using people for our advancement.

The difficulty is that writing for a public audience, or a practitioner audience, not only is not valued in academia but also is at times devalued. We recommend writing short, accessible versions of academic publications for participants and to consider publishing them in practitioner journals or in publications with a broad readership. Having made the recommendation, we also admit that we have not done well in this regard.

Policy

Research often has implications for policy. Making arguments in terms of the policy implications of the research forces the researcher to think beyond the bounds of description and interpretation to advocacy. This advocacy should come out of local concerns for children and those who work with them, answering the question, "How will these children benefit from my work, children who, in most cases, are in my own backyard?" Advocacy also should extend what is learned in the local setting to other readers in other places, who have the power to set certain types of action in motion.

Communicating to policy makers is formidable. It means communicating to yet another community with its own journals, meetings, and so on. It requires a critical translation of information so complex that it is often difficult to communicate it in readily accessible terms. It often demands that one think in "sound bites" to give the audience the tools to be able to see into the field too. It is more than good storytelling—it is focused communication done to leverage certain kinds of action.

Any influence that I (Daniel) have had on policy makers and policy has been not so much the direct result of something I have written as much as that what I have written has gained me access to policy makers face to face. For example, I have testified before legislative subcommittees, addressed State Education Boards, and met one on one with principals, superintendents, and other administrators. I must stress that the events described above have been more the exception than the rule and that they often have been as much the result of personal connections as scholarship. At times, I have been in very strange situations. I once found myself in a meeting with a high-ranking minister in the National Ministry of Education in Japan, being asked how Japanese schools should deal with the increasing incidence of "bullying" in middle schools. I know a little about Japanese early schooling but nothing about middle schools or bullying. I politely responded that I had no idea.

We both work with pre-service and in-service teachers. We both have done research in schools and have a strong vested interest in improving early schooling, especially improving it from the perspective of children. Margaret Donaldson, a developmental psychologist who did important work on young children's development in the context of schooling, made three main arguments throughout her work. The first is the importance of being able to understand how the world looks from the perspective of children. Her groundbreaking critiques of Piagetian tasks was based on this insight—children see tasks differently from the researcher. The second is that all knowledge begins as local knowledge in particular situations. The third is that the types of learning required in formal schooling are difficult for children, and that educators are seldom aware of this difficulty (Grieve & Hughes, 1990).

We believe that good interpretive work can expand these three important insights in ways that other kinds of research cannot and that, particularly in the area of early schooling, interpretive researchers have a lot to teach policy makers, not only about how schools should go about their business but also about how teachers, both pre-service and in-service, should be educated. The research described in this book is face to face, field-based, narrative, and theory building. These four terms also accurately describe what good teaching is about. We are not arguing that teachers should be trained to be interpretive researchers. They should be trained to become good teachers. Good teachers and good interpretive researchers, however, have much in common, and they should be able to communicate with each other well.

Validity

The very complexity of the validity notion in contemporary inquiry precludes any simplistic resolution that would apply across the various investigative procedures and diversity of circumstances of social research. What does seem clear, however, is that validity remains an essential and inescapable concern for qualitative study and that the interpretive products of ethnographic inquiry are, like any other scientific products, subject to appraisal for validity (Jessor, 1996, p. 9).

An initial draft of this manuscript did not have explicit sections related to validity. Beth did not feel comfortable talking about it, having read pages on the topic and having come away each time with a headache. The final version of this book dabbles with the topic in several places because very wise reviewers told us the discussion was incomplete without it. We agree but still undertake the conversation with a sense of uneasiness. We discussed validity briefly in Chapter 7 in the section on the importance of a good data record. Here we discuss limitations of the dominant research discourse on validity and make some suggestions for expanding the discourse to make it more useful.

Our concern with validity is the measurement baggage it carries and the awkwardness, given this baggage, of applying it to research that uses narrative description more than measurement description. Obviously, research should be "well grounded or justifiable," but we are not comfortable with the narrow criteria for well-groundedness or justifiability that a measurement perspective proffers.

Other qualitative researchers and theorists (e.g., Lincoln, 1995; Lincoln & Guba, 1985) have given up on the notion of validity, preferring to develop new criteria for judging interpretive research. Past experience in other situations, however, led us back to the term. The following discussion began in Beth's reflection on her work on readiness for schooling and switches to her first-person singular.

Readiness was a term that was located within practices and discourses of measurement and development-as-maturation. I initially tried to develop new vocabulary for this idea of fit between children and schooling, describing children with specific cultural, historical, and political contexts, but no one understood what I was talking about. Worse, I lost the "Hey, pay attention to me" flag that I had with the old word, "readiness." The term was so powerful, so important within the field of early childhood education, that I found that I had to use it, but I had to adapt it to my purposes. This approach gained me a place in the discussions about the fit between the child and the curriculum and forced me to articulate how my conceptions of readiness differed from the taken-forgranted ideas permeating the early childhood community. I am not sure how successful I was (from the sales of my book, I am not that confident), but it was a considered decision on my part. I take the same approach here.

The evolving concept of validity initially was located within activities related to measurement—does this measure what it is intended to measure? Discussion focused on methodological/technical concerns. The researcher labored to develop valid instruments by referring to the standard checklists of threats to validity.

I suggest an idea of validity that is populated by more participants than the traditional experimental validity or even the current consequential validity. This idea extends through the life span of the research process, through the development of written reports into the implications for practice, policy, and further research. From this perspective, validity refers to issues ranging from fieldwork techniques to implications in varied communities of practice. These communities include not only the site of research but also the broader research, policy, and practice contexts of those who read the research report to inform their actions. This is a very situated and relational approach to validity. Issues of validity are situated in a specific text and in the relationship that text has to various communities of practice. For example, an anthropologist will read a text differently than an educational psychologist, who will judge it differently than a social worker. This does not deny validity. Our point is simply that different people and different communities often will make different judgments.

Our discussion of validity portrays it through four interrelated dimensions: technical and methodological validity, interpretive validity, textual/narrative validity, and praxis-oriented validity.

Technical and Methodological Validity

What is done in the field and how it is done matters. An assessment of how well grounded research is needs to begin with the techniques used to generate data. The question should be: "Given the questions asked in this research, are the methods appropriate?" These methods would include general methodology (e.g., ethnography, life history, case study, etc.), sampling (cases, people, places, interactions, etc.), data generation techniques (style of observation, type of interview, etc.), and analysis strategy. No one set or combination of strategies will guarantee success, but some methods are more "right" than others for certain questions in certain situations. Methods matter—not only how you do what you do but also why. But discussions of validity should not end with methods.

Interpretive Validity

Data generation and data record construction leads to interpretations—what Erickson (1986) calls assertions—that describe and explain the relations and meanings in a given context. This aspect of qualitative research is doubly interpretive in that it seeks to describe meanings of participants through the creation of meaning by the researcher (Geertz, 1973). In the context of the research questions for this project, how do the interpretations relate to the methods used, data presented, and theories employed?

Key to assessing the validity of interpretations are the relations among methods, data, theories, and interpretations. We can only know certain things given a particular set of data generation activities. Carefully assessing what could be known from field activities is a first step. In addition, we must examine the links between evidence presented and interpretations—do assertions work within the boundaries set by the data? Although readers cannot possibly share all the knowledge generated by the researcher during a project, enough evidence needs to be shared so that assertions seem plausible.

Finally, interpretations need to be examined in relation to the theories used. Depending on the role of theory in a given project, theory could be used to support interpretations, it could practically determine interpretations, or it might be completely lacking in interpretations. From our perspective, the best theory-interpretation relation is one in which theory provides a framework for perceiving the data and provides leverage for interpretation. It is balanced, grounding interpretation within the intersection of theory and data.

Textual/Narrative Validity

A study could have an elegant design with rich data generated from multiple sources. Further, it could have generated important interpretations that explain interactions and meanings among participants. If however, the write-up misses chances to portray the complexity of the context or if it relies on sources of authority that are in conflict with its theoretical perspective, then the validity of the textual form needs to be called into question. How we present our work is just as important as how we develop our understandings, for in the end, our ability to help others understand our interpretations will rest on our ability to tell the story. The question of interest here is this: Within a set of research questions, how does the written format relate to the theoretical perspective taken and the understandings generated?

The validity of the text is a judgment related to the purposes and frameworks of the researcher as well as the needs and intentions of those who read the work. It requires congruence between the modes of authority used to frame the study and those utilized in its text. For example, a realist telling would not be appropriate in a study framed from a poststructural perspective. Further, the text of a qualitative research project should be shaped to the intentions and needs of those who need to hear the work—the audience. The language forms and textual formats of the academy are insular and inaccessible to those in the realms of policy and practice—and often are discounted as irrelevant. We need to learn to speak in ways so that others can hear what we have learned. Assessing the validity of texts is much more dialogic than the other forms of validity previously discussed, representing agendas of writers and readers.

Praxis-Oriented Validity

This aspect of validity relates to the basic question of why we do research. When we assess work in relation to praxis-oriented validity, the question we should pose is "How does this work create possibilities for new understandings of children's lives, and further, how does it promote action to that end?" This question extends the responsibilities for research to the most complicated level—we are forced to ask, "What good will this work do and for whom?"

When we consider this aspect of research, we contemplate research in context—examining how all parts of the research endeavor come together to provide openings for new ways of knowing and acting for children. It is a judgment that is situated within systems of value that will vary by individual and purpose. It is the least amenable to evaluation by checklist but certainly no less important than the more technically oriented concerns. The question of praxis-oriented validity should be negotiated and renegotiated throughout the life cycle of a research project, from the development of a question through the communication of interpretations to varied communities.

Praxis-oriented validity highlights the responsibilities inherent in the research endeavor, for all of us who produce, critique, and use research. It is a reminder that the work has ends other than the simple academic outcomes.

SUMMARY

Research extends beyond the practice of fieldwork or desk work—it gains momentum to serve purposes and constituencies that often are far from our imagination. In this chapter, we have tried to situate research in the varied contexts that shape its character and outcomes. In addition, we suggested ways of evaluating qualitative research with children that broadened the discussion beyond simple technical discussions.

We began this book by noting how little work exists that really listens and looks at the lives of children. We started writing more than 4 years ago and are pleased to report that the field is growing. More attention is being focused on children and their contexts, but it is still not enough. We hope that we have provided some ideas and tools for how you might undertake this important task—both reading and writing about children's lives.

REFERENCES

Achen, C. H. (1977). Measuring representation: Perils of the correlation coefficient. *American Journal of Political Science, 21*(4), 805-815.

Alderson, P. (1994). Researching children's rights to integrity. In B. Mayall (Ed.), *Children's childhoods observed and experienced.* London: Falmer.

Asher, S. R., & Gabriel, S. W. (1993). Using a wireless transmission system to observe conversation and social interaction on the playground. In C. H. Hart (Ed.), *Children on playgrounds: Research perspectives and applications* (pp. 184-209). Albany: State University of New York Press.

Atkinson, P. (1992). *Understanding ethnographic texts.* Newbury Park, CA: Sage.

Bakan, D. (1967). *On method: Toward a reconstruction of psychological investigation.* San Francisco: Jossey-Bass.

Bakhtin, M. (1981). *The dialogic imagination: Four essays by M. Bakhtin* (C. Emerson & M. Holquist, Eds.). Austin: University of Texas Press.

Baturka, N. L., & Walsh, D. J. (1991, April). *"In the Guinness Book of World Records it says that a girl stayed in kindergarten until she was 13": First graders who have been retained make sense of their world.* Paper presented at the annual meeting of the American Educational Research Association, Chicago.

Becker, H. S. (1996). The epistemology of qualitative research. In R. Jessor, A. Colby, & R. A. Shweder (Eds.), *Ethnography and human development: Context and meaning in social inquiry* (pp. 54-71). Chicago: University of Chicago Press.

Berger, P., & Luckmann, T. (1966). *The social construction of reality.* Garden City, NY: Doubleday.

Bernard, H. R. (1988). *Research methods in cultural anthropology.* Beverly Hills, CA: Sage.

Boulding, K. E. (1985). *The world as a total system.* Beverly Hills, CA: Sage.

Bradbard, M. R., Halperin, S. M., & Endsley, R. C. (1988). The curiosity of abused preschool children in mother-present, teacher-present, and stranger-present situations. *Early Childhood Research Quarterly, 3,* 91-105.

Bruffee, K. A. (1986). Social construction, language, and the authority of knowledge: A biographical essay. *College English, 48,* 773-790.

Bruner, J. (1986). *Actual minds, possible worlds.* Cambridge, MA: Harvard University Press.

Bruner, J. S. (1987). The transactional self. In J. S. Bruner & H. Haste (Eds.), *Making sense: The child's construction of the world* (pp. 81-96). London: Methuen.

Bruner, J. (1990). *Acts of meaning.* Cambridge, MA: Harvard University Press.

Bruner, J., & Haste, H. (1987). *Making sense: The child's construction of reality.* New York: Methuen.

Campbell, D. T. (1978). Qualitative knowing in action research. In M. Brenner, P. Marsh, & M. Brenner (Eds.), *The social context of method* (pp. 184-209). New York: St. Martin's.

Carney, T. F. (1990). *Collaborative inquiry methodology.* Windsor, Ontario: University of Windsor, Division for Instructional Development.

Cole, M. (1996) *Cultural psychology. A once and future discipline.* Cambridge, MA: The Belknap Press of Harvard University Press.

Conklin, H. C. (1954). *The relationship of Hanunoo culture to the plant world.* Ann Arbor, MI: University Microfilms.

Corsaro, W. (1985). *Friendship and peer culture in the early years.* Norwood, NJ: Ablex.

Cox, S. T. (1990a). Reconciling theory and data: In situ analysis in a study of oral storybook reading. In M. J. McGee-Brown (Ed.), *Processes, applications, and ethics in qualitative research* (pp. 358-367). Athens: University of Georgia Press.

Cox, S. T. (1990b). Who the boss?: Dynamic tensions in oral storybook reading. *International Journal of Qualitative Studies in Education, 3,* 231-252.

D'Amato, J. (1986). *We cool, tha's why: A study of personhood and place in Hawaiian second graders.* Unpublished doctoral dissertation, University of Hawaii.

Delamont, S. (1992). *Fieldwork in educational settings: Methods, pitfalls, and perspectives.* London: Falmer.

Denzin, N. K. (1978). *The research act: A theoretical introduction to sociological methods* (2nd ed.). New York: McGraw-Hill.

Denzin, N. K. (1989). *Interpretive interactionism.* Newbury Park, CA: Sage.

Denzin, N. K. (1994). The art and politics of interpretation. In N. K. Denzin & Y. S. Lincoln (Eds.), *Handbook of qualitative research* (pp. 500-515). Thousand Oaks, CA: Sage.

Donaldson, M. (1978). *Children's minds.* New York: W. W. Norton.

Eisenhardt, K. M. (1989a). Building theories from case study research. *Academy of Management Review, 14,* 532-550.

Eisenhardt, K. M. (1989b). Making fast strategic decisions in high-velocity environments. *Academy of Management Journal, 32,* 543-576.

Eisenhart, M. (1995). The fax, the jazz player, and the self-story teller: How do people organize culture? *Anthropology and Education Quarterly, 26*(1), 3-26.

Eisenhart, M. A., & Graue, M. E. (1990). Socially constructed readiness for school, *The International Journal for Qualitative Studies in Education, 3,* 253-269.

Emerson, R. M., Fretz, R. I., & Shaw, L. L. (1995). *Writing ethnographic fieldnotes.* Chicago: University of Chicago Press.

Erickson, F. (1986). Qualitative methods in research on teaching. In M. Wittrock (Ed.), *Handbook of research on teaching.* Chicago: Macmillan.

Erickson, F. (1989). *The meaning of validity in qualitative research.* Paper presented at the annual meeting of the American Educational Research Association, San Francisco.

Erickson, F. (1992, April). *Post-everything: The word of the moment and how we got here.* Paper presented at the annual meeting of the American Educational Research Association, San Francisco.

Erickson, F., & Schultz, J. (1977). When is a context? *ICHD Newsletter, 1*(2), 5-10.

Fendler, L., & Popkewitz, T. S. (1993). (Re)constituting critical traditions. *Educational Researcher, 22*(6), 24-26.

Fine, G. A., & Sandstrom, K. L. (1988). *Knowing children: Participant observation with minors.* Newbury Park, CA: Sage.

Finlan, T. G. (1994). *Learning disability: The imaginary disease.* Westport, CT: Bergin & Garvey.

Fischer, C., & Wertz, F. (1975). Empirical phenomenological analyses of being criminally victimized. In A. Giorgi (Ed.), *Phenomenology and psychological research* (pp. 135-158). Pittsburgh, PA: Duquesne University Press.

Fischer, K. W. (1980). A theory of cognitive development: The control and construction of hierarchies of skills. *Psychological Review, 87,* 477-531.

Flavell, J. H. (1982). Structures, stages, and sequences in cognitive development. In W. A. Collins (Ed.), *The concept of development: The Minnesota symposia on child psychology* (Vol. 15, pp. 1-28). Hillsdale, NJ: Erlbaum.

Ford, D. H., & Ford, M. E. (1987). *Humans as self-constructing living systems.* Hillsdale, NJ: Erlbaum.

Ford, D. H., & Lerner, R. M. (1992). *Developmental systems theory: An integrative approach.* Newbury Park, CA: Sage.

Foucault, M. (1978). *Discipline and punish: The birth of prison.* New York: Pantheon.

Fujita, M., & Sano, T. (1988). Children at American and Japanese day-care centers: Ethnography and reflective cross-cultural interviewing. In H. Trueba & C. Delgado-Gaitan (Eds.), *School and society: Learning content through culture* (pp. 73-97). New York: Praeger.

Garbarino, J. (1995). *Raising children in a socially toxic environment.* San Francisco: Jossey-Bass.

Gaskins, S. (1990). *Mayan exploratory play and development.* Unpublished doctoral dissertation, University of Chicago.

Gaskins, S., Miller, P. J., & Corsaro, W. A. (1992). Theoretical and methodological perspectives in the interpretive study of children. In W. A. Corsaro & P. J. Miller (Eds.), *New directions in child development* (pp. 5-23). San Francisco: Jossey-Bass.

Geertz, C. (1973). *The interpretation of cultures.* New York: Basic Books.

Geertz, C. (1983). *Local knowledge: Further essays in interpretive anthropology.* New York: Basic Books.

Geertz, C. (1986). Making experience, authoring selves. In V. W. Turner & E. M. Bruner (Eds.), *The anthropology of experience* (pp. 373-380). Urbana: University of Illinois Press.

Gelman, R. (1979). Preschool thought. *American Psychologist, 34,* 900-905.

Gelman, R., & Baillargeon, R. (1983). A review of some Piagetian concepts. In P. H. Mussen (Ed.), *Handbook of child psychology: Vol. 3. Cognitive Development* (pp. 167-230). New York: Wiley.

Gergen, K. J. (1985). The social constructionist movement in modern psychology. *American Psychologist, 40*(3), 266-275.

Gladwin, C. H. (1989). *Ethnographic decisions tree modeling.* Newbury Park, CA: Sage.

Glaser, B. G. (1967). The constant comparative method of qualitative analysis. In B. G. Glaser & A. L. Strauss (Eds.), *The discovery of grounded theory: Strategies for qualitative research* (pp. 101-116). Chicago: Aldine.

Glaser, B. G., & Strauss, A. L. (1967). *The discovery of grounded theory: Strategies for qualitative research.* Chicago: Aldine.

Glesne, C., & Peshkin, A. (1992). *Becoming qualitative researchers: An introduction.* White Plains, NY: Longman.

Goffman, E. (1974). *Frame analysis: An essay on the organization of experience.* Cambridge, MA: Harvard University Press.

Gould, R. A., & Potter, P. B. (1984). Use-lives of automobiles in America: A preliminary archaeological view. In R. A. Gould (Ed.), *Toward an ethno-archaeology of modern America.* Providence, RI: Brown University Press.

Graue, M. E. (1993). *Ready for what? Constructing meanings of readiness for kindergarten.* Albany: State University of New York Press.

Graue, M. E., & Smith, S. Z. (1996). Ventriloquating the meanings of mathematics. *Curriculum Studies, 4*(3), 301-328.

Greenspan, S. I. (1989). *Development of the ego.* Madison, CT: International Universities Press.

Grieve, R., & Hughes, M. (1990). *Understanding children: Essays in honor of Margaret Donaldson.* Cambridge, MA: Basil Blackwell.

Hall, E. (1982, January). Schooling children in a nasty climate: An interview with Jerome Bruner. *Psychology Today,* pp. 57-63.

Hall, G. S. (1883). The content of children's minds. *Princeton Review, 2,* 249-272.

Hall, G. S. (1901). Ideal school as based on child study. In *Journal of the Proceedings of the Fortieth Annual Meeting of the National Education Association* (pp. 474-488). Washington, DC: National Education Association of America.

Hart, W. (1994). "Children are not meant to be studied. . . ." *Our Schools/Our Selves, 5*(3), 6-27.

Haste, H. (1987). Growing into rules. In J. Bruner & H. Haste (Eds.), *Making sense: The child's construction of the world* (pp. 163-195). New York: Methuen.

Hatano, G., & Inagaki, K. (1986). Two courses of expertise. In H. Stevenson, H. Azuma, & K. Hakuta (Eds.), *Child development and education in Japan* (pp. 262-272). New York: Freeman.

Holloway, S. D., & Reichhart-Erickson, M. (1988). The relationship of day care quality to children's free-play behavior and social problem solving skills. *Early Childhood Research Quarterly, 3,* 39-53.

Hong, Y. (1995). *Teaching large-group time in a preschool classroom: The teacher as orchestra leader.* Unpublished doctoral dissertation, University of Illinois at Urbana-Champaign.

Howes, C. (1988). Same- and cross-sex friends: Implications for interaction and social skills. *Early Childhood Research Quarterly, 3,* 21-37.

Huberman, A. M., & Miles, M. B. (1994). Data management and analysis methods. In N. K. Denzin & Y. Lincoln (Eds.), *Handbook of qualitative research* (pp. 428-444). Thousand Oaks, CA: Sage.

Hymes, D. (1982). Ethnographic monitoring. In H. Trueba, G. P. Guthrie, & K. H. Au (Eds.), *Culture in the bilingual classroom: Studies in classroom ethnography* (pp. 56-68). Rowley, MA: Newbury House.

Inagaki, K. (1992). Piagetian and post-Piagetian conceptions of development and their implications for science education in early childhood. *Early Childhood Research Quarterly, 7,* 115-133.

Jackson, B. (1987). *Fieldwork.* Urbana: University of Illinois Press.

Jessor, R. (1996). Ethnographic methods in contemporary perspective. In R. Jessor, A. Colby, & R. A. Shweder (Eds.), *Ethnography and human development: Context and meaning in social inquiry* (pp. 3-14). Chicago: University of Chicago Press.

King, G., Keohane, R. O., & Verba, S. (1994). *Designing social inquiry. Scientific inference in qualitative research.* Princeton, NJ: Princeton University Press.

Kliebard, H. (1986). *The struggle for the American curriculum 1893-1958.* Boston: Routledge & Kegan Paul.

Kondo, D. (1990). *Crafting selves: Power, gender, and discourses of identity in a Japanese workplace.* Chicago: University of Chicago Press.

Kozulin, A. (1986). The concept of activity in Soviet psychology: Vygotsky, his disciples and critics. *American Psychologist, 41*(3), 264-274.

Krathwohl, D. (1993). *Methods of educational and social science research: An integrative approach.* New York: Longman.

Krieger, S. (1991). *Social science and the self: Personal essays as an art form.* New Brunswick, NJ: Rutgers University Press.

Kuhn, T. S. (1970). *The structure of scientific revolutions* (2nd ed.). Chicago: University of Chicago Press.

Lakatos, I. (1977). Falsification and the methodology of scientific research programmes. In I. Lakatos & A. Musgrave (Eds.), *Criticism and the growth of knowledge* (pp. 91-196). London: Cambridge University Press.

Leavitt, R. (1994). *Power and emotion in infant-toddler day care.* Albany: State University of New York Press.

Leont'ev, A. N. (1981). The problem of activity in psychology. In J. Wertsch (Ed.), *The concept of activity in Soviet psychology.* Armonk, NY: M. E. Sharpe.

Levi-Strauss, C. (1966). *The savage mind* (2nd ed.). Chicago: University of Chicago Press.

Lin, H.-F. (1993). *"Let's story!": Chinese preschoolers' joint exploration of two picture books.* Unpublished master's thesis, University of Illinois at Urbana-Champaign.

Lin, H.-F. (1995). *Science discourse in one American kindergarten classroom.* Unpublished doctoral dissertation, University of Illinois at Urbana-Champaign.

Lincoln, Y. S. (1995). Emerging criteria for quality in qualitative and interpretive research. *Qualitative Inquiry, 1*(3), 275-289.

Lincoln, Y. S., & Guba, E. G. (1985). *Naturalistic inquiry.* Beverly Hills, CA: Sage.

Luria, A. R. (1979). *The making of a mind.* Cambridge, MA: Harvard University Press.

Maclean, N. (1976). *A river runs through it and other stories.* Chicago: University of Chicago Press.

Mandell, N. (1988). The least-adult role in studying children. *Journal of Contemporary Ethnography, 16,* 433-467.

Mayall, B. (1994). Children in action at home and school. In B. Mayall (Ed.), *Children's childhoods observed and experienced.* London: Falmer.

McDermott, R. P. (1982). Rigor and respect as standards in ethnographic description. *Harvard Educational Review, 52,* 321-328.

McDermott, R. P., & Roth, D. R. (1978). The social organization of behavior: Interactional approaches. *Annual Review of Anthropology, 7,* 321-345.

Mehan, H. (1980). The competent student. *Anthropology and Education Quarterly, 11*(3), 131-152.

Mehan, H., Hertwick, A., & Meils, J. L. (1986). *Handicapping the handicapped.* Stanford, CA: Stanford University Press.

Miles, M. B., & Huberman, A. M. (1984). *Qualitative data analysis: A sourcebook of new methods.* Beverly Hills, CA: Sage.

Minick, N. (1989). Mind and activity in Vygotsky's work: An expanded frame of reference. *Cultural Dynamics, 11*(2), 162-187.

Mishler, E. G. (1986). *Research interviewing: Context and narrative.* Cambridge, MA: Harvard University Press.

Oakley, A. (1994). Parallels and differences between children's and women's studies. In B. Mayall (Ed.), *Children's childhoods observed and experienced.* London: Falmer.

Ottenberg, S. (1990). Thirty years of fieldnotes: Changing relationships to the text. In R. Sanjek (Ed.), *Fieldnotes: The makings of anthropology.* Ithaca, NY: Cornell University Press.

Pellegrini, A. D. (1987). Rough-and-tumble play: Developmental and educational significance. *Educational Psychology, 22*, 23-43.

Pellegrini, A. D., & Perlmutter, J. C. (1988). Rough-and-tumble play on the elementary school playground. *Young Children, 43*, 14-17.

Peshkin, A. (1982). The researcher and subjectivity: Reflections on an ethnography of school and community. In G. Spindler (Ed.), *Doing the ethnography of schooling: Educational anthropology in action* (pp. 48-67). New York: Holt, Rinehart and Winston.

Peshkin, A. (1988). In search of subjectivity: One's own. *Educational Researcher, 17*(7), 17-22.

Pianta, R. P., & Walsh, D. J. (1996). *High risk children in schools: Constructing sustaining relationships.* New York: Routledge.

Richardson, L. (1990). *Writing strategies: Reaching diverse audiences.* Newbury Park, CA: Sage.

Richardson, L. (1994). Writing: A method of inquiry. In N. K. Denzin & Y. S. Lincoln (Eds.), *Handbook of qualitative research* (pp. 516-529). Thousand Oaks, CA: Sage.

Rorty, R. (1979). *Philosophy in the mirror of nature.* Princeton, NJ: Princeton University Press.

Rorty, R. (1989). *Contingency, irony, and solidarity.* Cambridge, UK: Cambridge University Press.

Sacks, H. (1974). An analysis of the course of a joke's telling in the course of conversation. In R. Bauman & J. Sherzerf (Eds.), *Explorations in the ethnography of speaking.* New York: Cambridge University Press.

Sacks, H., Schegloff, E. A., & Jefferson, G. (1974). A simplest systematics for the organization of turn-taking in conversation. *Language, 5*, 696-735.

Sameroff, A. J. (1983). Developmental systems: Contexts and evolution. In P. H. Mussen (Ed.), *Handbook of child psychology* (Vol. 1, pp. 237-294). New York: Wiley.

Sanjek, R. (Ed.). (1990). *Fieldnotes: The makings of anthropology.* Ithaca, NY: Cornell University Press.

Schweinhart, L. J., & Weikart, D. P. (1995). *Significant benefits: The High/Scope Perry Preschool study through age 27.* Ypsilanti, MI: High/Scope Press.

Sechrest, L., & Flores, L. (1969). Homosexuality in the Philippines and the United States: The writing on the wall. *Journal of Social Psychology, 79*, 3-12.

Shotter, J. (1989). Social accountability and the social construction of "you." In J. Shotter & K. J. Gergen (Eds.), *Texts of identity.* Newbury Park, CA: Sage.

Sieber, J. E. (1992). *Planning ethically responsible research: A guide for students and internal review boards.* Newbury Park, CA: Sage.

Skinner, D. (1989, November). *Nepali children's formation of social selves.* Paper presented at the annual meeting of the American Anthropological Association, Phoenix.

Spindler, G. D., & Spindler, L. (1970). Fieldwork among the Menomini. In G. Spindler (Ed.), *Being an anthropologist: Fieldwork in eleven cultures* (pp. 267-301). New York: Holt, Rinehart & Winston.

Spindler, G. D., & Spindler, L. (1987). *Interpretive ethnography of education: At home and abroad.* New York: Holt, Rinehart & Winston.

Spodek, B. E. (1993). *Handbook of research on the education of young children.* New York: Macmillan.

Spradley, J. (1979). *The ethnographic interview.* New York: Holt, Rinehart & Winston.

Stake, R. (1995). *The art of case study research.* Thousand Oaks, CA: Sage.

Stanley, B., & Sieber, J. E. (Eds.). (1992). *Social research on children and adolescents: Ethical issues.* Newbury Park, CA: Sage.

Strauss, A. L. (1987). *Qualitative analysis for social scientists.* Cambridge, UK: Cambridge University Press.

Thorne, B. (1993). *Gender play: Girls and boys in school.* New Brunswick, NJ: Rutgers University Press.

Ting, H. (1992). *A child on the edge: Silent rejection.* Unpublished master's thesis, University of Illinois at Urbana-Champaign.

Tobin, J., & Davidson, D. (1990). The ethics of polyvocal ethnography: Empowering versus textualizing children and teachers. *International Journal of Qualitative Studies in Education, 3,* 271-283.

Tobin, J. J., Wu, D. Y. H., & Davidson, D. H. (1989). *Preschool in three cultures: Japan, China, and the United States.* New Haven, CT: Yale University Press.

Tsai, M. (1993). *The unintelligible voices that make sense: Ting-ting and Ying learning to become preschool students.* Unpublished doctoral dissertation, University of Illinois at Urbana-Champaign.

Turiel, E. (1989). The social construction of social construction. In W. Damon (Ed.), *Child development today and tomorrow.* San Francisco: Jossey-Bass.

Van Maanen, J. (1988). *Tales of the field: On writing ethnography.* Chicago: University of Chicago Press.

Vellutino, F. (1987). Dyslexia. *Scientific American, 256*(3), 34-43.

von Bertalanffy, L. (1968). *General system theory.* New York: George Braziller.

Vygotsky, L. S. (1987). Thinking and speech. In R. W. Rieber & A. S. Carton (Eds.), *The collected works of L. S. Vygotsky: Vol. 1. Problems of general psychology.* New York: Plenum. (Original work published 1934)

Wacksler, F. C. (1986). Studying children: Phenomenological insights. *Human Studies, 9,* 71-92.

Walsh, D. J. (1991). Reconstructing the discourse on development appropriateness: A developmental perspective. *Early Education and Development, 2,* 109-119.

Walsh, D. J. (1992, December). *Implications of a post-Piagetian perspective for early childhood education: Helping children make sense.* Paper presented at the Taipei Municipal Teachers College Conference on Early Childhood Education, Taipei, Taiwan.

Walsh, D. J. (1993, April). *Time to move on: A few thoughts on a post-Piagetian/cultural psychology.* Paper presented at the annual meeting of the American Educational Research Association, Atlanta.

Walsh, D. J., Tobin, J. J., & Graue, M. E. (1993). The interpretive voice: Qualitative research in early childhood education. In B. Spodek (Ed.), *Handbook of research on the education of young children.* New York: Free Press.

Wasser, J. D., & Bresler, L. (1996). Working in the interpretive zone: Conceptualizing collaboration in qualitative research terms. *Educational Researcher, 25*(5), 5-15.

Webb, E. J., Campbell, D. T., Schwartz, R. D., & Sechrest, L. (1966). *Unobtrusive measures: Nonreactive research in the social sciences.* Chicago: Rand McNally.

Weitzman, E. A., & Miles, M. B. (1995). *Computer programs for qualitative data analysis.* Thousand Oaks, CA: Sage.

Werner, O., & Schoepfle, G. M. (1987a). *Systematic fieldwork: Vol. 1. Foundations of ethnography and interviewing.* Newbury Park, CA: Sage.

Werner, O., & Schoepfle, G. M. (1987b). *Systematic fieldwork: Vol. 2. Ethnographic analysis and data management.* Newbury Park, CA: Sage.

Wertsch, J. (1979). Introduction. In J. V. Wertsch (Ed.), *Culture, communication, and cognition.* New York: Cambridge University Press.

Wertsch, J. (1985). *Vygotsky and the social formation of mind.* Cambridge, MA: Harvard University Press.

Wertsch, J. V. (1989). A sociocultural approach to mind. In W. Damon (Ed.), *Child development today and tomorrow.* San Francisco: Jossey-Bass.

Wolcott, H. F. (1981). Confessions of a "trained" observer. In T. S. Popkewitz & B. R. Tabachnick (Eds.), *The study of schooling: Field based methodologies in educational research and evaluation* (pp. 247-263). New York: Praeger.

Wolcott, H. F. (1990). *Writing up qualitative research.* Newbury Park, CA: Sage.

Wolf, J. (1994). *Doing day care.* Unpublished master's thesis, University of Illinois at Urbana-Champaign.

Wolf, J. M. (1995). *If you haven't been there, you don't know what it's like: Life at Enchanted Gate from the inside.* Unpublished doctoral dissertation, University of Illinois at Urbana-Champaign.

Index

ABOUT THE AUTHORS

M. Elizabeth Graue, a former early childhood special education and kindergarten teacher, is Associate Professor in the Department of Curriculum and Instruction at the University of Wisconsin-Madison. She received her PhD in research methodologies at the University of Colorado at Boulder in 1990. Her dissertation, *Socially Constructed Readiness for Kindergarten in Three Communities,* won awards from the American Educational Research Association for qualitative research methods and for early childhood education. It was later published as *Ready for What? Constructing Meanings of Readiness for Kindergarten* (1993). She has continued to do research on beliefs about readiness, with a particular focus on academic redshirting, instructional assessment, and parent relationships with public schools. She is Associate Editor of the *Review of Educational Research* (1996-1999) and has published work in *Early Childhood Research Quarterly, Early Education and Development, Educational Policy, Journal of Curriculum Studies,* and *Urban Education.* She is married to Clark Landis and has two sons, Sam and Max.

Daniel J. Walsh is Associate Professor of Early Childhood Education at the University of Illinois at Urbana-Champaign. He received his PhD from the University of Wisconsin-Madison in 1985. His interest in interpretive research began with two courses on the ethnography of schooling he took with George and Louise Spindler at Wisconsin. He spent a dozen years as a prekindergarten and kindergarten teacher, the majority of those years in the Chicago public schools. His research has focused on policy and practice in early public schooling, teachers' perspectives as contexts for development, post-Piagetian developmental theory, and research methodology. He is past Associate Editor of the *Early Childhood Research Quarterly* and has published in various journals, including *Journal of Curriculum Studies, Teachers College Record, Educational Foundations, Educational Evaluation and Policy Analysis, Early Education and Development,* and *Psychological Bulletin.* He is the author, with Robert Pianta, of *High Risk Children in Schools: Constructing Sustaining Relationships.* He is married to Naneera Vidhayasirinun and has two children, Buck, 4, and Scooter, 11. He spends as much time as he can on his bicycle and ice skates, preferably with the three people just mentioned.

ABOUT THE
CONTRIBUTORS

Deborah Ceglowski is Assistant Professor of Early Childhood Education in the Department of Curriculum and Instruction and Outreach Coordinator for the Center for Early Education and Development at the University of Minnesota. A former program specialist with Head Start, she received her PhD at the University of Illinois at Urbana-Champaign. She is a recipient of a Bush Leadership Fellowship and the Mary Catherine Ellwein dissertation award from the American Educational Research Association. Ceglowski's research interests include qualitative studies of the impact of policies on teachers, parents, and children and employing alternative writing strategies in research.

Anne Haas Dyson is Professor of Language, Literacy and Culture in the School of Education at the University of California, Berkeley. A former teacher of young children, she studies the social lives and literacy learning of schoolchildren. Among her publications are *The Need for Story: Cultural Diversity in Classroom and Community* (co-edited with Celia Genishi), *Social Worlds of Children Learning to Write in an Urban Primary School*, which was awarded the NCTE's David Russell Award for Distinguished Research, and *Writing Superheroes: Contemporary Childhood, Popular Culture, and Classroom Literacy*.

269

David E. Fernie is Professor of Early Childhood Education in the School of Teaching and Learning, The Ohio State University College of Education. His interests include children's play, their understanding and use of media/technology, and the ethnographic study of preschool classrooms.

Rebecca Kantor is an Associate Professor in the School of Teaching and Learning, College of Education at The Ohio State University (OSU). Her research interests include language and social processes in early childhood settings, children's social worlds and friendships, and preschool ethnography. After 14 years as director of the Sophie Rogers Lab School at OSU, she now serves as its Curriculum Adviser.

Robin Lynn Leavitt is Associate Professor and Chair of the Educational Studies Department at Illinois Wesleyan University. She received her PhD in Educational Policy Studies from the University of Illinois at Urbana-Champaign. She is the author of *Power and Emotion in Infant-Toddler Day Care* and several book chapters and articles on day care. Leavitt's research is interpretive and focuses on the everyday lived experiences of young children in early childhood settings.

Peggy J. Miller is Professor of Speech Communication and Professor of Psychology at the University of Illinois at Urbana-Champaign. She received her PhD from Teachers College, Columbia University. She is interested in everyday discourse as a medium of socialization and has written extensively on narrative practices in families from a variety of cultural groups. She is the author of *Amy, Wendy, and Beth: Learning Language in South Baltimore* and (with Wendy Haight) *Pretending at Home: Early Development in a Sociocultural Context*. She is co-editor (with William Corsaro) of *Interpretive Approaches to Children's Socialization* and co-editor (with Jacqueline Goodnow and Frank Kessel) of *Cultural Practices as Context for Development*.

Hsueh-Yin Ting is Associate Professor and head of the Center for Early Childhood Education at National Hsin-Chu Teachers College in Taiwan. She received her PhD in the Department of Curriculum and Instruction from the University of Illinois at Urbana-Champaign. Her master's and doctoral research focuses on peer relationships in early childhood classrooms. Her interests in the interplay between culture and individual also led her to do a study exploring how school culture shapes teacher education.